A SOCIAL STRATEGY

A SOCIAL STRATEGY

HOW WE PROFIT FROM SOCIAL MEDIA

MIKOŁAJ JAN PISKORSKI

PRINCETON UNIVERSITY PRESS

Princeton & Oxford

Requests for permission to reproduce material from this work
should be sent to Permissions, Princeton University Press

Published by Princeton University Press, 41 William Street,
Princeton, New Jersey 08540

In the United Kingdom: Princeton University Press, 6 Oxford Street,
Woodstock, Oxfordshire OX20 1TW

press.princeton.edu

LIBRARY OF CONGRESS CATALOGING-IN-PUBLICATION DATA

Piskorski, Mikołaj Jan.

A social strategy : how we profit from social media / Mikołaj Jan Piskorski.
          pages cm

Includes bibliographical references and index.

ISBN 978-0-691-15339-1 (alk. paper)

1. Internet marketing. 2. Social media—Economic aspects. 3. Online social
networks—Economic aspects. I. Title.

HF5415.1265.P57 2014

658.8'72–dc23   2013035547

British Library Cataloging-in-Publication Data is available

This book has been composed in Sabon Next LT Pro and Ideal Sans

Printed on acid-free paper ∞

Printed in the United States of America

10 9 8 7 6 5 4 3 2 1

CONTENTS

PREFACE

I vividly remember sitting in my office at the Stanford Graduate School of Business in April 2003 when two men knocked on my door asking if they could have a word. By then I had done a fair amount of research on offline social networks and had written a paper on how social networks can help venture capitalists gain recognition. As a result, many newly minted (and always impeccably dressed) venture capitalists dropped in on me, looking for additional insights. I figured these two fell in the same category—except they weren't dressed as sharply.

It turned out, though, that they weren't venture capitalists at all; they wanted to talk to me about a company they were about to launch, one that involved online networking. A number of similar companies had sprung up in the area, and their founders had all secured Stanford professors who studied social networks as their advisors. As the most junior professor on campus who studied social networks, I was the only one unspoken for, and so these two gentlemen sought me out to be their sounding board.

Their site, soon to be released to the public, would let people create professional profiles to display their educational and work achievements and publicly indicate their business relationships. People could then use the online network to offer or seek consulting engagements, expertise, or financing.

The idea sounded interesting to me, but I did not believe it was going to succeed. "Why reinvent the wheel?" I thought. "We already know that networks work very well, and people already get jobs through networks." In fact, a classic sociological work by Mark Granovetter (1974) had long ago demonstrated that a significant percentage of jobs are obtained through personal networks. Clearly, offline networks do what they are supposed to do, and have done so for centuries, so why would we need to network online? I was polite with my comments, but I was politely *negative* and we parted ways.

Later that day, as I was driving back home to San Francisco on Interstate 280, I continued to think about just how much I did not like the online networking idea. Then, as I was approaching the intersection with Route 92 that takes you to Half Moon Bay, and admiring the fog rolling over the Santa Cruz Mountains, it dawned on me that I was wrong. I remember thinking: "We have all of these theories in sociology—about how networks work, how they help us, and how they are better than markets. But what if these networks do not perform as the theory says? What if there are many social interactions that would make people happier, but these interactions simply do not happen? We have no theory that tells us when social relationships might *not* work. And if there are many missing social interactions, then there is a huge opportunity for new ventures to help people interact with one another! My visitors were right and they were onto something really big!"

By the time I got to San Francisco, I was completely convinced that I needed to contact the two men, retract most of what I had said, and ask them to meet with me again. I emailed them as soon as I got home, and the two gentlemen, Reid Hoffman and Konstantin Guericke, agreed to meet again. Just a few years later, their company, LinkedIn, had prevailed over its erstwhile competitors. Within eight years, LinkedIn reported $65 million profit on $500 million revenue and debuted on the New York Stock Exchange with one hundred million users and a $10 billion valuation. When this book was going into print, the company was valued at $25 billion. Sadly, I had nothing to do with the company's success. (In fact, I have no formal paid relationships with any of the companies discussed in this book.) But the interaction with Hoffman and Guericke changed my research trajectory for the next ten years. I document this research in this book.

LinkedIn's Critical Choice

LinkedIn's road to success was not straightforward. Indeed, in the summer of 2005, Reid Hoffman found himself facing a critical decision regarding the company's future. By then, the company had amassed five million users, but it had very little revenue to show to investors. Furthermore, it had only five million dollars in cash reserves, which would allow it to survive for just another nine months without an infusion of cash from venture capitalists. Given about a six-month lead required to obtain financing, LinkedIn had to start generating revenue quickly, or the terms of financing would be very unfavorable.

In deciding how to generate revenue, Hoffman had to make sure that he did not undermine the basic principles that had allowed the company to attract users. For example, LinkedIn had always encouraged users to form online connections only with people they actually knew offline. It also allowed members to contact only those members who were no more than four degrees of separation, and every time someone wanted to contact someone else on the platform, the chain of friends connecting the sender and the receiver had to approve the communication. This fostered a trustworthy online environment and reduced the incidence of spam, which helped LinkedIn prevail over competitors.

The company also had to be mindful about its superusers—individuals who were so committed to the site that they used a separate computer dedicated only to their LinkedIn activities. Often referred to as "networkers," these users had established many online relationships on LinkedIn and played critical roles in connecting other users by forwarding their requests.

Hoffman and his team entertained two options. The first entailed keeping the existing free service intact, but offering a fifteen-dollar subscription for a bundle of eight new services that would help LinkedIn members search the site and manage interactions more effectively. This option garnered significant support because it helped the site's most active users, the networkers. It also offered the promise of steady cash-flow streams associated with monthly subscriptions.

The second option called for allowing members to contact each other directly, regardless of whether they were connected to each other through intermediaries. LinkedIn would charge a fee for such communication—roughly equivalent to ten dollars per message. The company had received some requests for this functionality and estimated it to be a profitable option. Many people worried, however, that pursuing this option could lead to the platform's demise. First, if anyone could contact anyone, then there would be much less need for the networkers—the most active site members—who would probably abandon the site. Second, allowing users to contact anyone on the network would violate LinkedIn's basic premise—its commitment to privacy—potentially leading to massive user defection.

I will reveal what the company chose in a moment, but before I do, I want you to make the call yourself:

Which option would you choose?

I ask this question every time I teach the Competing with Social Networks class to Harvard Business School MBA students and to various experienced business managers in the executive education programs. And every time I do, my heart stops beating for a moment as I expect everyone in the class to pick the second option—the one that LinkedIn chose. It is so much harder to teach when all students pick the option the company chose . . . and yet it never happens!

Even eight years after the event, with lots of information on LinkedIn readily available on the Internet, 60 percent of my students vote against the second option largely because it seems to violate the privacy and trust of the people who joined the site to begin with. Many students, particularly in the executive education sessions, claim: "I would never want to be on a site like this where I can be spammed with messages." Only 15 percent of students support it. And the remaining 25 percent say that neither option offers profitability for LinkedIn.

So, *was* LinkedIn wrong to adopt the second option? Evidence suggests the contrary—the company did very well as a result. In implementing the strategy, the company opted for a subscription model rather than a fee per message, but the imputed price per message was roughly the same. And although the ability for anyone to contact anyone else on the platform for a fee did drive away the networkers, their defection did very little to curb the platform's success.

Ultimately, the second option worked well for LinkedIn because it opened up a communication channel between recruiters and people in long-term employment relationships who may be looking for new jobs. Most people in this situation face a huge normative restriction—it is often not appropriate for them to look for new jobs openly while they are still working. Those who violate this norm can lose their jobs or be passed over for promotion. It is exactly for this reason that many people in long-term employment relationships do not put their résumés on Monster.com—a popular job-seeking website—lest their own company's HR department spot it. This normative restriction prevents these people from engaging in mutually beneficial interactions with recruiters, which in turn can prevent them from getting better jobs.

On LinkedIn, however, it *is* appropriate to list one's educational and work achievements and open oneself up to overtures from recruiters. Displaying this information on that platform does not violate the norm because the information is also used for LinkedIn's other functionality—networking with friends and business associates. Employees can use such networking activities to generate benefits for companies where they currently work and thus justify their presence on LinkedIn. So, even though company leaders know that they might lose their employees through LinkedIn, they also know that they can get a lot of benefits by having employees on that platform. As a consequence, most companies do not object to their employees being on LinkedIn.

In effect, LinkedIn overcame the norm that prevents people from going on the market while still employed. This enticed numerous employed job seekers, who in turn attracted recruiters to the site. The latter paid LinkedIn a lot of money to be able to access these employed candidates who are very hard to find in the offline world and on other online sites. To date, LinkedIn continues to generate most of its revenues this way.

Concepts Presented in This Book

LinkedIn's 2005 decision illustrates many of the central themes and concepts in this book. I'll introduce them very briefly now—putting the key concepts in italics. First, LinkedIn identified a mutually beneficial social interaction that does not take place—that between employed people and recruiters that could result in the former getting better jobs and the latter recruiting excellent candidates. I will refer to such mutually beneficial social interactions that do not take place as *social failures*. LinkedIn also recognized that the interaction it wanted to address does not occur because of normative restrictions. Various normative restrictions that prevent us from engaging in social interactions will be of central importance throughout the book.

Second, LinkedIn developed a *social solution* that minimized the salience of this norm, and allowed people to make themselves visible to recruiters and thus engage in mutually beneficial interactions. It did so by helping people interact with business acquaintances, and leveraged that solution to give people an excuse to interact with people they did not know without violating the norm. Throughout the book, we will underscore that social solutions work best when they overcome social norms that prevent mutually beneficial interactions offline.

Third, LinkedIn's example shows us that when a firm provides a valuable social solution, it can ask the beneficiaries to do something that benefits the firm in return. In LinkedIn's case, this amounted to paying the firm money. This insight will be particularly useful in the second part of the book when we study more traditional companies, such as Nike or American Express. These companies have built their own social solutions or leveraged existing ones to help their customers interact with others. In return, these firms ask that these customers do something beneficial for the firm, such as buying more expensive products or doing customer acquisition on the firm's behalf. I will use the concept of *social strategy* to capture the idea that firms can lower their costs and/or increase their customers' willingness to pay by helping their customers develop better relationships.

Social failures, *social solutions*, and *social strategy* are the essential concepts on which this book is based. Chapter 1 explains how the book will explore and use these concepts to understand why certain social platforms have failed while others have succeeded, and how the surviving social platforms compete with each other.

CHAPTER 1

The Arc of the Book

Why do some social platforms flourish while others die? What is a social strategy, and what distinguishes a strong social strategy from a weak one? To begin to examine these concepts in depth step back for a moment and consider the meteoric rise of online social platforms. The first set of dedicated online social platforms launched in 1995 when Classmates made its appearance, and then SixDegrees followed in 1997. Neither gained significant traction, and both closed quickly. Then, when Friendster launched in 2003, followed by MySpace and Facebook, the social revolution stormed the Internet. By the time this book was in press in late 2013, Facebook, the largest online social platform, had amassed more than 1.25 billion users, who made more than a trillion connections and uploaded more than 240 billion photos.[1] Twitter—a U.S.-based social platform providing real-time communication between friends and strangers—had garnered 232 million users.[2] eHarmony, one of the leading online matchmaking sites, with more than one million paying users, claimed to be responsible for almost 5 percent of all new heterosexual marriages in the United States.[3] Meanwhile, in China, WeChat, a mobile text and voice communication software, with some Facebook-like functionalities, boasted more than 500 million active users.[4]

Initially, social platforms were considered a passing fad. But given the breadth of adoption, few now doubt that they fulfill important social needs. And upon reflection, the popularity of these platforms is not surprising. Most of us have friends. Platforms that enable us to interact with them easily therefore have understandable appeal. Moreover, at various points in our lives, most of us want to make new friends or find a partner, and before the advent of social platforms, there were few large-scale outlets for meeting these social needs. So when technology allowed social platforms to emerge and a critical mass of people became aware of the possibilities, pent-up demand quickly translated into broad adoption.

In other ways, however, the popularity of these platforms is deeply surprising. After all, before these platforms took off people used to meet new people in the offline world and maintained relationships with friends, and no one lamented the absence of an online social platform. This begs the question: Why *do* we need online social platforms to interact with others when we can interact in the offline world?

Social Failures

To answer this question, I argue that there are many interactions in the offline world that we would like to undertake but cannot. These missing interactions represent unmet social needs, or *social failures*. In some cases, these social failures relate to inability to meet new people—I will refer to these as "meet" failures. In other cases, they pertain to the inability to share private information or social support within the context of existing relationships—I will refer to them as "friend" failures. These failures lie at the heart of why people are attracted to social platforms, and we will review them in more detail in chapter 2.

Social Solutions

In chapter 2, we will also examine how to build social features that, when put together, create successful *social solutions* that allow people to meet strangers or deepen their existing friend relationships in ways they could not do on their own. As we do this, we will seek to distinguish between strong social solutions that truly address social failures from weak social solutions that do little to alleviate social failures. We will use this distinction to help us understand why some social platforms have won over others.

Subsequently, we will turn to broader strategic questions and examine competitive interactions between different types of social solutions. Such analysis can help us answer questions such as: What stops Facebook from replicating LinkedIn's solutions and adding them to its current offering? Or, more generally: Why do we not see one all-encompassing social platform that provides social solutions to all of our social failures?

To answer such questions, I argue that there exist powerful strategic trade-offs that cause two or more social solutions to be less effective when they are provided by the same platform. To avoid these negative implications, social platforms will refrain from copying solutions provided by other types of platforms. When this happens, different types of platforms with non-overlapping solutions will coexist. As we will see in later chapters, it is exactly such trade-offs that prevent Facebook from replicating what LinkedIn is doing. They also stop one large social platform from providing all types of solutions.

Strategic trade-offs can arise in many different ways. In this book, however, I focus on trade-offs that arise between different ways of helping us interact with people we do not know and with those we already do. Specifically, I will show that platforms that offer "meet" solutions face trade-offs between: (1) allowing private interaction with a few strangers, (2) allowing private interaction with many strangers, or (3) permitting unlimited public interaction with strangers. These are illustrated on the vertical axis of table 1.1, together with examples of platforms that exemplify these choices. Chapters 3 and 4 will discuss these trade-offs in detail using the examples of eHarmony, OkCupid, and Twitter, respectively. This discussion will help us understand why eHarmony, which offers private interaction with a limited number of strangers, would not be as effective if it also allowed private interaction with many strangers. Similarly, it will identify when platforms offering private interaction functionalities, such as a dating site, may wish to refrain from providing public interaction functionalities—something that Twitter provides.

In contrast, as shown on the horizontal axis of table 1.1, platforms that offer "friend" solutions face a trade-off between helping users to interact with a small number of their closest friends or with a large

Table 1.1. Strategic Trade-offs among Social Platforms

		"Friend" solution	
		Many friends	Few close friends
"Meet" solution	Limited interaction with strangers	Facebook	mixi
	Private interaction with few strangers	LinkedIn	eHarmony
	Private interaction with many strangers	Friendster	OkCupid
	Public interaction with many strangers	MySpace	Twitter

number of their friends and acquaintances. As we will see in chapter 5, where we will study Facebook and mixi, these interaction choices lead to distinctive positioning, preventing one type of platform from replicating the appeal of the other.

Finally, we will focus on platforms that provide solutions to help people meet strangers but also facilitate interactions with friends and acquaintances. In chapter 6, we will use LinkedIn and Friendster as examples of such platforms, and show that they generate user behaviors that would be unacceptable on platforms like Facebook. This will help us explain why Facebook makes it so difficult for us to interact with strangers, which in turn allows LinkedIn to compete in a distinct manner. We will end our analysis in chapter 7 with MySpace, which provided solutions for users to interact with a broad set of friends but also allowed them to interact publicly with many strangers, leading to user behaviors that would undermine the efficacy of platforms offering other solutions.

Social Strategy

Having understood what makes social solutions work and how they compete with one another, the second half of the book focuses on how businesses that cater mainly to our economic needs, such as Ford or Procter & Gamble, can leverage social platforms for competitive advantage.

Many companies have already tried to do this by acquiring fans on Facebook or followers on Twitter, and broadcasting promotional messages to them. Despite the apparent promise, the results of such actions are often disappointing. Either companies fail to engage their customers or, when they do, they find it difficult to convert that engagement into real sales.

I attribute this relative lack of success to the fact that such broadcasting actions do not help people do what they like to do on such platforms—interact with others to solve their social failures. Instead, these commercial messages interfere with the process of making human connections. To see why, imagine sitting at a table having a wonderful time with your friends, and then suddenly someone pulls up a chair and asks, "Can I sell you something?" You would probably ignore that person or ask him to leave immediately. This is exactly what is happening to companies that try to "friend" their customers online and then broadcast messages to them.

But companies *can* successfully leverage social platforms for competitive advantage. To do so, they simply need to help people do what they naturally do on social platforms: engage in interactions with other people that they could not undertake in the offline world. To continue the earlier analogy, companies can walk up to that table and say, "Hi! Can we help you become better friends with the people you are with?" When companies provide a social solution that addresses unmet social needs, they can then ask people to undertake certain corporate tasks, for example, contribute free inputs, produce goods for the company to sell, or market or sell these goods on the company's behalf. By performing these tasks, people lower the companies' costs, or increase their ability to charge higher prices, which translates into greater competitive advantage. I will refer to the confluence of social benefits and greater competitive advantage as a successful *social strategy*.

Chapter 8 introduces this concept in more detail and examines two key decisions that arise when developing a social strategy: Should such a strategy aim for higher willingness to pay or for lower costs? And should the company achieve this goal by providing a "meet" solution or a "friend" solution? I then dedicate one chapter to each of the four possible configurations of social strategy that result from answering these questions (see table 1.2).

Specifically, chapter 9 examines Zynga's social strategy, which aims to lower costs by facilitating relationships between people who already

Table 1.2. Types of Social Strategies

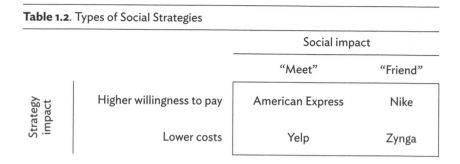

		Social impact	
		"Meet"	"Friend"
Strategy impact	Higher willingness to pay	American Express	Nike
	Lower costs	Yelp	Zynga

know each other. Chapter 10 looks at Yelp's social strategy, which seeks to reduce costs by promoting relationships between people who did not previously know each other. Chapter 11 introduces us to the social strategy that encourages a higher willingness to pay while facilitating new relationships, and shows us that established firms, such as American Express, can pursue many social strategies at the same time. Chapter 12 rounds off this analysis by reviewing some of the preceding types of strategies, and adding one, used by Nike, that increases willingness to pay while strengthening existing relationships.

To help managers prepare to construct their own social strategies, chapter 13 focuses on the process of social strategy development at the *Harvard Business Review*. Chapter 14, the conclusion, summarizes the book.

Key Choices I Made about the Book's Content

Every author makes choices when writing a book. I would like to highlight three choices I made. First, I chose to introduce a number of my own terms rather than using existing ones. For example, other than in the subtitle, I chose not to use the term *social media*. This is because to me the term implies content creation and broadcasting. As we will see later, such activities comprise only a small percentage of how people engage with others online. Instead, I opt to use the term *social platforms*, to underscore that people connect online, using whatever means, in whatever form, primarily to improve their relationships with others. I also avoid the term *online social networks* because that term implies interacting with one's existing set of friends and acquaintances. People often meet new people online, however, and for this reason I prefer to use the all-encompassing term *social platforms*.

Second, I chose to downplay the histories of various social platforms and the personalities of the executives who ran (and run) them. I cover those details in the Harvard Business School cases I have written on these companies. Instead, in this book, I concentrate on examining various social platforms against a common framework. Doing so allows me to highlight, compare, and contrast their similarities and differences with ease. (By the time you finish the first part of the book, you will see more similarities than differences between eHarmony, Twitter, and Facebook.)

Finally, in writing the book, I explicitly excluded all social platforms hailing from China. When the book was written, Chinese users could not access many of the Western social platforms, such as Facebook, Twitter, or YouTube. This allowed a multitude of Chinese social platforms to emerge and meet the social needs of Chinese Internet users. Documenting this complex ecosystem requires a separate book—one that I hope to write soon!

The Book's Audience

This book is primarily aimed at scholars interested in understanding why we use social platforms, how these platforms compete with each other, and how more traditional firms can leverage social platforms for competitive advantage. I hope that the ideas presented here will inform both sociology and strategy, and encourage their further integration. Specifically, I hope that my colleagues in sociology will benefit from understanding the kinds of social platforms that are likely to emerge in the future. And I trust that my colleagues in strategy will be convinced that puzzling over the details of social behavior can have a tremendous impact on how firms compete in the marketplace.

Separately, I hope that this book will help practicing managers. I suspect that most managers will be drawn to the second part of the book, where they can find examples of what companies have done to increase their competitive advantage using social platforms. I do recommend, however, that before implementing any social strategies managers read the first part of the book. Doing so will help them with a task that may be unfamiliar but is absolutely essential to designing an effective social strategy: identifying the unmet *social* needs of their customers. No social strategy will succeed without identifying those unmet social needs correctly.

To help practicing managers, as well as people who advise them, succeed in the marketplace, I have built a dedicated social platform for this book, which can be accessed through a link at http://press.princeton .edu/titles/10190.html.[5] The platform will allow you to deepen your insights into social strategies, examine the success of social strategies that were developed after this book was written, and, most important, interact with other managers to learn from one another's experience.

Finally, I trust that this book will be of interest to social platform users. We all use these platforms differently but we cannot observe how others use them. As a consequence, we are often forced to infer what others are doing by using our own behaviors as a template. This book will allow us to "look under the hood" objectively and examine how user behavior differs across different platforms and individuals. I hope that, armed with this knowledge, readers will be better able to use any given social platform to its fullest potential and avoid common pitfalls. At the same time, better understanding of how and why we behave as we do may dispel some myths surrounding online social platforms and help those who are staying away from them to realize the opportunities these platforms offer.

CHAPTER 2

Social Failures and Social Solutions

Every insight, suggestion, and lesson in this book hinges on the concept of social failures. Social failures are interactions that do *not* occur, but would make two people better off if they did. Some failures entail being unable to meet strangers, such as a potential spouse or a hobby buddy. These are the "meet" social failures. Others entail failed interactions within existing relationships. These are the "friend" social failures. These failures include inability to discuss everyday matters, give psychosocial support to each other, convey affect, or simply display certain information without having to engage in a conversation.

Social failures arise because of *interaction costs*. To see how, consider an interaction between two people that generates benefits for each of them. As long as these benefits are higher than what each could obtain by engaging in other activities, the relationship is mutually beneficial. Now, consider the possibility that costs related to the interaction exist. These can arise, for example, if the two people are far away from each other, or when the two people experience significant discomfort when initiating the interaction. If these interaction costs exceed the benefits from the interaction, the interaction will not take place, and a social failure will emerge.

There are a number of different types of interaction costs. Each of them can work alone or in tandem with others to prevent an interaction from happening. To identify these costs, consider a simple framework, shown in table 2.1, that distinguishes between four types of interaction

Table 2.1. Reasons for and Types of Interaction Costs That Underlie Social Failures

	Types of interaction costs			
	Breadth	Display	Search	Communication
Economic reasons				
Social reasons				

costs. As the framework shows (and as we'll discuss in more depth later) each type of interaction cost can arise for economic or social reasons.

The first set of interaction costs arises when people cannot easily access others, which limits the number of relevant individuals with whom interaction is possible. This requires people to engage in costly actions to increase the breadth of people who might be the right match for them. I refer to these as *breadth* interaction costs. When these costs exceed the expected value of the interaction, the interaction will not take place and a social failure will occur.

Breadth interaction costs occur for economic reasons, for example, when people live far away from each other or have nonoverlapping time schedules. Suppose there is a woman in Australia who would make the perfect spouse for you, but the two of you are far from each other. For you to meet this woman, you would have to incur the cost of traveling to Australia and trying to find her there. The high cost of doing so prevents the mutually beneficial interaction from occurring.

The social reasons for breadth interaction costs include normative restrictions on social contact. For example, there might be a man who lives next door to you who would make the perfect spouse for you, but you live in a country where it is simply inappropriate for you to approach men when you are single. For you to meet this man, you would have to incur the cost of violating the pervasive norm. If this cost is substantial, you will refrain from engaging in this act, the mutually beneficial relationship will not form and a social failure will occur.

The second set of interaction costs arises in the context of unilateral interactions in which one actor would like to convey personal information to another to create value for both, but faces restrictions against doing so. These restrictions require an individual to engage in costly actions to display relevant information to others, and for that reason, I refer to this set of costs as *display* interaction costs. When these costs exceed the expected value of the interaction, the interaction will not take place and a social failure will occur.

Display interaction costs can also occur for economic and social reasons. To see these economic reasons, consider that you may want to show your brand new house to your friends, and they may want to see it, but it is quite costly to invite each of them to see it. As a consequence, only a few of them will, while the rest will remain uninformed. For social reasons, consider the possibility that you want to show your new house to your friends, but you refrain from doing so for fear of coming across as boastful. If the costs of being seen this way outweigh the potential benefits, you will not engage in these display behaviors.

The third set of interaction costs arise in the context of unilateral interactions in which one actor would like to obtain personal information from another to create value for both, but there are restrictions against such behavior. To overcome these restrictions, people have to engage in costly search efforts, and for this reason I refer to these interaction costs as *search* interaction costs. When these costs exceed the expected value of the interaction, it will not take place and a social failure will occur.

For an economic example of search interaction costs, suppose that you are attending a large party and you are interested in exploring the possibility of establishing a romantic relationship with another guest, but you are not sure who else at the party is unattached. It would take a lot of effort for you to approach each person at the party and look for clues of their relationship status. As a consequence, you refrain from doing so, and thus fail to identify a person who would make a great partner for you. For a social example, suppose that you actually wanted to take the time to walk from person to person to figure out who at that party is single, but you know you would come across as very awkward if you did so. To avoid such social costs, you do not engage in the search behaviors, but as a consequence, you fail to identify a person who would make a great partner for you. A social failure has occurred.

The final set of interaction costs arises in the context of bilateral interactions in which both actors want to convey personal information to each other to generate value, but find it difficult to do so. These costs arise, for example, when people communicate with each other, and so I refer to these as *communication* interaction costs. For an economic reason for a communication interaction cost, consider a scenario where you want to talk with your dad about how your entire family could vacation together, but you expect that your dad will have very different views from yours, and as a result, you are certain that the conversation will take a long time. Since you are really time-constrained, you choose not to have the conversation at all, and you forgo the family vacation altogether. For a social cause, continue the earlier example, but now suppose that it is normatively inappropriate in your culture to question your parents. To avoid the costs of violating the norm, you avoid the conversation, choose not to go on the vacation, and social failure emerges.

Throughout the book, we will use the distinction between these four types of interaction costs, and the two types of causes that underlie each of them, to help us identify and evaluate various types of solutions for social failures.

Interaction Costs Vary across People, Relationship Types, and Approaches

The magnitude of the four types of interaction costs varies greatly across people. Consider, for example, different types of people looking for spouses or long-term partners. Ethnic minorities seeking a spouse of the same ethnicity, or sexual minorities seeking a spouse of the same gender, encounter a smaller breadth of potential candidates during their everyday activities. As a consequence, they will experience higher breadth interaction costs. Or consider people who live in countries where norms of modesty restrict their ability to display personal information to others. These people will have to come up with creative ways of displaying this information to their potential spouses and, as a consequence, experience much higher display interaction costs.

Furthermore, there exist significant differences in search interaction costs related to age. In high school and college, for example, these interaction costs are relatively low, as many students in high school and college environments are also looking for relationships. Once we enter the workforce, however, identifying others who are looking for a relationship gets harder. As we enter our thirties, the cost of finding a spouse increases even more, and it continues on that upward trajectory as we get older. Finally, men and women face different communication costs. In most cultures, women are subject to normative restrictions that prevent them from pursuing men for romantic relationships (Cate and Lloyd 1992). Throughout the book, we will use these kinds of differences to examine whether and to what extent various solutions to social failures help those who are most affected by interaction costs.

Moreover, the magnitude of the four types of interaction costs varies across relationship types, and the different ways in which people pursue any given type of relationship. Consider, for example, the process through which people meet new people (we will consider the process of interacting with friends later in the book). There are at least three different ways of achieving this goal: (1) by engaging in a common *activity*, such as school, work, or a hobby, (2) by asking *brokers*, such as friends or paid professionals, to make introductions, or (3) by going to a *marketplace*, such as a bar, and trying to meet others at this venue. Each of these processes entails very different interaction costs across the four dimensions.

Consider breadth costs first. Activity-based methods of establishing relationships require relatively little effort, as people already spend a great deal of time engaged in work- or education-based activities. Most activities, however, restrict interactions to a limited set of people, implying that people will often be unable to establish new relationships that fit them. As a consequence, this method of establishing new relationships will entail substantial breadth interaction costs. Broker-based means of establishing new relationships afford greater breadth than is possible through activities. This is because one's friends are likely to know people outside one's core set of activities, and can match one with those other friends and acquaintances. Similarly, specialized third-party brokers are likely to have access to broader sets of potential matches than individuals can get to know on their own, through their own activities. And finally, marketplace-based methods of establishing relationships allow for even greater exposure to more people of different types, allowing people to find others who fit them well. Thus, marketplace-based methods will entail the lowest breadth interaction costs.

Next, consider display interaction costs. Activity-based methods of meeting others make it easy to display personal information to others in the context of engaging in a particular activity, such as work or a hobby. The activity generates a straightforward excuse to provide others with information and makes it quite difficult to provide others with inaccurate information. Thus, the activity-based method of establishing a relationship entails the lowest display interaction costs. Broker-based methods of establishing a relationship also make it quite straightforward to display truthful information to others. However, since it is the brokers rather than the actual individuals who display the information to potential targets, there is a greater potential for error if the brokers misunderstand or misrepresent personal information to the target. As a consequence, broker-based methods are subject to higher display interaction costs. Finally, in marketplace settings, there is no personal vouching for information, and so there are strong incentives to display incorrect information to maximize chances of success. As a consequence, marketplaces are subject to the highest display interaction costs.

Now consider search costs. Activity-based methods of establishing a relationship give people an opportunity to observe others as they perform various tasks, interact with people, and deal with and resolve conflict. This vantage point enables great insights into who might be a good fit, a better fit, or a great fit, or not a fit at all! Search interaction costs, then, are usually low for activity-based meet situations. Broker-based methods entail higher search costs, as it is the brokers, rather than the individuals, who are doing the search, raising the possibility that they will omit candidates who would actually be good matches. Marketplaces, not surprisingly, are subject to the highest search interaction costs.

Finally, consider communication costs. Activities make it fairly easy for people to interact. For example, suppose two coworkers want to become friends, but both refrain from directly asking to do so for fear of being rebuffed. Since they engage in a common activity on a repetitive basis, however, it is easier for them to transition to become friends. As a consequence, activities are relatively free of communication costs for establishing new relationships. Broker-based methods also entail relatively few communication costs, as brokers can identify who is looking for a new friendship and introduce interested parties. Finally, marketplace-based processes are subject to relatively high communication costs because the individuals who want to establish relationships need to do this on their own, and to the extent that they are afraid of being rebuffed, significant communication costs are likely to arise.

The assertion that **interaction costs vary across types of people, relationships, and approaches** will form the first of the four main claims I will examine in the first part of the book.

Social Failures and Existing Theory

To understand social failures better, it may help to consider the concept of *market* failures, discussed at length in the field of economics (Bator 1958; Coase 1937; Grossman and Hart 1986; Williamson 1985). There are some basic similarities between the two concepts. Market failures, like social failures, are transactions that do not occur, but would make people better off if they did. And they, too, arise when transaction costs associated with a particular exchange exceed the value of that transaction.

The two concepts are also similar in that economic theory has identified at least four types of transaction costs that are akin to the four types of interaction costs we identified earlier. First, economic theory has argued that transaction costs arise when potential traders are far away from each other and cannot access each other easily. When this happens, there is insufficient breadth of people to trade with in a particular market (Williamson 1996), and traders have to incur a cost to increase it. Second, transaction costs can also arise when it is difficult to display trustworthy information about the quality of goods on the market (Spence 1974). When this happens, traders have to engage in costly actions to signal the veracity of their claims. Third, transaction costs arise when it is hard to search for information about the quality of goods sold (Akerlof 1970). In such circumstances, traders again have to incur search costs to ascertain that the quality of goods sold is commensurate with their price. Finally, transaction costs arise when traders communicate and bargain with each other to establish terms of trade and later enforce them (Grossman and Hart 1986). These four types of transaction costs correspond to the four types of interaction costs I outlined earlier.

The two concepts differ, however, in that economic theory has largely focused on economic causes of transaction costs, but has not paid a lot of attention to the social underpinnings of such costs. In contrast, the discussion of social failures includes both social and economic sources of interaction costs. It is my hope that future research in economics will address more social underpinnings of transaction costs.

Separately, the concept of social failures is also related to the wealth of sociological research on social exchange. Specifically, social exchange theory, as summarized by Coleman (1990) and extended by Molm (1997), assumes that people possess resources that they trade for resources they need. It then argues that not all mutually beneficial exchanges take place (Marsden 1983), which is tantamount to social failures. Since that theory did not identify the cause of these exchange restrictions, subsequent work sought to fill this gap. Specifically, researchers argued that these restrictions arise when people involved have not previously engaged with each other (Casciaro 2008; Kollock 1994; Lawler and Yoon 1996; Molm, Takahashi, and Peterson 2000), are demographically different from each other (Kossinets and Watts 2009; McPherson, Smith-Lovin, and Cook 2001), or perceive the gains from trade to be distributed unequally (Marsden and Friedkin 1993; Molm 1997; Piskorski and Casciaro 2006). These analyses have not, however, provided a unified theory of how these exchange restrictions arise—something I endeavor to offer in this book.

Furthermore, the concept of social failures implicitly underpins many social network theories, which argue that people who occupy a particular network structure will be at an advantage over those who do not (Ingram and Roberts 2000; Powell, White, Koput, and Owen-Smith 2005; Uzzi 1997). To see why, consider that for these theories to hold in equilibrium, it has to be the case that the disadvantaged people cannot easily replicate the network structure of the advantaged ones (Safford 2008; Schrank and Whitford 2013). Otherwise, everyone will have the same relationship structure, and the benefit of possessing it will disappear. However, social failures limit people's ability to engage in all mutually beneficial relationships, and thus stop people from replicating the most beneficial network structures. This allows people in advantageous network structures to retain the benefits of occupying those structures.

This argument is particularly salient for the structural hole theory, which argues that people connected to individuals who do not have relationships with each other are at an advantage over others (Burt 2005). If the theory is correct, then everyone should build relationships with people who are not connected to existing friends. But if everyone successfully does that, nobody will be at an advantage (see Buskens and van de Rijt 2008 for a formal proof). It is only when social failures exist and some people cannot form networks rich in structural holes that the benefits of this network structure can persist.

Finally, the concept of social failures is directly related to accumulating evidence on the apparent poverty of social exchanges and relationships in the United States. For example, McPherson, Smith-Lovin, and Brashears (2006) have reported that up to one-quarter of Americans lack a person to confide in. Putnam (2000) argued convincingly in *Bowling Alone* that the quality of interpersonal relationships is declining and that substantial opportunities exist to improve the state of social relationships in the United States. Social failures are a strong undercurrent in this work. With a robust understanding of the causes of these trends—and ongoing research on how those causes evolve—sustainable solutions may come into focus more readily.

Social Solutions

To alleviate social failures we use social solutions. These solutions should provide a set of four social functionalities, each of which acts to reduce breadth, display, search, and communication interaction costs. These functionalities can be easily understood within the context of, say, a dating site. Functionalities that ensure that a lot of people who are actually interested in dating show up to the dating site fall under the breadth category. Those that collect personal information about these individuals and then display it publicly for others to see are display functionalities. The ability to search for and view these data is a search functionality. And the ability to interact privately is a communication functionality. Put together these functionalities form a social solution.

There are two important considerations in building effective social functionalities. The first is to ensure that the functionality reduces both the economic and the social causes of the interaction cost. The second is to be mindful that the social functionalities seeking to reduce some interaction costs can introduce new interaction costs that did not exist beforehand. I expand on these assertions below.

REDUCING BOTH ECONOMIC AND SOCIAL CAUSES OF AN INTERACTION COST

To see a functionality that solves economic and social causes of interaction costs, consider the ability to search for personal information on a dating site. Such functionality reduces the economic interaction costs related to search, as individuals can cheaply acquire information about numerous others. At the same time, it reduces the social interaction costs related to search by allowing people to acquire this information without having to engage in the potentially embarrassing act of asking for it.

In a less optimal scenario, a social functionality will reduce economic interaction costs but do little to reduce social interaction costs. Consider an emailing functionality on a dating site. The functionality allows people to communicate with each other without being physically present at the same time, thereby reducing economic interaction costs as they relate to communication. It does little, however, to reduce the social cost associated with initiating contact when it is normatively inappropriate to do so, thereby keeping the social interaction costs unchanged. As a consequence, such functionality will not be as powerful as one that addresses both the economic and the social interaction costs.

In the worst-case scenario, a social functionality will reduce economic interaction costs, but will do so by increasing the social costs.

To see how, return to the dating site example and focus on the norm that makes it inappropriate for certain individuals to initiate interactions with others. Within this environment, consider a communication functionality that allows people to indicate interest in starting an interaction without having to write or say anything. This functionality reduces economic interaction costs by allowing people to start interacting without writing long messages. But, it makes the norm restricting contact initiation even more salient, because now people can no longer use text to justify why they initiate an interaction. As a consequence, the social interaction costs might actually increase. When this happens, the functionality will likely facilitate few new interactions.

These considerations are particularly important if only certain groups of people are affected by the normative restrictions. Suppose, for example, that the normative restriction against initiating contact and the concomitant social interaction cost affect only women. If this is the case, men will find it easy to start interactions with women they like, but women might not be able to approach men they like, resulting in more social failures affecting women. A social functionality that effectively addresses the norm, and alleviates both the economic and the social interaction costs, will allow women to start interactions. When this happens, the ability to start interactions is effectively equalized between the two sexes.

In contrast, when a social functionality reduces only the economic interaction costs but does nothing to alleviate social interaction ones, women will still be at a disadvantage. And so, the resulting pattern of interactions will be as skewed as it was without the social functionality. Finally, when a social functionality reduces the economic interaction costs but does so by increasing social costs, women will be at a greater disadvantage. When that happens, the resulting pattern of interactions will be even more skewed than it was without the functionality. Thus, if we care about helping those who face largest problems forming relationships, we need to build functionalities that reduce both social and economic interaction costs.

Indeed, the assertion that **social functionalities have to address both the economic and the social causes of interaction costs** will form the second of the four main claims that I will examine in the first part of book.

BEING MINDFUL OF POTENTIAL NEW AND UNEXPECTED INTERACTION COSTS

When building effective social functionalities it is important to bear in mind that they can introduce new interaction costs that did not exist beforehand. We use the term *derivative costs* to refer to these unexpected consequences. These costs can affect those who were initially the presumed beneficiaries of the social functionality, but they can also affect third parties who do not benefit from the functionality.

To see how some derivative costs arise, consider a "friend" solution provided by platforms like Facebook. On the one hand, such platforms reduce the cost of displaying information to friends and acquaintances. At the same time, they potentially force individuals to disclose the same information to all of their friends, preventing those individuals from portraying themselves differently to different people. Such information may undermine the poster's relationship with some of his friends, creating derivative costs. To avoid these costs, people will limit the type and amount of information they share. Indeed, if these derivative costs exceed the benefits people obtain through the social solution, they will refrain from using the solution altogether.

To see another type of derivative costs, consider a situation in which an individual is in an exclusive relationship with someone, and then, thanks to a social solution, finds another person with whom he is more compatible. Even though this solution has helped the newly formed couple, it has generated derivative monetary and psychic costs for the person who is left behind. Whereas the newly formed couple could in principle compensate the former partner for the monetary costs, it is very difficult to furnish compensation for psychic costs. As a consequence, social functionalities may impose important derivative costs on third parties for which full compensation will not be possible. To prevent that from happening, firms may—and in my opinion should—refrain from providing such solutions.

SOCIAL SOLUTIONS AND TRADE-OFFS BETWEEN THEM

Armed with an understanding of what it takes to provide an effective social functionality, we can focus on effective social solutions which aggregate these functionalities. As I suggested earlier, people vary in the kinds of interaction costs they experience. For example, some people experience significant breadth costs, others experience search costs, and others will be affected by display or communication costs. Some people will experience combinations of the four: breadth, display, search, and communication costs. To ensure that a social solution appeals to the largest possible set of people, it should incorporate all types of social functionalities to reduce all types of interaction costs. If it does so successfully, it will appeal to those people who are affected by individual types of interaction costs as well as to those who are affected by many types of interaction costs.

To see why this is important, consider a social solution that reduces only breadth and display interaction costs, but does little to reduce search and communication costs. Such a solution will appeal to people who are affected by breadth and display costs but relatively unaffected by search and communication costs. It will not appeal, however, to those who experience the latter set of costs. And that gap will provide an opportunity for another social solution—one that minimizes all types of interaction costs—to prevail. Such a solution will appeal to all types of people, and therefore will outcompete one that provides only certain types of social functionalities.

Indeed, the assertion that those **social solutions that combine breadth, display, search, and communication functionalities outperform those that provide only some of these functionalities** will form the third of the four main claims that I will examine in the first part of book.

Having said that, I will argue that the foregoing rule will not apply if there exist powerful strategic trade-offs associated with social solutions. These trade-offs make it very difficult for a social solution to feature a particular type of functionality without undermining the efficacy of other types of functionalities it has. Many such strategic trade-offs exist, and I will dedicate a great portion of this book to documenting them. I start by outlining two primary trade-offs that arise in the process of providing "meet" solutions, and discuss the trade-offs that pertain to "friend" solutions later in the book. **The existence of strategic trade-offs between social solutions will form the fourth main claim that I will examine throughout the first part of book.**

The first strategic trade-off related to "meet" solutions arises between minimizing search costs and minimizing communication costs. To see this trade-off at work, consider a solution that allows everyone to search and access everyone else on a given platform, and compare it to one that allows users to see only a limited set of others. The former solution reduces the search interaction costs more than the latter one does. After all, the more strangers a user can see, the more likely the user is to find people whom the user considers great matches for a new relationship. This solution limits, however, the platform's ability to reduce communication costs. To see why, consider that when every user can search for and contact everyone else, users will be inundated with numerous requests for contact from others. As a consequence, users will be less likely to respond to such requests for contact, and so it will be more difficult for the social solution to reduce communication costs.

In contrast, when the "meet" solution allows users to see and contact only a limited set of strangers, they will find fewer strangers with whom they would like to establish a new relationship. Such a solution will not, therefore, be as effective at lowering search costs. However, since everyone gets to see and contact fewer people, users will also have fewer people contacting them, and as a result, they will be more likely to respond to any requests for contact. So the social solution will do a better job at reducing communication costs.

This situation implies a trade-off in that a "meet" solution that allows everyone to search and communicate with everyone will significantly reduce search costs at the expense of a lesser reduction in communication costs. In contrast, a solution that allows users to search for and interact with only a few others will not reduce search costs much but will have a greater effect on lowering communication costs. This trade-off allows firms to make different strategic choices, which will then attract different types of people. Specifically, those people who are particularly affected by search costs, but not by communication costs, will gravitate toward the solution that does not restrict contact. Those people who are not affected by search costs, but are affected by communication costs, will gravitate toward the solution that does restrict contact. We will discuss this choice in more detail and illustrate it empirically in the next chapter, using OkCupid and eHarmony as examples.

The second major strategic trade-off for companies providing "meet" solutions arises between minimizing interaction costs related to public interactions and minimizing those related to private ones. To understand this trade-off, consider the benefits and the costs of public interaction as compared to private interaction. When two people interact with each other publicly, others can watch that interaction and gather information to help them identify the individuals these others should interact with. Furthermore, many people are more comfortable joining a public conversation than they are engaging in a private interaction with someone they don't know. Finally, some people may wish to engage in public interactions when they want certain others to witness what they have to say, in situations when approaching these particular others privately would be difficult or socially awkward.

Despite these advantages, public interaction has also a number of shortcomings as compared to private interaction. For example, most people are afraid of engaging in a personal public interaction in which they are asking a certain other party for a response. The potential embarrassment if the other person does not reciprocate in kind is offputting. What's more, people who already know each other may refrain from interacting publicly, reasoning that the kinds of things they want to share with friends should not be seen by strangers.

Given that public and private interactions have very distinct benefits and costs, it stands to reason that a "meet" solution could simply offer the ability to interact both privately and publicly. In fact, many do. Some platforms, however, prefer to offer only private interaction ability. This is because when people can interact both privately and publicly there is always a chance that if the private interaction remains unanswered or derails for some reason, one of the parties can publicly lash out at the other, causing the latter embarrassment. Such concerns would be particularly salient in the context of dating, for example. And so, to prevent such situations from occurring, some "meet" solutions may actually preclude people from interacting with each other publicly. We will discuss this choice in the next chapter and again in chapter 4, where we examine it in the context of Twitter, which chose to provide a solution for public and private interaction between strangers.

The Social-Solution Concept and Existing Theory

Just as the concept of social failures bears similarities to the concept of market failures, the concept of social solutions bears many similarities to economic solutions that alleviate market failures. Specifically, a number of papers and books in economics have argued that firms and other organizations, such as governments, can act to minimize economic transaction costs and thus facilitate exchanges that would not occur through markets (Coase 1937; Hart 1995; Williamson 1996). The argument in this book closely parallels that argument; in the same way that organizations can solve certain economic failures, organizations such as LinkedIn or Facebook can alleviate certain social failures.

Social solutions are also similar to economic solutions in that they both generate derivative costs. For example, a substantial amount of literature in economics has argued that alleviating market failures by undertaking them within the realm of organizations reduces the incentives to exert effort (Williamson 1985). If this reduced effort limits the value of the transaction to the point that it no longer makes economic sense, a derivative failure arises (Hart and Moore 1990).

There is, however, an important theoretical difference between the two concepts, and it relates to the ability to compensate third-party individuals for derivative failures. An effective solution to a market failure generates monetary benefits. Since these are easily transferrable, part of them can be used to compensate parties who experience derivative failures and are negatively affected by the solution. As a consequence, an effective solution to a market failure can always make two people better off without making someone worse off. In contrast, an effective solution to a social failure generates social benefits. Unlike monetary benefits, benefits from better social relationships cannot always be transferred to others. Thus, if third parties are affected by a derivative failure, it is possible that they will not be fully compensated. As a consequence, a solution to a social failure may sometimes make two people better off while making someone else worse off.

Equipped with a thorough understanding of social failures and the solutions that seek to remedy them, we can now start testing the ideas proposed so far. To do that, we turn to an empirical study of OkCupid and eHarmony.

CHAPTER 3

"Meet" Solutions

eHarmony and OkCupid

To see the ideas outlined in chapter 2 in action and test their merit, consider the world of online dating platforms. Market demand for such services is huge. In the United States in 2010, for example, there were roughly 90 million unmarried Americans 18 years or older and 40 million of those considered themselves active daters. Roughly 30 percent of people 35 to 44 years of age were unmarried, and 17 percent of all unmarried people were 65 years or older.

To meet this demand, thousands of online dating sites have emerged since the mid-1990s, giving their users unrestricted search functionalities. Most of them failed to gain requisite size and died quickly, but some, such as Match, Yahoo! Personals, OkCupid, and Plenty of Fish, have survived. A smaller set of companies entered the market by giving users limited search functionalities and brokering relationships between strangers. eHarmony, the first such company, and Chemistry, another entrant in this category, are two leading surviving platforms in this segment. By 2013, one in ten Americans had tried online dating, and one-quarter of online daters had met a current or past partner online.[1]

In this chapter, we'll look at how two of these companies, OkCupid and eHarmony, reduced breadth, display, search, and communication costs, and I will explain in some depth my research methods and analysis. Although both companies have survived up to 2013, our analysis will reveal that OkCupid has performed much worse on a number of social and economic criteria than eHarmony. Many of these outcomes can be traced directly to the claims in the previous chapters.

The data in support of these claims encompass qualitative evidence of these companies' strategies and quantitative evidence of user activity on the two platforms. The qualitative evidence encompasses interviews with eHarmony's executives, archival research on eHarmony and OkCupid, and analysis of the companies' websites. The quantitative evidence for OkCupid is based on a dataset I purchased from the company. The dataset documents personal characteristics of 1,804,993 users (1,493,205 of whom live in the United States) who logged in to the site between October 1, 2010, and December 15, 2010, or were visited by another user or received a message from another user. The dataset also contains information on which users viewed or messaged which users. To protect user privacy, the company encoded the data to make it impossible to identify the users in the offline and the online world, which included removing responses to all open-ended parts of the profile and links to user pictures.

The quantitative evidence for eHarmony is based on a dataset I obtained from the company in return for unpaid consulting. For the dataset, I chose a random sample of 1,804,933 eHarmony's heterosexual users who logged into the site during the same time period, October 1–December 15 in 2010, or were matched by the company with others, or were visited by another user or received a message from another user. The dataset also contains information on which users were matched with each other, which ones chose to view the match, and which ones messaged others. As before, all data were encoded to make it impossible to identify the users.

Breadth

Let's start with a brief description of OkCupid, which was launched in 2003 by four Harvard math majors as a platform for heterosexual and homosexual dating. The site did not require that users pay a membership fee, making it easy for users to join and message each other. But this decision forced the company to rely mostly on banner advertising for its revenues. With this business model, the founders reckoned they would need at least eight million users and two million regular daters, who would log in at least once during a six-week period, to deliver a profit. Yet, four years into the company's existence, the site was not even close to approaching these numbers.

In late 2007, the company launched a sister site, CrazyBlindDate. com. Users of that site filled out a set of questions to help match them to other users, and then indicated at what times and in what neighborhoods they would be available for a date. When the site found a match, it would text both parties to see if they were still available. If they were, dates would be scheduled in public venues, and users were given a dedicated text messaging number thirty minutes before their date to communicate with each other anonymously. The setup was catchy enough to attract attention from radio stations, whose on-air personalities talked it up during prime commuting hours.

Despite the initial traction, the CrazyBlindDate site soon fizzled out. However, CrazyBlindDate publicity drew attention to OkCupid, whose number of users started to grow at a much faster pace. Encouraged by the effects of radio on user acquisition, the founders put tens of thousands of dollars into this medium in certain metropolitan areas. Constrained by its financial resources, the company was unable to increase its advertising efforts over time. Nonetheless, the radio advertising attracted the attention of bloggers and other journalists, who fueled word-of-mouth publicity for the site. This allowed OkCupid to become the first link that users saw on Google when they searched on the term *online dating*, which again helped the site acquire users.

In 2011, the eighth year of its operation, the company reached its goal of getting two million regular daters, and was able to generate slightly less than five million dollars in revenue. Banner advertising continued to generate most of the revenue, with the remainder coming from a five-dollar optional subscription that gave members "A-List" status. By comparison, however, OkCupid's top free online dating competitor, PlentyOfFish.com, had 250,000 users logging in each day and revenues of about ten million dollars. Ashley Madison—a site for married people seeking extramarital affairs—claimed to have three and a half times more registered users than OkCupid.

This description of OkCupid's approach indicates that even though the company managed to grow its membership, it did not really have a well-articulated strategy for reducing breadth interaction costs. Instead, it relied on a series of fortuitous events, such as uptake by radio DJs and bloggers, as well as by Google, to help it grow. Reliance on these methods meant that the company took a long time to reach its membership goal, and even then could not become larger than many of its competitors. Clearly, OkCupid could have done much better to alleviate failures related to breadth. Discouraged by the growth potential, the founders of OkCupid in 2011 sold the site to IAC, the parent company of Match, a paid dating site, for less than one hundred million dollars—a small sum given how many active users the site had.

OkCupid's lack of a well-developed breadth functionality becomes even more salient when we compare that platform with eHarmony. eHarmony was founded in 2000 by practicing psychologist Dr. Neil Clark Warren and his son-in-law. The site focused on singles seeking a serious relationship, but for its first nine years of existence, it offered services only to the straight community. (As part of the settlement of a New Jersey discrimination case, it began offering services to lesbian women and gay men in 2009.)

At the beginning, eHarmony grew slowly, but in August 2001, it was featured on a Christian radio program, and subsequently gathered one hundred thousand registrations in just a few weeks. In 2003, the company started to buy substantial advertising time on TV and radio, and by the end of that year, it had three million registrations, of which 40 percent were considered active users.

Each year, eHarmony continued to increase its advertising budget significantly, and by 2011, the company was spending slightly more than 40 percent of its revenue on advertising, to the tune of one hundred million dollars, with 75 percent of that spend going to TV and radio ads. Throughout its history, the company featured the same advertising theme and format—testimonials from happy couples who had found love through eHarmony, in short upbeat segments. For TV ads, the couple was always featured in front of a plain white background and accompanied by Natalie Cole's song "This Will Be." These advertising campaigns allowed eHarmony to persuade more than one million people every year to pay a subscription fee to communicate with other members. More than 60 percent of members were women; and people over age 45 constituted the fastest-growing segment of users.

This brief description of eHarmony's strategy shows that the company took a very methodical approach to reducing breadth interaction costs. It not only spent a lot of money to address these costs but also emphasized final outcomes featuring people who used the site successfully and got married.

To understand the implications of the two companies' choices as they related to breadth interaction costs, I examined user geographies, ages, and heights for the two sites and compared them to the underlying population of single people between the ages of 18 and 65. To do that, I collected data from the Household Relationship and Group Quarters Population table from the 2010 census. Then, for every two-digit group of ZIP codes I calculated how many single people live in that ZIP code group as a percentage of all single people in the United States and how many OkCupid users hail from that two-digit ZIP code group as a percentage of all OkCupid users in my database. I compared these two percentages for every two-digit ZIP code group and found that certain ZIP code groups are vastly overrepresented. Specifically, ZIP codes in Northern California (the 94 group), New York (10), Massachusetts (02), and Washington state (98) had at least twice as many OkCupid users as would be expected on the basis of the number of single people in those ZIP code groups. In contrast, ZIP code groups in Maine (00), Florida (33), Texas (77), South Carolina (29), and Tennessee (38) had at least two times fewer OkCupid users than would be expected on the basis of single people in those ZIP code groups. (Tables showing these results are available online and can be accessed through a link on http://press .princeton.edu/titles/10190.html.)

To better understand the kinds of areas that are over- and underrepresented on OkCupid, I shifted to analysis at the level of the first three ZIP code numbers, and examined the difference between the percentage of users hailing from a particular three-digit ZIP code group and the percentage of single people in that ZIP code group as a function of a number of different explanatory variables. One of the key variables predicting this difference is population density—the higher the density, the more users OkCupid has compared to the single population. The overrepresentation in densely populated areas suggests that OkCupid is attractive in areas where breadth interaction costs are already low. The underrepresentation in sparsely populated areas suggests that Ok-Cupid is not reducing breadth interaction costs in low-density areas, where breadth interaction costs are presumably highest. To make this more specific, I calculated how many additional users OkCupid would need in those underrepresented areas to give users in those areas the same chance of meeting others as users in a proportionally represented state have. That number came out to 250,000 additional users—a large number, given that the dataset has approximately 1,500,000 users in the United States.

To measure the efficacy of eHarmony's efforts, I repeated the exercise of comparing the percentage of all U.S. single people who live in a particular three-digit ZIP code group with the percentage of eHarmony users from that three-digit ZIP code group. The results show very little geographic over- and underrepresentation. If anything, there is slight overrepresentation of eHarmony users in low-density areas. This suggests that eHarmony provides real social solutions by helping people meet in areas where they would otherwise have a difficult time meeting each other.

I repeated this comparative exercise for age and height distributions on the two sites. For age, I calculated how many unmarried people there were in a particular age bracket as a percentage of all unmarried people under the age of 65 in the United States, as reported in the 2010 census. Then for each of the two sites, I calculated the number of people in equivalent brackets on the site as a percentage of all people under the age of 65 on that site and then subtracted the population percentage from the site percentages. As shown in figure 3.1, I found that OkCupid attracts many more people ages 20–39 than would be expected on the basis of the underlying population, but attracts many fewer over age 40 than in the underlying population. In contrast, eHarmony is not very popular with 20- to 24-year-olds. Beyond that age, however, eHarmony

**Deviation from
expected value (%)**

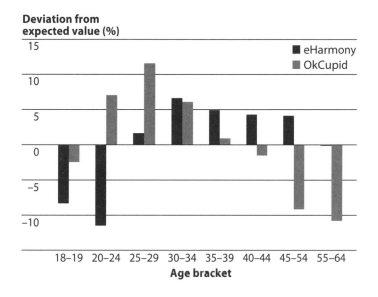

Figure 3.1. Distribution of user ages on OkCupid and eHarmony

boasts a much more evenly distributed population. It appeals to the 25–39 crowd, much as OkCupid does, but it also has more people over 40 than expected on the basis of underlying population, and it has exactly the percentage of 55- to 64-year-olds we would expect. Given that it is presumably harder for people in their forties, fifties, and sixties to find others to date, eHarmony reduced breadth interaction costs for those who face the highest costs of that nature in the offline world.

Finally, I repeated the exercise for user heights. To do this, I calculated how many men there were between 57 and 82 inches tall, in one-inch increments, as a percentage of all men between 57 and 82 inches in height in the United States, as reported in the 2010 census. Then for each of the two sites, I calculated the number of men in equivalent brackets on the site as a percentage of all men between 57 and 82 inches tall on that site. Then I repeated the exercise for women.

The results? As shown in figure 3.2, both sites had fairly good coverage of people across the height spectrum. But there were some interesting differences. Specifically, OkCupid had fewer than expected

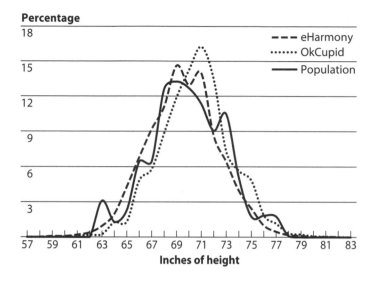

Figure 3.2. Distribution of heights on OkCupid and eHarmony

men shorter than 68 inches, but more than expected men taller than 68 inches. In contrast, eHarmony had more than expected men who are less than 66 inches tall, and women under 63 inches tall, but fewer than expected men taller than 66 inches and women taller than 63 inches. Given that people notoriously exaggerate their height on dating sites, these numbers represent upper-bound estimates of heights on these sites. So once again, we see that eHarmony provided better social functionality by appealing to people who would ordinarily face higher breadth interaction costs in the offline world.

With broad geographic and demographic coverage, it was no surprise that eHarmony had substantial social impact. A set of studies commissioned by eHarmony found that ninety individuals who had met on eHarmony got married each day in the United States in 2005. That number had increased to 236 by 2007, representing 2 percent of new marriages in the country, and again to 542 by 2010, or roughly 5 percent of all new marriages in the United States.[2] At that point, eHarmony claimed to be responsible for almost 25 percent of all of the marriages of people who met their spouses online.

Display

Next, let's tackle display costs—those related to displaying personal information to others. Both sites provided functionalities to reduce these costs, but did so in very different ways. When users first logged into OkCupid, the site asked them to fill out their personal information, which included their self-reported sex, age, location, sexual orientation, relationship status, ethnicity, height, body type, diet, smoking, drinking and drug habits, religion, star sign, education, job type, income, attitudes toward children and pets, and languages spoken. Although users were encouraged to provide these data, they were not required to do so to use the site. Neither was it a requirement that users answer several open-ended questions such as: "What I am doing with my life is . . ." or "I am really good at . . . ."

To help users identify their best matches, OkCupid also prompted them to answer other questions, such as: "If you had to name your greatest motivation in life thus far, what would it be?"; "Which makes for a better relationship?"; "How often do you brush your teeth?"; "Is it a requirement that you communicate every day with your significant other (via phone, text, in person, whatever)?"; and "How often do you keep your promises?" Every question came with a prepopulated set of answers for the user to choose from. For every question, OkCupid also asked the user which answers he or she would accept from potential matches, and how important their matches' questions were to them. Answers to these questions were then used to develop a "match percentage," which steered users to higher-potential partners by identifying those people who gave the right answers to questions the user had deemed most important.

eHarmony also asked its users to provide basic demographic characteristics, lifestyle data, and what they expected from their partner. Unlike OkCupid, however, it required answers to these questions for the user to be able to use the site. Furthermore, unlike OkCupid, which merely encouraged people to fill out answers to questions, eHarmony required that customers fill out a questionnaire as a prerequisite of service. At the time this book was written, the questionnaire contained more than 250 questions that were designed to cover what eHarmony considered the twenty-nine measures of compatibility. Despite its length, eHarmony claimed that fourteen million people completed the questionnaire during the first seven years of the company's existence. Furthermore, unlike OkCupid, which allowed everyone to participate in the service, eHarmony used the questionnaire to screen users for eHarmony, and decide which prospective customers to reject up front. Upon filling out the relationship questionnaire, as many as 20 percent of prospective customers were not offered eHarmony memberships. My interviews with company executives revealed that by 2008, that percentage had amounted to more than one million people who sought membership but failed to become paying customers, and had cost the company an estimated $10 million in membership fees each year. Most people who were rejected either were already married or underage, or had been divorced more than three times.

Taken together, we can see that both companies' up-front requirements sought to reduce display interaction costs. After all, in the offline world, it is difficult and socially awkward to carry around a long list of personal characteristics and show it to every potential partner we meet. Equally, it is difficult to carry the list of one's own preferences and ask others how they fit against it. Both of these platforms solved those failures by asking individuals questions about their personality and what they seek in others, thereby reducing display interaction costs. Between the two sites, however, eHarmony reduced these costs more, in that it insisted that users provide this information to be able to use the site. This approach translated into higher profile completion rates. For example, 60 percent of OkCupid users did not have any pictures as compared to 31 percent of eHarmony users. Thirty percent OkCupid users did not disclose their race online, but only a small percentage of eHarmony users did not do so. Finally, almost 25 percent of OkCupid members did not provide any responses to open-ended questions, while on eHarmony less than 10 percent of members did not provide a short blurb about themselves. This suggests that eHarmony reduced display interaction costs more effectively than OkCupid did.

Search

The differences between OkCupid and eHarmony became even starker as I considered functionalities that reduce search interaction costs. Ok-Cupid's search functionality allowed users to specify characteristics of their preferred match, such as sexual orientation, age range, distance from the user, time of last log in, whether they require that the match have at least one photo posted, and the potential matches' relationship status. The site returned a list of users who satisfied the criteria, along with a mini-profile of each person including a small photograph, the person's username, age, gender, sexual orientation, and relationship status, a four- to five-line "blurb," and a percentage rating (based on the data entered) that indicated the likelihood of a good match.

Users could then click to see the target's full-length profile, which revealed the target's answers to the profile segment questions, and also offered additional information, including the target's height, his or her preferences regarding smoking, drinking, and drugs, and the time of his or her last log in. Users could also click a "two of us" tab that revealed a target's answers to OkCupid questions from the optional questionnaire discussed in the previous section. The user could choose to view all of these data either anonymously or openly. In the latter case, every visit left an electronic footprint informing the owner of the viewed profile, who visited them, and when. Upon seeing who visited them, the owners of target profiles could reciprocate a visit, anonymously or openly, and/or send the original viewer a message.

The ability to search on a number of observable criteria and visit profiles of those who are a potential fit, to acquire more information about them without their explicit permission and potentially even without their knowledge, reduced a number of search interaction costs. After all, in the offline world, it is difficult to acquire information about others. Doing so generally requires an extensive conversation with potential targets. Therefore the site reduces the economic causes of such costs. But it also reduces the social causes of such costs. After all, in the offline world, it is very socially awkward to ask people all these personal questions.

We can actually examine the extent to which this functionality reduces search interaction costs by testing whether it is used by those who are most affected by interaction costs in the offline world. Existing literature suggests that, in marketplaces, people choose partners on the basis of initial attractiveness, which depends on a number of easily observable individual characteristics, such as wealth, education, and personal attractiveness (e.g., Hitsch, Hortaçsu, and Ariely 2010). In contrast, individuals who are less wealthy, less educated, older, shorter, or heavier will find it harder to attract a mate. Those people will also have a hard time with their initial inquiries being rebuffed in the offline world. As a consequence, they are most likely to experience difficulties acquiring information about others. Thus, if OkCupid truly reduced search interaction costs, then the users who were most likely to experience those in the offline world should have been most likely to visit others' profiles on the site.

According to my empirical analyses, that is exactly how it plays out (see models 3.1 to 3.6 in the online appendix). Specifically, I found that shorter men were more likely than their taller peers to view women's profiles. This finding is consistent with the observation that shorter men are likely to be considered less attractive to women (Hitsch, Hortaçsu, and Ariely 2010), and so they more likely experience greater interaction costs gathering information about women in the offline world. Thus, online functionality that allows them to do this freely will be useful to them.

At the same time, I find that taller women were more likely than their shorter peers to view men's profiles. This finding is consistent with the observation that taller women find it harder to attract a mate in the offline world, which implies greater costs of gathering information. Thus, online functionality that allows them to do this freely will be attractive to them.

The same pattern held for age and body type. Both older men and older women (who again experience higher search interaction costs in the offline world) were more likely than younger people to engage in viewing profiles of members of the opposite gender. Finally, OkCupid members who described themselves as overweight were more likely to view profiles of others than those who described themselves as athletic. All of these results suggest that people who encountered the highest search interaction costs offline were most attracted to OkCupid's search functionalities, suggesting that the platform truly reduced these interaction costs.

eHarmony took a very different approach to solving search failures in that it did not allow users to browse profiles at all. Instead, it fed the answers from the relationship questionnaire into a "matching algorithm" that sought to identify similarities between members—focusing on areas such as intellectual ability and emotional stability. Every day, eHarmony generated new matches for its users—up to seven per user per day with the average being closer to three. In most cases, both parties were informed about the match at exactly the same time and could review basic demographic characteristics about each other (in some cases, the match was revealed to only one user). Initially, the company did not even allow members to share their photographs as part of that initial review, though the company has changed its policy since, and by the study period had begun allowing photos to be shared along with basic information. Then, the individuals could decide whether to start communicating. If one of them decided not to pursue the match, both sides were informed and the match was considered "closed."

Since eHarmony gave users far fewer choices, I hypothesized that the company reduced search interaction costs by less than OkCupid did. To understand the effects of this restriction, I chose a day at random and took all of the acts of viewing others on each platform. Then I calculated what percentage of people who logged in that day viewed more than one other user, two users, and so on. The results indicate that there seemed to be very little evidence that eHarmony's restrictive practices made a tremendous amount of difference to how many people users viewed. Roughly the same percentage of users (about 75 percent) viewed more than one user both on OkCupid and eHarmony. Beyond that, the viewing patterns were actually more favorable on eHarmony. Specifically, 50 percent of eHarmony users viewed at least four profiles, while 50 percent of OkCupid users viewed only three profiles. As many as 37 percent of eHarmony users viewed more than six profiles, while only 29 percent of OkCupid users viewed more than five profiles. After that point, the trend reversed—for example, only 10 percent of eHarmony users viewed more than ten profiles, but 18 percent of OkCupid users did so. The crossover point is not surprising—a vast majority of eHarmony users received no more than seven new matches a day, implying that to have more than seven matches to view at one time, the user would have to be absent from the site for at least one day. Taken together, these results suggest that eHarmony's approach did not substantially reduce the amount of viewing. In fact, the median users viewed more profiles on eHarmony than he or she did on OkCupid. eHarmony did, however, reduce the likelihood that users would look at very many profiles.

Subsequently, I examined whether eHarmony's search functionality helped those who were most affected by search interaction costs in the offline world, in the same way OkCupid did (see models 3.7 to 3.10 in the online appendix). As was the case with OkCupid, I found that shorter men were more likely than taller men to view women's profiles. At the same time, taller women were more likely than shorter women to view men's profiles. The same patterns held for age and body type. Both older men and older women were more likely than younger people to view profiles of members of the opposite sex. Finally, eHarmony members who described themselves as overweight were more likely to view others' profiles than those who described themselves as athletic. These results are in line with what we found on OkCupid and suggest that people who faced the highest interaction costs in the offline world were most helped by eHarmony's search solutions.

Even though both OkCupid and eHarmony provided equally powerful social solutions for the person initiating the search, there are reasons to believe that the two sites differed in efficacy from the perspective of the person viewed. Specifically, on OkCupid, users were unconstrained regarding whose profile they get to view. As a consequence, they were likely to gravitate to people who possess external characteristics that are generally considered more attractive, skipping those who could be great matches but do not exhibit those external characteristics. eHarmony, in contrast, decided who could see whom and thus could ensure that everyone on the system was afforded equitable visibility. Statistical analyses confirm these outcomes. When I calculated the number of views obtained by people of a certain height as a percentage of all views received and then compared it to the percentage of people of that height, I found that the values were almost identical for eHarmony, implying that the likelihood that one's profile would be viewed is almost independent of one's height. In contrast, I found that on OkCupid, shorter men, and similarly certain shorter women, would receive fewer views than we would expect on the basis of how many people were in those categories.

Taken together, these results suggest that even though eHarmony provided functionalities that in theory should reduce the search interaction costs by less than OkCupid, in reality the difference between the two sites was not that large. eHarmony reduced search costs as well as OkCupid did for people who are interested in searching only for a few people, and was at a disadvantage only for people interested in searching for many others. This disadvantage was offset to a certain extent, however, by the fact that eHarmony was able to get users to look at a broader variety of users.

Communication

We now turn to understanding communication functionalities for Ok-Cupid and eHarmony. Since both platforms offer fairly complex communication features, we will cover a lot of material in this section.

OkCupid

There were at least two different ways in which one OkCupid user could initiate a communication with another. First, when a user undertook a search for others and identified the target user, he or she could compose an open-text message to that person for free. The sender could not see when or whether the message had been read, but because a sender could see when the intended recipient last logged in, he or she was able to infer whether the target had at least had an opportunity to read the message. If the target sent a reply message, the two parties could continue to interact, and if the online communication was successful, it transitioned to the offline sphere, and in some cases into a successful relationship. By allowing a user to initiate communication even if the recipient was engaged in other activities, this functionality reduced communication costs caused by economic considerations.

Second, users could use a *quickmatch* feature, whereby OkCupid chose a target for the user, and then showed the user a modified version of that target's profile, predominantly showcasing the target's photos. The user was encouraged to rate the target's profile on a scale of one to five. If the user chose to rate the target four stars or above, the system *automatically* emailed the target, informing him or her about the rating. If the user rated a target three or below, the site would not send an email message; it would simply advance the user to another target's profile. Targets who received an automatic email had the option to respond to the user and transition to communicating in the offline world if both agreed to do so. This functionality reduced communication costs caused by economic factors even more. Not only could a user contact another when the latter was unavailable, but it was also now faster to do so, because it was easier to send a message to the target by clicking on a rating button than by composing a message to the target.

Despite reducing communication costs caused by economic factors, neither functionality reduced communication costs caused by social factors. To see why, start with women and consider the normative restrictions they face in romantic marketplaces. Perhaps the most salient norm in this context contends that women should refrain from initiating communication with men (Cate and Lloyd 1992; Dickson, Hughes, and Walker 2005; McElhany 1992; Miller, Perlman, and Brehm 2009). This is problematic when a woman wants to reach out to a man who has not noticed her, but if contact were established, the two would hit it off and would enter into a relationship. Because the woman feels it is inappropriate to initiate communication, she never does so and the mutually beneficial relationship never materializes, resulting in a social failure.

The emailing function does little to suppress the normative restriction on initiating communication. A woman reaching out to a man via email is still sending a very strong signal of interest—something that she might feel she is normatively not supposed to do. As a consequence, she is unlikely to send the message, leading to communication costs not being fixed on OkCupid. The situation gets even worse when we consider quickmatch. Since there is no personal message attached to the initial quickmatch communication, the woman has no means of justifying that initial message. That forces women to be even more direct in their approach than they would be through, say, a regular email message. Thus, a woman is even less likely to message a man after she saw him through quickmatch.

Empirical data from OkCupid are consistent with this claim. First, as shown in table 3.1, even though women viewed more men's profiles than men viewed women's, women actually sent fewer initial messages than men did. Furthermore, regression analysis shows that women were much less likely to use quickmatch feature than men as their preferred mode of initiating contact (see model 3.5 in the online appendix). These differences became even bigger as normative restrictions became even more pronounced. Consider, for example, older women, who are particularly subject to normative restrictions preventing them from initiating contact (Dickson, Hughes, and Walker 2005; McElhany 1992). As I reported in an earlier section, these women were more likely than younger women to look at men's profiles. It is precisely these older women, however, who were least likely to initiate contact with men. Older women were also less likely to use the quickmatch feature, suggesting that it did little to alleviate the normative restriction.

OkCupid's inability to reduce communication costs caused by social factors pertains to men, too. To see why, consider that the emailing functionality lowers the cost for men to message women. Since initiating contact for men is considered socially legitimate, men send many more requests for contact than they would in the offline world. As a result, however, women become inundated with messages, and find it hard to click through and study every profile of every man who sent her a message to see if there is a fit. Being inundated with messages, recipients might have to rely on easily observable characteristics and reply only to those who score high on these criteria. When this happens, men who do not score well on these criteria will see their messages go unanswered, which will lead them to send fewer messages in the future.

Again, empirical data are consistent with this dynamic (see model 3.2 in the online appendix). Specifically, men who are shorter, older, or overweight were less likely to send messages to women than those who

Table 3.1. Sex Differences in Viewing Profiles and Initiating Messages on OkCupid

	Number of profiles of opposite sex viewed	Number of initial messages sent to members of opposite sex
Straight men	26	27
Straight women	35	21

are taller, younger, and more athletic. We could interpret these results to mean that shorter, older, or overweight men are simply less interested in communicating with women. That's unlikely to be true, however, given our earlier findings that shorter, older, and overweight men are actually *more* likely to search for women. This suggests that OkCupid interaction functionalities did less to reduce communication costs—particularly those that arise for social reasons.

The situation gets even worse when we consider the quickmatch functionality. Despite making communication more efficient, this functionality did little to reduce communication costs that arise for social reasons. To see why, consider again the older, shorter, or overweight men who have less courage to message women. As daunting as composing an email message could be, at least men who are not expecting a response can take the time to compose more elaborate messages to improve their chances of receiving a reply. The quickmatch feature, however, sent a standardized message to the target. As a consequence, men who were not expecting to receive a response were not able to write, say, witty text to compensate for their visible characteristics. Thus, they were less likely to message women through this function. Only men who felt that they would obtain a response both offline and online would use this functionality. Once again, this functionality did very little to reduce communication costs caused by social factors. Indeed, my empirical results confirm these predictions. Even though the quickmatch feature increased the rate at which men messaged women, it did so only for men who were young, tall, and athletic, who did the least searching on the platform. Older, shorter, and less athletic men were reluctant to use this interaction feature, even though, as I documented above, they were the most avid searchers.

Both email and automatic messages expressing interest seem like natural choices to get people to interact, and yet neither reduced communication costs that arise for social reasons. To help us understand what kinds of functionalities may actually reduce these costs, let's examine the *quiver* and *visitors* features that alleviated some of the shortcomings of the basic messaging functionalities provided by OkCupid.

The *quiver* feature provided a user with the names and brief bios of three people ("targets") that OkCupid's analysis had identified as having the potential to hit it off with the user. For every target, the site displayed a small photo, demographic information, and a short blurb. Underneath each profile, there were two buttons, one leading the user to the target's full profile, and the other saying "I'm not interested." If the user visited one of the targets, quiver recommended that he or she send a message to the target. Clicking on "I'm not interested" removed the profile from the user's quiver list.

Although it is unclear why OkCupid introduced this feature, there are plenty of reasons to believe that the functionality reduced some of the communication costs caused by social norms that women face. Specifically, it allowed a woman to compose a message to a man and justify doing so by stating that the site recommended that she reach out to him. And in fact, the site would display a short sentence attesting to the fact that the recipient of the message was placed in the sender's quiver. In this way, a woman could downplay the fact that she was interested in the man, and emphasize that fact that she was following the recommendation that the site gave her. By externalizing the decision to write to the man, the woman diminished the perception that she was "violating" the norm on initiating contact, probably making it easier for her to reach out (cf. Cate and Lloyd 1992).

Indeed, data show that women were most likely to message men via the quiver feature (see model 3.5 in the online appendix). Furthermore, older women were particularly more likely to message men they saw in their quiver. Since older women are likely subject to the biggest stigma against initiating contact, this result lends additional credence to the claim that quiver worked by removing social stigma. Finally, as shown in model 3.6 online, men were no more likely to message women they saw in their quiver than they were to message a woman they found elsewhere on the site. The fact that quiver appears to have had no effect for men strengthens the claim that quiver had a positive effect on women's rate of messaging by lessening the stigma, rather than through an alternative mechanism such as giving the user some assurance that she would receive a response. Having said that, it is important to bear in mind that the results also indicate that quiver did not completely equalize messaging between younger and older women. Even though older women viewed more profiles than younger women did, they still messaged less than their younger peers.

Finally, we examine the *visitors* feature, which showed users the identities of others who looked at their profiles and decided not to delete the electronic record of their visit. Even though the functionality was available both to men and women, it reduced the communication costs faced by men more. This is because if a woman visited a man's profile and did not delete the record of her visit, the man could surmise that the woman had ascertained at least a basic level of fit and was sufficiently curious about the man to click through to his full profile. In the words of one male OkCupid user I interviewed: "If I see a woman visited my profile, I am thinking, she saw my picture, and the little blurb about me, and something must have attracted her to me. So chances are, if I write to her, she might write me back." Since the functionality gave an implicit assurance that the sender would receive a response, it was likely to have the strongest impact on those facing the highest communication costs arising out of rejection. Hence, these men were most likely to message a woman after seeing her visit his profile. Indeed, data show that men were much more likely to write to a woman upon seeing her profile in the visitors' list (see model 3.2 in the online appendix). Furthermore, men who were shorter, older, or overweight were particularly likely to write to the women in their visitors' list.

Of course, it is possible that men wrote to women who visited their profiles not because it alleviated concerns regarding receiving a reply, but because these women were in some way better matches for them. If this were true, however, we would also expect that men who visited women's profiles would also be better matches for those women, and so the women would write to those men more frequently too. Our results, however, indicate that this is not the case. Women were no more likely to write to men they saw in their visitors' list than they were to write to a man they found on the site in general, and their level of concern with receiving a reply had little if any effect on their likelihood to write.

Thus, the visitors feature worked at least in part by alleviating concerns of receiving a reply. Having said that, however, it is important to bear in mind that the results also indicate that the visitors feature did not close the gap in messaging between shorter, older, and more overweight men and their taller, younger, and more athletic counterparts.

Taken together, this analysis indicates that OkCupid has a very mixed record when it comes to reducing communication costs caused by social factors, with people who face the biggest obstacles in communicating in the offline world still facing obstacles on OkCupid. Even though the quiver and visitors features provided some help for those who were most affected, they never managed to level the playing field.

eHarmony

eHarmony took a very different approach to lowering communication costs. First, to communicate with one's matches, a user had to buy a subscription (OkCupid was free to use). And, compared with other online personal sites that operated in this manner, eHarmony's fees were high—up to 25 percent higher than other firms' fees. Furthermore, even with a subscription, members were not allowed to communicate with each other directly, but were encouraged to use a formal, guided communication process. Members could elect to bypass this process, but only 10 percent had ever used that option. eHarmony's founders instituted this process because they believed that people, when left on their own, would not have meaningful conversations that would lead to strong relationships. As Greg Waldorf, eHarmony's CEO between 2006 and 2011, put it to me in an interview: "People gravitate to the most superficial questions, like sports or activities, not to what really matters in relationships. Instead, you need to give people a way to talk about deep issues such as children, finances and ideal locations, without the social stigma."

eHarmony's guided communication process had four distinct characteristics. First, members could not contact everyone else on the platform. They could contact only the people who were chosen for them by eHarmony. Second, to initiate communication with one of those people, each member in the pair was asked to select five easy-to-answer questions from a list provided by eHarmony, and send those questions to their match. Once both parties answered the questions, they were asked to exchange their personal list of "must haves" and "can't stands." Finally, they were required to ask one another three additional open-ended questions, either from a list or of their own design, to allow a more detailed description of their values to emerge. Only after that stage could the two individuals engage in what eHarmony calls "open communication," and send each other open-ended, unscripted emails in preparation for a face-to-face meeting. At any point in the guided communication process, either party could opt to stop further contact. And, in fact, most did; only 20 to 30 percent of eHarmony matches ended up in open communication.

Clearly, this elaborate process was not designed to minimize communication costs that are economic in nature. But what about reducing communication costs that arise out of social considerations? To see those, it helps to return to our discussion of how such social costs differ between men and women when it comes to dating. We'll start with women. Recall that women face significant normative restrictions on initiating interaction. eHarmony overcame those restrictions in two ways. First, by not letting users browse among other users, and instead recommending contacts, the site legitimized and depersonalized the choice that the woman made in contacting a man. Second, by requiring individuals to follow a communication protocol, eHarmony further depersonalized the initial exchange of information, allowing women to contact men and communicate with them under the guise of following a process that requires them to behave in a particular way. What's more, the fact the questions were serious, rather than flirtatious, and that they sought to separate men on the basis of values and opinions about lifestyles and choices, put women in a more powerful position. Specifically, it set them up to choose between potential suitors, rather than having to work to woo a man, which is normatively more difficult.

To test these ideas, I studied the likelihood that a random sample of women would message men they received as a match on eHarmony and subsequently chose to view. The results are consistent with this interpretation (see model 3.10 in the online appendix). Specifically, I found that on eHarmony, older women were actually *more* likely than younger women to message men. This is a reassuring finding, given that earlier we found that older women were more likely than younger women to look at men's profiles on eHarmony. These results are particularly powerful when we compare them to data on OkCupid. There I found that older women were *less* likely than younger women to message men, even though older women were actually more likely than younger women to look at men's profiles.

Now consider the normative restrictions faced by men, and recall that they might refrain from initiating interaction because they fear their advances will be rejected, even if in reality they would be accepted. This problem is most likely to occur for older, shorter, or overweight men. As I discussed earlier, OkCupid, which allowed everyone to email everyone else, did not alleviate the problem for those men. eHarmony limited the ability for people to message others. As a consequence, women receive many fewer messages from men, and were therefore more likely to respond. This in turn encouraged the men who are most afraid of rejection to go ahead and send a message.

Data again are consistent with my claims and provide a stark contrast to what we saw on OkCupid. Specifically, on eHarmony, older, shorter, and more overweight men are actually more likely than other men to message women (see model 3.8 in the online appendix). This is in line with what we discovered with respect to viewing behaviors—these men are more likely to look at women's profiles on eHarmony than are younger, taller and more athletic men. In contrast, on OkCupid, older, shorter, and more overweight men are less likely to message women, even though these are precisely the kinds of men who are most likely to look at women's profiles.

Conclusions and Implications

The key objective of this chapter was to bring to life four key claims from chapter 2. First, we saw that various types of interaction costs exist and are not distributed equally. This insight was highlighted when we examined who is most likely to look at profiles of others on dating sites and discovered substantial differences. Second, we saw that social functionalities must attend to both the economic and the social causes of interaction costs. This point became salient when we examined Ok-Cupid and eHarmony, which reduced search interaction costs by allowing people to view personal information about others without having to ask them for it. This point was also driven home when we saw what happens when social solutions fix only the economic but not social sources of interaction failures. Such functionalities will be less likely to facilitate mutually beneficial interactions, particularly for those who need the most. Third, the comparison of the strategies of OkCupid and eHarmony lent some support for the claim that social solutions need to reduce interaction costs related to breadth, display, search, and communication. This was very clear in the case of eHarmony, which attended to all four types of interaction costs. OkCupid, in contrast, had done little to reduce breadth and communication costs. Finally, the comparison of the two case studies helped us identify a strategic trade-off in the provision of social solutions. eHarmony limited its ability to reduce search costs, particularly for those people who want to look for many others, to make sure that it excels at lowering communication costs. This allowed the company to differentiate itself from other solutions, such as OkCupid, which focused explicitly on minimizing search interaction costs but then was unable to reduce communication costs.

CHAPTER 4

"Meet" Solution

Twitter

In this chapter we continue to test the key predictions of the framework, but do so in the context of a "meet" solution that allows for public interaction between strangers.

As I outlined in chapter 2, such interaction offers unique advantages as compared to private interaction in that it helps third parties join conversations with ease. At the same time, public interaction is fraught with interaction costs, particularly when a public interaction between strangers derails and everyone can observe this. People might refrain from public interactions in anticipation of these costs, and if they forecast such costs incorrectly, social failures in public interaction with strangers will emerge.

This opens up an opportunity for a social solution to step in, lower interaction costs, and facilitate mutually beneficial interactions. To illustrate one such social solution, we examine Twitter—an online social platform launched in early 2006. The platform allows Internet users to establish accounts and share status updates up to 140 characters in length (known as tweets). Although tweets could be made private, most users make them public for the world to see. To judge the efficacy of Twitter as a social solution I will use qualitative analysis of Twitter's product strategy gathered from archival research and examination of the Twitter site. I will also use quantitative evidence based on three waves of data collected in 2009, including profiles of more than three hundred thousand Twitter users, information about who they followed and who followed them, and the content of their tweets.[1] The study employed automated and manual techniques to denote whether the users were male (34 percent of users were identified as such), female (41 percent), or corporate accounts (25 percent). It also tracked a subsection of these users for a period of six months to understand how their behavior changed over time. To put these results in context, I will compare them to equivalent results from OkCupid and Pinterest.[2]

Before I start, it may help, however, to clarify an important point that will be salient to readers who use Twitter frequently. On the one hand, such readers are likely to have experienced a situation in which they were exchanging tweets with someone, and all of the sudden a stranger joined the conversation, bringing new content to the discussion. Indeed, many users I have interviewed have told me that this is when they experienced their "Twitter moment" and understood the "true value of Twitter." On the other hand, many readers will also know that this does not happen very often. Instead, most of the activity on Twitter entails broadcasting by a few, consumption by many, and relatively little interaction. These competing views of Twitter can be easily reconciled by making a distinction between Twitter having the *capacity* to facilitate public interaction, and Twitter actually providing the right functionalities to encourage people to engage in such interactions frequently. Indeed, much of what follows will suggest that Twitter has provided few functionalities to encourage people to interact publicly, resulting in relatively few such interactions.

Background

Twitter started out as a podcast directory company, called Odeo, founded by Noah Glass and Evan Williams in 2005. At some point, Jack Dorsey, an Odeo engineer, presented an idea that was unrelated to the company's main business but nonetheless intrigued its leaders. He suggested that Odeo develop a system that would allow people to post short status updates to let their friends know what they were doing. Odeo's leaders liked the idea, and the engineers built a prototype in two weeks. Soon everyone at the company started using it.

When the service was released outside the company, however, users preferred to interact with people they did not know. As tweets could be viewed by anyone, most people found it awkward to have a conversation with their friends when the entire world could be watching. Instead, they preferred to have a public conversation with strangers online, which others could join as they saw fit. And because Twitter displayed tweets as soon as they were posted, it was possible for people who did not know each other to have conversations across the globe in real time.

Breadth

From its inception, the company allowed users to post and read messages through numerous channels. Users could send and receive tweets via the text-messaging functionalities on their cellphones. They could read tweets via a Really Simple Syndication (RSS) feed, or via graphical units embedded on third-party websites. In September 2006, Twitter introduced its Application Programming Interface (API), which allowed third-party programmers to build applications that drew on Twitter's database. Early applications using the API included Twitter Peek, which displayed Twitter updates in a small application window, and Twapp, which sent updates to a user's computer taskbar. By the end of 2009, the Twitter API was used by more than two thousand applications, some of which were sold through venues such as Apple's App Store.

The ability to access Twitter content from numerous sources did not translate into substantial traffic for the company, however. This is because very few people knew what Twitter was back then. The company never advertised, instead it relied on offline and online word of mouth. For example, as early as July 2006, the blogger Om Malik advertised the service on his blog. In 2007, the South by Southwest Interactive Festival in Austin, Texas, recognized Twitter with the "Best Blog" award. Even with all of this publicity, Twitter had garnered no more than eighty thousand users. Clearly, the early fame on the Internet did not allow Twitter to grow big quickly.

The number of users began to grow a little bit faster when Twitter attracted substantial attention from traditional media. For example, when massive wildfires broke out in San Diego in October 2007, engulfing more than three hundred square miles and destroying more than one thousand homes, many people turned to Twitter to report what was happening and to find information from neighbors about what was happening around them. To help people access that information, the *Los Angeles Times* put a Twitter feed on its front page and frequently used the tweets to inform its own reporting. Even then, however, despite these third-party sites advertising Twitter, the site still did not enter the mainstream, receiving only between four hundred thousand and 1.2 million visitors by the end of 2007.[3] By comparison, sites such as www.gun.net, a venue for online discussions about guns, or whatsyourdeal.com, an online forum for shopping coupons, had similar traffic levels.

Twitter's real breakthrough happened when TV finally took note. CNN News in 2008 was the first official broadcast network to do so, when it integrated Twitter into its iReport program, a citizen journalism initiative that allowed people from around the globe to contribute pictures and video of breaking news stories. Then, later in 2008, CNN launched a program called *Rick Sanchez Direct* that featured a ticker of tweets across the screen as host Sanchez commented on them. Many newspapers and other TV media derided CNN's approach, calling it childish, irresponsible, and nonjournalistic. However, the integration of CNN and Twitter worked incredibly well for both entities, allowing Sanchez to become quite a celebrity while generating notoriety for Twitter.

Twitter became a permanent fixture on CNN as the result of a horrific event: the terrorist attacks in November 2008 in Mumbai, India. During the course of the attacks, which lasted several days, users flooded Twitter with updates, including details about activity in the area as well information regarding casualties. CNN constantly broadcast this information on TV, demonstrating the power of Twitter to deliver real-time information from people to people across the globe. After that, the number of Twitter users started increasing dramatically, with five thousand to ten thousand new users joining every day. By March 2009, that rate increased to almost one hundred thousand new users per day, allowing the service to finish the year with a staggering sixty million users (see figure 4.1 for U.S. figures). About half of those users were 18-to 34-year-olds and, in an average month, they accessed Twitter fourteen times and spent seven minutes on the site. At that point, 40 percent of Twitter web traffic came from the United States, followed by Japan, 23 percent; Spain, 7 percent; and the United Kingdom, 6 percent.

This brief description of Twitter indicates that the company did not have an explicit strategy to provide breadth functionalities. Thus, Twitter is very different from eHarmony and akin to OkCupid. However, Twitter differs from OkCupid in that the former accidentally provided a powerful complement to large existing media platforms who took it upon themselves to advertise Twitter. If this had not been the case, Twitter would not have grown to the size it did. This is an important point, as firms seeking to build social platforms to help people meet should not expect to be able to replicate Twitter's reach. Very specific factors explain how Twitter achieved its size, and unless a company can provide a complement to the existing platform with a large reach, it should not count on growing to the size of Twitter as cheaply as Twitter did.

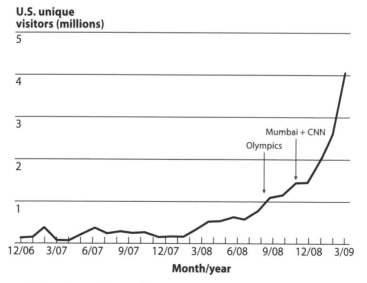

Figure 4.1. U.S. unique visitors to Twitter

Display

To use Twitter a person had to sign up and choose a username, and was then given the option to provide his or her name, photograph, location, URL, and a short bio. These data were then shown on the user's public profile located at http://www.twitter.com/username. My data indicate that approximately 60 percent of users did not upload their picture, though only 20 percent did not provide some sort of name. Twitter did not allow users to provide their sex, age, and other demographic characteristics.

Although Twitter users had limited opportunities to display their characteristics in an orderly fashion for others to see, they could express themselves through tweets. These tweets, most of which did not have an intended recipient in mind, could express daily musings, particular points of view, or links to webpages. As soon as a user posted a tweet, it was displayed on his or her profile page, together with all of the user's previous tweets in reverse chronological order. By default, the tweets were visible to everyone on the Internet (including Twitter nonusers), but users had the option to restrict the visibility of their tweets. My data indicate that fewer than 10 percent of Twitter users kept their tweets private.

Users did not necessarily have to compose their own content. They could forward, or "retweet," others' tweets by prefacing the message with "RT." In response to users' behavior, in 2009 Twitter automated the retweeting process, introducing a Retweet button. People who followed someone who used the Retweet feature would see the original tweet in their timeline, accompanied by a short blurb "Retweeted by [username of the retweeting user]."

The ability to compose and display tweets addressed the economic causes underlying display interaction costs. Specifically, in the offline world, the ability to communicate information to others critically depends on these others being present to receive the information or explicitly visiting the place where that information might be displayed. When these others are absent, they will not obtain the information, which will prevent mutually beneficial interactions from taking place. Since Twitter recorded and archived users' tweets, it allowed others to access information provided by the user at any point, which served to reduce these display interaction costs.

In contrast, Twitter did much less to address the social causes underlying display interaction costs. To see these, consider that when people display information publicly they are often afraid that this information will not garner others' interest, will be perceived as inappropriate, or will be misinterpreted by others. This can then lead these others to ignore the people displaying the information or, worse, criticize them for what they displayed. These concerns become even more pronounced when individuals are asked to express themselves in the public sphere. In a private conversation, it is easier to tailor the information and minimize the risk of displaying something inappropriate to others. That is much harder to do in a public setting, and individuals may prefer not to display anything at all than to bear interaction costs if their public display of information is misinterpreted or ignored. Unfortunately, Twitter has provided no functionalities that would reduce these concerns, and as a consequence it did little to alleviate social causes of display interaction costs.

Failure to do so had concrete implications for the kinds of users who felt comfortable with Twitter's display functionalities. Specifically, users who did not believe that the information they display would be ignored, or perceived as boastful, would use the functionality a lot. In contrast, those for whom these concerns loomed large would refrain from using it. It is actually relatively easy to identify types of users in both categories. Organizations, celebrities, politicians, and other public figures, who are widely known to others, are unlikely to be concerned that their messages will be ignored or perceived as boastful. In contrast, regular people, who are unlikely to be known by others, find it quite difficult and awkward to discuss and display their personal thoughts in public. Indeed, this is exactly the pattern of usage we see on Twitter.

Furthermore, given that there are very few users in the former category but many users in the latter category, we would expect that only a very small proportion of users actually engage in display behaviors. Indeed, data I collected support this claim: almost 40 percent of users in the dataset did not have even a single tweet, and 90 percent had fewer than ten tweets. The median number of tweets was one, but the average number of tweets per user was thirty-three, suggesting a tremendous skew in the data. These numbers suggest that Twitter did a fairly poor job of eliciting self-disclosure from many people who chose to register for the service.

The argument that Twitter did not address the social causes underlying display interaction costs begs the question of what the platform could have done to address those costs. Perhaps the simplest thing that Twitter could have done is to give people more guidance about the kinds of things they should post. That way, users would be less afraid that they were posting things that others would find inappropriate or uninteresting. Although we cannot directly measure the impact this would have on contribution patterns, we can extrapolate from other sites that elicit public information from users but do so in a more guided fashion. Consider, for example, how Twitter compares to OkCupid, the platform studied in the previous chapter.

On the face of it, we would expect that OkCupid would find it harder to elicit public information. To use the site, users had to disclose much more private information than on Twitter and compose complete paragraphs about themselves rather than individual sentences. OkCupid, however, provided users with a much more structured environment in which to provide relevant information. By giving individuals certain prompts, the site freed users from the concern that they would write something that would be deemed uninteresting or inappropriate for potential readers.

The data suggest that such a structured environment does indeed elicit broader display of information. Since OkCupid users did not express themselves in short bits of information, like tweets, I converted the length of OkCupid profiles into tweet equivalents by taking the number of characters in a user's OkCupid profile and dividing it by the average tweet length (roughly 100 characters). I found that roughly 50 percent of OkCupid users provided more than ten tweets' worth of information about themselves. In contrast, only 10 percent of Twitter users wrote more than ten tweets. The data suggest that the more structured environment on OkCupid makes more of its users display more information than Twitter's users do.[4]

Alternatively, Twitter could have encouraged people to express themselves through media other than words and sentences. For example, Twitter could have developed more explicit functionalities for users to share pictures. Pictures convey more information than words and can be interpreted in a number of different ways. This might alleviate the posters' fear that the information they display would be perceived as useless or inappropriate. Furthermore, there are already many pictures taken by others that are available on the Internet. The fact that other people took these pictures would make it less likely that users would be criticized for posting them, and so users should be less afraid of posting those pictures.

Although we cannot directly observe what would happen if Twitter explicitly encouraged people to express themselves through pictures, we can examine Pinterest—another platform that did exactly that. Pinterest gained notoriety in 2011 by allowing people to "pin" or share images that they uploaded to or found on the Internet. Viewers could then click on the pictures and be taken to their source on the Internet. Data on the number of "pins" by users in the study's sample group confirm our claims in the previous paragraph. Consistent with expectations, only 10 percent of Pinterest users had not posted a single pin to their page, as compared to the 40 percent or so Twitter users who had not tweeted even once. The pattern persisted throughout the range of pins posted. Indeed, data showed that 30 percent of Pinterest users had more than one hundred pins as compared to a mere 2 percent of Twitter users who have more than one hundred tweets. Thus, Pinterest, with its emphasis on pictures rather than words, allowed a broader set of people to contribute content.

Search

Not only did Twitter face substantial issues related to eliciting content, it also built very few functionalities that would help users be found by others. Indeed, when Twitter first launched, it did not even offer the ability to search through others' tweets. Instead, Summize, a third-party developer, ended up developing and offering a search engine for tweets. Summize enabled users to type in keywords, and the search engine would then return a limited list of tweets matching those keywords from the previous ten days or so. Each tweet surfaced contained the Twitter handle of the user who wrote it, allowing the searchers to click through to that user's profile and begin to follow that user. In 2008, Twitter acquired Summize, integrated it into its service, and made it available at http://search.twitter.com. At one point, Twitter put the search bar on its web landing page, but then chose to remove it, thereby diminishing the search functionality as a central part of the Twitter experience.

What's more, the tweet search functionality used words, rather than topics of conversation. So if a user happened to select a slightly unusual word to describe the topic of the tweet, for example, *canine* instead of *dog*, that tweet would not be surfaced to others looking for a conversation on dogs. To counteract that language issue, Twitter users themselves developed a tagging system, which used the "#" symbol, followed by the topic being discussed (e.g., a tweet might read, "The #weather in Boston is quite amazing today"). Some users found it easier to search Twitter by topic, since they could simply enter a tag of their choosing into the search engine to find all tweets containing that tag.

But others found it difficult to know what tag to use, or found it off-putting to see hashtags inside otherwise properly formed sentences. Indeed, my interviews with novice users indicated that they felt intimidated by the complex syntax of Twitter. Imagine, for example, what a novice user would make of the following tweet: "I would like to talk more about #socialmediaresearch." This feeling of intimidation reduced the likelihood that a novice user would be willing to tweet.

In 2009, Twitter started aggregating the use of hashtags and listed the most popular ones as links first on the Twitter home page, and then next to the user newsfeed. Users could then click on the links and see the list of recently posted tweets with these tags. My data indicate, however, that only a very small proportion of users included hashtags in their tweets. This suggests that using hashtags to identify overall thrust of conversations on Twitter is unlikely to be representative.

Ultimately, therefore, Twitter's search functionalities were a poor substitute for searching on a site by interest or by other observable criteria. Thus, Twitter's search functionalities provided poor solutions to search interaction costs.

Communication

Users on Twitter could communicate in three different ways. First, a user could express interest in another user by requesting to "follow" that user. If the user requested to follow someone who kept his or her profile public, such a request was approved automatically. Those who chose to make their profiles private had to approve the follow requests. Upon approval, Twitter added the requester's username to the list of the approver's followers, and the approver's username to the requester's list of accounts followed. Both lists, as well as information on the total number of accounts followed, were publicly available for third parties to see. The approving user could, but did not have to, reciprocate the request. Some users were quite happy to do so, while others sought to be followed by many but wanted to follow few in return. Twitter used the follower list to assemble a list of recent tweets from all the accounts the user followed and would show them in reverse chronological order as a newsfeed.

The ability to follow others addresses both the economic and the social causes of communication costs. Specifically, it can be fairly awkward to initiate an interaction with someone for fear of our advances being rebuffed. On Twitter, however, it was possible to start such an interaction without any fear. A user could simply follow another to indicate interest in that user without worrying that the target would refuse to provide the information or reject the advances.

Viewed this way, this functionality shared some similarities with OkCupid's visitors feature we discussed in the previous chapter. Both were unidirectional passive expressions of interest; neither required the recipient to acknowledge it or accept it (with the exception of private profiles); but both gave that person the option to do so. Yet, despite the apparent similarity, data suggest that Twitter's following feature was not used broadly. Take the number of users people followed on Twitter and compare that information with OkCupid's data on viewing others. Approximately 18 percent of Twitter users signed up and never followed anyone. In comparison, only 10 percent or fewer users signed up for OkCupid and yet never examined anyone's profile during the three-month study period (see figure 4.2). This pattern held for the entire numerical scale.

It is possible that the difference in rates at which users followed others on Twitter and viewed others on OkCupid can be explained by the fact that following others requires more effort. But consider following people on Twitter to a more demanding activity on OkCupid, namely, messaging others. Eighteen percent of OkCupid users never messaged anyone during the three-month study period, which is exactly the same number as the percentage of Twitter users who never follow anyone. Progressing down the numerical scale, the difference between Twitter and OkCupid reappears. For example, 41 percent of OkCupid users messaged more than ten others, but only 27 percent of Twitter users followed more than ten people. Given that it is presumably more difficult to compose an email to someone on a dating site than it is to follow someone on Twitter, these results suggest that Twitter did a very poor job of encouraging people to interact on the site in this very light-touch way.

This difference is even more acute when one examines the extent to which users were actually followed on Twitter. Data show that 30 percent of Twitter viewers were not followed by anyone, whereas only 14 percent of OkCupid users had never been viewed by anyone (see figure 4.3). This pattern became even more pronounced when progressing down the numerical scale. Thus, for example, a staggering 98 percent of Twitter users had fewer than thirty followers, but only 58 percent of OkCupid users had been viewed by fewer than thirty people.

Again, the difference could be explained by the fact that following people is more onerous than viewing them on a dating site. But consider messaging behaviors on both sites: only 14 percent of OkCupid members, both men and women, never received a single message, as compared to the 30 percent of Twitter users who were not followed by anyone. The OkCupid percentage was consistently lower than the comparative Twitter percentage across the numerical scale. Once again, Twitter's following functionality did not perform as well as OkCupid.

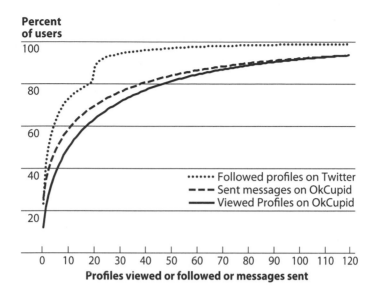

Figure 4.2. How many profiles users followed on Twitter

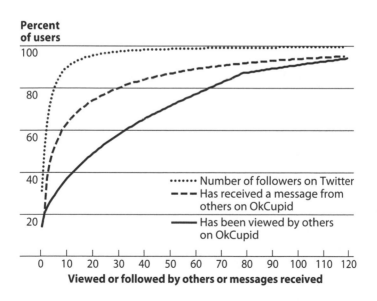

Figure 4.3. How many followers users had on Twitter

The second communication functionality on Twitter allowed users to send messages to each other, and make them visible to third parties. To do that, users started a tweet with an @ sign followed by the username of the person they wanted to address. For example, a congratulatory message addressed to a Twitter cofounder, Ev Williams, would read "@ev Twitter is great!" Users could also place the @ sign in the middle of the tweet when they wanted to reference another user. For example, a user who wanted to tell the world that he is attending a conference with two of his friends might tweet: "Attending a great conference with @klakhani and @guptsunil."

The use of @ messaging was not something that Twitter developed—it arose spontaneously between users. When such messaging became a norm, however, Twitter developed a separate newsfeed that allowed every user to see tweets that mentioned his or her Twitter username preceded by the @ sign. My data indicate that on average over a three-month period, users sent out three @messages to others and received one @message. However, as we have seen with many other Twitter results, fewer than 10 percent of users sent or received an @ message, implying that only a small subset of users felt secure enough to communicate publicly with others while third parties were watching.

Twitter's third communication functionality (known as a "direct" message on Twitter) allowed users to write a 140 character private message to anyone who followed them. As such, this functionality was akin to writing a private message on OkCupid. These messages were accessible to the recipient under a separate tab in the user interface, but were not publicly viewable. I do not have data on the usage of this feature, but it is highly unlikely that users would message others privately at a rate that is higher than following them in the first place. This suggests that private messaging was concentrated in a small number of users.

How Poor Search Functionalities Affected Communication on Twitter

The fact that Twitter provided three different types of communication functionalities, and yet their usage was so concentrated in a small subset of users, begs the question of why this is the case. One explanation lies in the potential for following behaviors to introduce derivative costs. For example, on Twitter, if one user explicitly followed another, then that information was displayed for everyone to see. If these third parties discovered that the user followed someone these parties found unacceptable, they could change their opinion about the user, which could undermine their relationships with the user. To prevent that from happening, it is possible that users limited the number of others they followed.

Although this explanation is plausible, I do not think it is sufficiently strong to help us understand why so many users followed so few others or were followed by them. Instead, I believe that it is the very weak search functionalities on Twitter that explain why so few people used the communication functionalities. To see why, consider that for me to communicate with a user, I first need to be able to find that user. But, as discussed earlier, Twitter did little to help users to find others, which in turn made it very difficult for them to communicate with many others.

I do not have direct data on search behaviors to support this point. This forces me to rely on indirect data to provide some evidence consistent with this assertion. I do this by explaining why women on average had 11.4 followers as compared to 13.4 followers for men (a 15 percent difference), an empirical regularity I detected in the Twitter data. Understanding how this difference comes about will shed some light on the interaction between search and communication functionalities.

There are at least three possible reasons women attract fewer followers than men do. First, women may hold fewer positions of power in society, and as a consequence have less information to contribute. Second, it is possible that women have similar amounts of information, but poor search functionalities make it hard to find women and obtain information from them. Finally, it is possible that women have the same information and it is easy to search for them, but people choose not to do it, possibly due to discrimination.

To understand which of the three mechanisms explains why women are followed less on Twitter, I first looked at whether women contributed less content or were less active. Here, I found that women followed as many people as men, tweeted with the same frequency as men, wrote tweets of similar length, use similar words, and used @messages at the same rate. Thus, the data suggests it is unlikely that women were followed less because they contributed less content.

To examine whether discrimination was at work, I used regression analysis (see model 4.1 in the online appendix), and found little support for that explanation. Users who had their profile more fully filled out attracted more followers, but there was no difference for men and women (even for pictures). Similarly, users who tweeted more got more followers, and that effect was exactly the same for men and women. If anything, women got more followers for using hashtags and links than men did.

Given that women produced as much content as men, and their content production converted into getting followers at least at the same rate as it did for men, we are left with the second mechanism: the difficulty of finding people on Twitter. With poor search functionalities, what probably happened is that people came to the site and chose to follow the people they already knew in the offline world and considered worthy of following. Given that those people in the offline world were likely to be men, men received more followers online. Users could attempt to find women to follow, but given that Twitter offered poor search functionalities, they were unlikely to succeed. As a consequence, they ended up following fewer women. If Twitter developed better functionalities to help people search for content they care about, however, women would get followed more.

In fact, evidence from my empirical analyses suggests that when content contributed by women was explicitly retweeted by others, women gained more followers than men did (see models 4.2 and 4.3 in the online appendix). Similarly, women were more likely to attract reciprocal followers when they followed someone. Both of the findings suggest that when users engaged in activities that compensated for the lack of search functionalities, women did actually obtain more followers. Unfortunately for women, Twitter never explicitly designed its system to ensure that men and women are followed at the same rate.

More broadly, these results underscore one of the key insights established in chapter 2—namely, that for social platforms to be successful they should to attend to all types of interaction costs (unless doing so entails a costly trade-off). Our analysis of Twitter is consistent with this claim. Here, we found that Twitter provided poor search functionality, which severely undermined the efficacy of the numerous communication functionalities the platform offered and thereby limited the success of the platform. This not only limited the scope of people who used these communication features, but it also ended up affecting those people who are having most trouble having their views heard in the offline world.

Conclusions

Taken together, the foregoing analysis lends further credence to the four key claims I made in chapter 2. First, we saw again that interaction costs are not distributed equally—most of us face substantial display and search costs when interacting in public, and a small minority of people, such as celebrities, experience them much less. Second, we saw that social functionalities must attend to both the economic and the social causes of interaction costs. This became particularly important when we examined display functionalities on Twitter, which did little to address the latter class of costs and thus led very few people to display content. Third, as I discussed in the previous paragraph, we saw that social solutions need to reduce interaction costs related to breadth, display, search, and communication. Finally, our analysis highlighted the presence of strategic trade-offs in the provision of social solutions related to "meet" solutions. Given the liabilities of public interaction I described, it would be hard to believe that platforms such as eHarmony or OkCupid would benefit from introducing public interaction functionalities. The presence of this trade-off allows the two types of platforms to remain distinct and prevents each from incorporating features of the other.

In addition, the analysis reveals concrete insights into Twitter as a company. On the one hand, Twitter is clearly a success story, which culminated with the company filing for an initial public offering (IPO) in the fall of 2013. Without a doubt, the platform has also had an incredible impact on many people, helping them coordinate uprisings against repressive regimes, warning them of impending dangers, and providing them with an invaluable news source. On the other hand, even as the company was ready to sell its stock to the general public, its own pre-IPO documents as well as industry observers pointed to three types of strategic problems that Twitter needed to address to become a true success in the long run.

First, despite its initial success, Twitter experienced problems maintaining its user growth rate. Indeed, the company had set itself an internal goal of attracting more than 400 million members by the end of 2013, but in the fall of 2013 it only had 240 million users. Although there are many potential explanations of why Twitter has experienced much slower growth than it expected, our description of Twitter's breadth strategy underscores one: Twitter was lucky to acquire traffic from large media platforms despite having no explicit strategy. Now that these media have delivered all the members they could, Twitter again found itself with no explicit breadth strategy, which limited its growth. Without developing one, it is hard to see how the company will restart its aggressive growth.

Second, company insiders report that Twitter suffers from a significant churn problem, with users sampling the product but then leaving, never to return. Once again, this problem is easily understood within the context of our discussion of display and search functionalities. Given how hard users find it to disclose information about themselves, and how difficult it is for them to find relevant others on Twitter that they cannot find elsewhere, it is not surprising that users test the site but then leave it quickly. Again, unless Twitter fundamentally changes the way in which users display and search for information, it is hard to believe that churn problem will go away quickly.

Finally, Twitter faces the problem of generating significant revenue per active user. In the last half of 2012 and first half of 2013, the company's made slightly in excess five hundred million dollars, or roughly seventeen cents per active user per month. With such low revenues per user, Twitter clearly could not be considered a runaway monetization success, and simple analysis reveals why. Take Twitter's ability to monetize commercial advertising on the site, which the company started doing by having firms pay to make sure that users are exposed to those firms' tweets. Even though firms find this feature attractive, they are unwilling to pay much for it because they cannot easily target the advertising to the right users. That is not because Twitter could not build targeting functionalities; instead, it has to do with the fact that Twitter simply does not possess the requisite data to target those users. Twitter has very little data about user demographics or interests. Furthermore, most users contribute so little content about themselves that it is hard to figure out what users are interested in. And given the poor search capabilities, most users end up following the same types of accounts, making it difficult to infer their true preferences.

Of course, Twitter could have been making money on other functionalities, but this is hard, too. Consider the possibility of using Twitter to perform data analytics to reveal what products people like, predict election results, or help people better understand economic drivers. Indeed, a slew of companies have already emerged promising exactly that on the kind of publicly available data I used for this chapter. Twitter is charging these companies for these data. Before we believe that companies will pay for it in the long term, however, we better believe that Twitter data are representative of the underlying population or at least the direction of bias is known. Unfortunately, with so few people contributing content to Twitter, and the majority of tweets being concentrated in a minority of users, it is very difficult for the company to make this claim credible. This is perhaps why, for every academic paper suggesting that Twitter can predict economic outcomes of interest such as ticket sales, many others show that Twitter's ability to predict anything of interest is low. With this in mind, it is clear that the company will have to continue to evolve its product to ensure that it can monetize its customer base.

CHAPTER 5

"Friend" Solutions

Facebook and mixi

In chapter 2, we introduced a general framework for understanding social failures and social solutions, and in chapters 3 and 4 explored it in detail in the context of meeting strangers. In this chapter, we examine "friend" social failures and solutions that arise when interacting with people we know. To do that, we examine various interaction costs that arise in such relationships and consider them in the now-familiar categories of breadth, display, search, and communication. For each category, we examine how to build functionalities to address interaction costs, examine the kinds of strategic trade-offs that arise in building these functionalities, and illustrate these considerations using data from two "friend" solutions: Facebook and mixi. These two platforms made very different strategic choices and ended up with very different outcomes. I'll review them briefly here, before we take a deeper dive.

Facebook was launched in February 2004 by Harvard undergraduate Mark Zuckerberg and two of his roommates as an alternative to Harvard's printed student directory. As Zuckerberg explained the site's main premise: "People already have their friends, acquaintances, and business connections. So rather than building new connections, what we are doing is just mapping them out." Within a month, nearly three-quarters of the students at Harvard had registered, and Zuckerberg's sights were set on expansion. Four months after its launch, Facebook was serving about thirty college networks and 150,000 users. In 2005,

Facebook expanded to high schools, and by the end of that year, 5.5 million users signed up. Subsequently, Facebook allowed people with work emails to sign up, and then allowed everyone on the platform.

By May 2007, Facebook had 27 million users, and by the end of October 2008 that number had grown to about 125 million. It reached 175 million by February 2009, 400 million by early 2010, 800 million by September 2011, and 900 million by March 2012. At that point, more than 55 percent of the users were female, and 80 percent hailed from outside the United States. Almost 45 percent of these users visited the site at least six times a week, and 55 percent accessed the site through mobile devices. In 2012, the company went through its initial public offering. A month after that event, its market capitalization was $60 billion. That number dropped to $45 billion, before reaching more than $130 billion in the fall of 2013.

mixi traces its origins to 1997, when Kenji Kasahara, then a 22-year-old student at the University of Tokyo, started an online job-posting site called "Find Job!" The site enjoyed initial success but also drew the attention of large, established offline recruitment companies. As those organizations entered the online market, the company quickly started facing stiff competition. Seeking new opportunities, Kasahara turned in a different direction, morphing Find Job! into a "friend" platform that launched in the same month that Facebook did, February 2004. The new site's name stood for "mix" (interact) and "i" (person), and was pronounced "miku'shi" in Japanese. mixi insisted that new users could join only if they were invited by existing users and possessed a Japanese phone number, thereby effectively precluding any growth overseas. Most users accessed the site through mobile devices. Indeed, in early 2005, some nineteen million people, or roughly 25 percent of the Internet-using population in Japan, were accessing the Internet exclusively through mobile devices—an unusually high number for a developed country at that time.

By the late summer of 2006, the site had more than 7 million users, at which point the company offered its shares on the public market at a valuation of almost two billion dollars. mixi continued to grow, reaching 11 million users in 2007, and 21 million users (or around 20 percent of Japan's population of Internet users) by the end of 2010.

By mid-2012, however, the number of active users had dropped to 15 million, at which point the company was valued at $251 million, or roughly $16 per user. That year Facebook also surpassed mixi in terms of the total number of users in Japan.

Clearly, the two companies experienced very different outcomes. In what follows, we will draw on the framework established in chapter 2, and apply it to "friend" platforms to help us identify the root causes of the difference. As we do this, we will rely on qualitative data regarding the companies' choices and quantitative data documenting user behavior. The quantitative data for mixi came from the company, and comprised a list of all clicks from all the users who logged into the site during a six-day window in October 2010. These data were complemented with data on all online relationships between all mixi users, as well as all users' demographic data. These data were unique in that they covered both PC and mobile traffic, offering visibility into the differences in behaviors of users sitting in front of their machines and those on the go. I obtained these data from the company in a format that protected users' identities. The quantitative data from Facebook comprises public-source data compiled by compete.com and a detailed dataset, collected with Jerzy Surma of the Warsaw School of Economics, that tracked Facebook use among 220 members who were university students and graduates in and around Warsaw, Poland. Although the latter data are not representative of the overall Facebook population in that users in this sample are more likely to produce content, as I will discuss later, this bias ultimately provides further support for many of our findings.

Breadth

Breadth interaction costs in existing relationships arise when two people would benefit from interacting with each other, but rarely come into contact with each other. The primary economic costs related to breadth are distance and busy schedules. Social costs span a wider spectrum of possibilities. For example, they arise when someone believes that his acquaintances no longer find him interesting to talk to. In other cases, people might refrain from connecting with others because they want to reestablish only a casual relationship and are afraid that their attempts at connecting will force them into repeated interactions. Finally, people may refrain from reconnecting with friends when they suspect that those friends might be upset that they have not been in touch for such a long time. These concerns are particularly likely to arise between family members, or when the relationship between the two people in question used to be strong at some point.

To alleviate these costs, "friend" solutions allow people to articulate their relationship with others, usually by having one person initiate the online relationship and the other person approve the request. Subsequently, each person would then be privy to more information about the other person than they could see before the connection was established. Establishing a connection in this way does not force individuals into an interaction. It merely sets the stage for people to interact with each other, which could then result in an interaction. Importantly, this type of connection also does not force individuals to continue their interactions indefinitely. Instead, individuals can come in and out of the interaction as they please.

There are substantial benefits to building social functionalities that facilitate maximum breadth. First and foremost, "friend" solutions with large breadth will grow faster. This is because "friend" solutions grow when users invite their friends to join the platform. When the solution is narrow in breadth, and people interact with only a small number of close others, they will invite only a few other people. Furthermore, since a user's closest friends probably know one another, they will have very little need to invite new people. In contrast, when the breadth functionality makes people connect to numerous others, every user can invite many new users to the platform. Those who accept these invitations will in turn invite their friends and acquaintances, most of whom will not be friends of the original inviter, resulting in much faster growth.

These differences were salient for Facebook and mixi. For example, Facebook was created in a university environment, where users connected to people they know, as well as to mere acquaintances who attended the same university. As the site opened up to everyone, the company embarked on a strategy to encourage users to increase the number of friends they had. For example, every time someone became online friends with someone else, that information would be quickly disseminated to those users' friends, who would then often request to establish a link to these new connections, too. The company also analyzed the structure of connections between its users and, using the principle that people who have many friends in common are likely to know each other, recommend new relationships. Facebook also offered users the ability to upload their address books, thus helping the company to identify people they already knew on the site. Once Facebook gathered enough email addresses, it was able to help users who had recently signed up by scouring those users' email addresses in the address books of others and recommending whom to friend.

The mixi site took a completely different tack, and suggested that people establish relationships on the site only with their closest friends. For this reason, mixi's leaders did not engage in many online link-building strategies. Furthermore, the site did not require that users display their real names or use their real pictures (and many users indeed did not). This identity obfuscation allowed users to prevent acquaintances from finding them, and thus avoid a potentially embarrassing situation in which someone could find them and issue a friend request, thereby pressuring them to accept an online relationship they would rather not form.

These differences translated into very tangible network size differences. For example, on Facebook, the average user had 190 online relationships in 2011,[1] but on mixi that year, an average user had only 27 relationships. Furthermore, only 10 percent of all Facebook users had fewer than 10 connections (Ugander, Karrer, Backstrom, and Marlow 2011), while on mixi almost 50 percent of users had fewer than 10 ties. Facebook users also had fewer friends who were friends with each other. There, only 12 percent of possible relationships between friends existed (Hampton, Goulet, Marlow, and Rainie 2012), as compared to 35 percent on mixi. Given these numbers, it is not difficult to see why Facebook was able to grow so much faster than mixi.

Facebook and mixi's breadth strategies also had substantial effects on the sites' geographic coverage in their countries of origin, both in terms of percentage of Internet users in a particular area who used the service and in terms of the average number of online friends that users had across different areas. My own research indicates that in the first couple of years of their existence, both Facebook and mixi had low penetration rates in areas of low population density, and users in these areas had fewer online friends. By 2011, however, Facebook had reached fairly equal penetration across the U.S. states and users' number of on-line friends had begun to equalize regardless of the population density in that state. In contrast, mixi's penetration and the number of online friends across different prefectures was still tightly correlated to the population density in any given prefecture in 2011.

For example, users from the Tokyo area (with more than 5,500 inhab-itants per square kilometer) accounted for 18.5 percent of mixi users, but only 12.8 percent of the Japanese population of Internet users. This means that mixi had almost 50 percent more users from Tokyo than one would expect if mixi had equal rates of penetration across various prefectures. Furthermore, mixi users in the Tokyo area had as many as 35 more friends than did users in prefectures with the lowest average number of online friends. The Kyoto, Osaka, and Hyogo prefectures (with an average of 1,145 inhabitants per square kilometer) also had 20 percent more mixi users than would be expected on the basis of equal penetration. Users in these prefectures had an average of 17 more friends than did users in prefectures with the lowest average number of online friends. Finally, users who lived in prefectures such as Shimane, Nagano, Akita, and Iwate (all of which had fewer than 170 inhabitants per square kilometer) had only two-thirds the number of connections one would expect if mixi had equal rates of penetration across various prefectures.

To understand why, consider the relationship between popula-tion density and relationship strength in the offline world. For two people to be close friends with each other in the offline world, they generally need to spend a fair amount of time with each other. But in areas with low population density, there are fewer opportunities to meet people in the offline world, which will lead to fewer close relationships in these areas (Simmel 1970; Fischer 1973). By contrast, people do not need to spend a lot of offline time together to be ac-quaintances. So even people who live in sparsely populated areas can still have as many acquaintances as those in densely populated ones, as long as they establish contact with people who do not live close to them.

This simple mechanism helps us understand why we observe an association between population density and site growth on mixi, but not on Facebook. On mixi, users by and large invite only their closest friends. Since people in low-density areas have fewer close friends, they will make fewer strong connections in the online world. In contrast, on Facebook users become online friends both with close friends and with acquaintances, so, as Facebook continued to grow, those in low-density areas were able to reach out to increasing numbers of acquaintances outside their areas, and achieve a similar number of online connections as did Facebook users in high-density areas.

This dynamic also helps us understand why, on mixi, low-density areas retained lower penetration, but on Facebook, penetration equalized between low-density and high-density areas. Consider that sites like mixi and Facebook grow because existing users invite new users, or new users join in expectation of interacting with existing users. On mixi, because users ask only their closest friends to join, users in low-density areas will probably invite only a few new people to join their networks each year, while those in high-density areas will invite more, thereby creating disparity between the two types of areas. In contrast, on Facebook, where users interact with closest friends and with acquaintances, users in low-density areas will invite or be invited at similar rates as those in high-density areas, thereby closing the gap between the two types of areas.

Despite all of these benefits, there are also a number of liabilities that arise when the social functionality has substantial breadth. Consider what happens when the functionality starts off facilitating relationships only with one's closest friends, but then expands to include coworkers, acquaintances, and other people we do not know well. Once that expansion occurs, the nature of the functionality changes dramatically, because the kinds of interactions we are willing to have with close friends are very different from the kinds of interactions we are willing to have with acquaintances. As a consequence, such functionality will prevent certain types of interactions that we might want to have with our closest friends. Put differently, providing narrow breadth functionality will address one set of interaction costs related to the close interactions we have with close friends. Providing substantial breadth functionality will address interaction costs related to acquaintances, but will not address those related to close interactions. I discuss these considerations in the next section.

Display

Display interaction costs arise when people face difficulties conveying information to others. These costs have their roots in both economic and social reasons. The economic reasons for display costs center around the difficulty of conveying information to others when those others are not available to see the information. The social reasons stem from a single overarching norm, according to which we should interact in a way that benefits others. This general norm prohibits, for example, boasting or talking about oneself, unless doing so directly benefits the person we are talking to (Goffman 1967). Instead, it is much more acceptable to behave in a way that benefits that person (Collins 2004). It is exactly for this reason that certain social interactions begin with a gift, individuals paying compliments to others, or telling them information that is directly relevant to them.

Although this norm prevents many unnecessary interactions, it can also lead to social failures. This is particularly when both sender and the receiver would stand to benefit, but the sender does not know it, and therefore anticipates incurring display costs related to violating the norm. Take, for example, a situation in which you are discussing your most recent vacation with your friends. Some of your friends may actually wish to find out more about your holiday than you have shared, but you might not be aware of their desire. As a consequence, you might withhold information for fear of coming across as boastful and incurring interaction costs. Your mistaken belief that your friends are not interested in particular information will lead to a social failure.

Display functionalities reduce these interaction costs by allowing people to post content on their own profile, which their online friends can then come and see. We will refer to this as posting primary content. This simple solution addresses the economic causes of display costs by allowing people to display content to their friends without their friends physically being there. Furthermore, it alleviates the social concerns underlying display interaction costs. To see how, recall that these costs arise because individuals believe that they will display information that others would not want to see. With this functionality, individuals simply put the content out there, and then interested parties can choose to acquire it or not. It is impossible, in this scenario, for anyone to impose information on another and commit the mistake of conveying information to someone who does not want to see it. This lowers the display interaction costs.

It is also possible for display functionalities to reduce display costs by helping people comment on their friends' primary content, either by writing something about it or by "liking" it. We will refer to such content as *secondary content*. Perhaps the most important function of secondary content is to validate that the original information was useful to those who saw it. This assures the person who shared the information that he or she did not violate the norm, and should therefore continue to share more information with friends.

As much as functionalities for displaying primary and secondary content lower interaction costs, they can also generate derivative costs. To see these costs, consider a set of pictures you took on Friday night while having fun with your friends. You would probably like your closest friends to see these pictures, but you would not want some of your work-related acquaintances to see them because in those relationships you are supposed to represent yourself only as a committed professional who would never do anything to taint your employer's reputation. If you believe that the negative costs of making that content available to work acquaintances outweighs the benefits of displaying it to friends, you will probably refrain from sharing it altogether.

Another set of derivative costs arise because posting primary content can give rise to secondary content, which is then visible to the friends of the original poster. Suppose you wanted to share a particular picture from your childhood, but you are afraid that some of your friends may provide secondary content in the form of inside joke commentary. Although the commenting friends may wish to use your post as an opportunity to reach out to you, their commentary may be interpreted incorrectly by third parties, which may then negatively affect your relationship with those third parties. Anticipating the possibility of these derivative costs, you might withhold contributing the photo in the first place.

The magnitude of these derivative failures depends on the type of the breadth functionality. On social platforms with narrow breadth solutions, it is unlikely that any primary content they will contribute, or secondary content provided by online friends, will be deemed offensive to anyone. This will limit derivative costs introduced by the display functionality. In contrast, derivative costs are more likely when the platform offers great breadth, where the average users' online network is bigger and more varied. In this case, it is more likely that some primary content will be appropriate for some online friends but not others. It is also more likely that the secondary content provided by some online friends will be offensive to other online friends, leading to more derivative failures.

These considerations are relevant to mixi and Facebook as both provided display functionalities that allowed users to express themselves to others by uploading pictures, posting status updates, and writing diaries or notes. But users of each site behaved very differently in displaying content.

Some of the differences in display behaviors could be attributed to culture. For example, Japanese norms of humility made it less likely that mixi users would post pictures of themselves, either as their main profile picture or elsewhere. Instead, they posted pictures of objects, animals, or buildings they liked or visited. Indeed, the effects of this cultural norm were quite pronounced: as many as 66 percent of mixi users in the research sample did not have a single picture on their profile and only 22 percent had more than 10 (the "top 10 percent" in terms of posting pictures had 75 pictures or more). In contrast, almost all Facebook users in the research sample had posted at least one picture, 80 percent had posted more than 10, and the "top 10 percent" in terms of picture posting had 630 pictures or more.

Other differences could be more clearly attributed to the fact that mixi provided a narrow breadth functionality, while Facebook provided wide breadth. This difference was particularly salient for posting written text. Specifically, on mixi, during the six-day observation period, roughly 10 percent of users posted at least one status update or a diary (generally a longer contribution). On Facebook, during the same six-day window, only 5 percent of users contributed written text. Furthermore, almost all of the written content on Facebook came in the form of short status updates. Only 30 percent of posts on mixi were short status updates, however, with diaries comprising the remaining 70 percent. As noted earlier, these diaries were generally longer posts, often spanning many paragraphs and documenting in detail what had happened at work, home, or school, what the writers had for dinner, what they bought, or what their other friends did. They often contained very personal content, which included accounts of setbacks or problems users were experiencing, together with implicit or explicit requests for help from friends.

It is tempting to attribute the popularity of diary writing on mixi at least in part to Japanese culture. Public "journaling" has been a fairly common practice in Japan for centuries, with many people swapping diaries with others. Empirical evidence suggests, however, that the fact that only a restricted set of people saw these journals was a key reason why users posted them. Specifically, data show that mixi users with more friends actually contributed fewer, rather than more, diaries. Furthermore, when a user already had a lot of friends, every additional friend made it even less likely that the user would contribute a diary. The magnitude of this negative effect was partially attenuated when the user had friends who knew each other. Even if all of the user's friends knew one another, however, adding a new friend who knew the user's every online friend still reduced the likelihood that the user would contribute more impersonal diaries. In contrast, mixi users with more friends posted more impersonal content, such photos and status updates (see models 5.1 to 5.4 in the online appendix).

I found further evidence linking how comfortable users were displaying private content and how many people could see that content on Facebook. There, I found that users with larger networks post more status updates, pictures, and links, but as soon as they surpassed a particular number of friends, usually in excess of two hundred, the addition of every new online friend made them display less content. This is consistent with our earlier claims. Although having many friends encourages Facebook users to share status updates and pictures, passing a certain threshold in terms of number of friends results in users sharing less information (see models 5.11 to 5.14 in the online appendix). Furthermore, the inflection point at which Facebook users begin to hold back on their posts depends on the nature of that content, as illustrated schematically in figure 5.1. Specifically, as users' total number of friends increases, they contribute less written content in the form of status updates. As the number of friends increases even further, users start posting fewer pictures, but they still continue to display more links. Finally, as the number of friends increases even further, users post fewer links to external sites.

I found the same pattern of results for secondary content. During the same six-day observation period on Facebook and mixi, only 4 percent of Facebook users contributed secondary content. In contrast, 16 percent of mixi users contributed secondary content. Furthermore, when I examined the entire history of Facebook posts in the sample, and tracked how many of those posts received a comment, I found that almost 40 percent of written posts received no comments or likes from

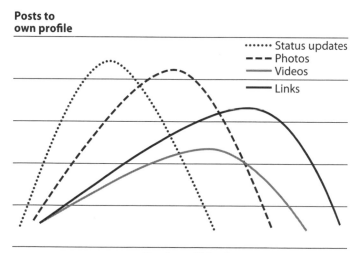

Figure 5.1. Posting different types of content on Facebook

others, 15 percent received one, 10 percent received two, 7 percent received three, and the remaining 28 percent received four or more comments or likes. In comparison, on mixi, only 30 percent of written posts, including diaries, received no comments or likes from others, 22 percent received one, 12 percent received two, 10 percent received three, and the remaining 26 percent received four comments or more. And all of these comments on mixi happened within six days of posting the content! Clearly, users on mixi posted more secondary content than Facebook users did.

I also found that secondary content was more important to the production of primary content on Facebook than it was on mixi. To see why, consider two mechanisms through which secondary content, such as comments and likes, will encourage users to write more. First, users may get personal utility from obtaining affirmation from others (an effect that one would expect to be quite similar on mixi and Facebook). Second, by obtaining comments and "likes" from others, users may become more secure that the information they are providing is truly useful to their friends. To the extent that people care about not violating the norm of conveying information that does not benefit their friends, knowing that the information is actually valuable to their friends will increase the likelihood of providing content. That's likely to be more important on Facebook, where users have much bigger networks and therefore will be more afraid of posting content that may be considered inappropriate. So, for that reason, one would expect that secondary content would be more important to eliciting primary content on Facebook than on mixi.

Indeed, results from both sites are consistent with this claim (reported in models 5.1 to 5.4 and 5.11 to 5.14 in the online appendix). Both mixi and Facebook users who received more comments on the content they posted were more likely to post content in the future. Furthermore, results indicate that the effect of secondary content on eliciting primary content was stronger on Facebook than it was on mixi. This meant that the same number of comments on a post of a Facebook user generated a much larger number of comments in the future than it did on mixi.

Taken together, this pattern of results suggest that display functionalities are subject to a trade-off between "friend" solutions that provide narrow breadth functionalities and those that provide wide breadth functionalities. Specifically, when the social solution provides narrow breadth functionality, then display functionalities are capable of eliciting very personal content. As the size of the network grows, however, the relevance of personal content such as status updates and personal pictures declines, leading users to post less of it. This is less likely for "recycled" content, such as links to other sites, which is much less personal in nature. But even that approach has its limits, and the amount of this impersonal content displayed shrinks as online network size increases too much.

The existence of the trade-off requires that social solutions offering significant breadth supply additional functionalities such as "privacy controls" that allow users to display their primary content to some of their friends, while hiding it from others. With privacy controls, users are likely to post more content because they are assured that only selected people will see particular pieces of content, thus limiting the possibility of derivative costs. Privacy controls also ensure that only those friends who see the primary content can provide secondary content, and that the secondary content is visible only to friends who could see the primary content. With such limited visibility, users will be less concerned that one friend will contribute secondary content that will be interpreted by another friend in a way that reflects poorly on the user. As a consequence, users will be more apt to post primary content when they can use privacy controls.

Indeed, Facebook was clearly aware of the need to provide such privacy controls. In 2007, the company introduced a functionality that allowed users to assign their friends to multiple lists and make every piece of content that users posted visible only to people on one or more lists. With time, Facebook expanded that functionality and allowed users to make a particular piece of content visible to individual people, regardless of whether they were on any privacy lists. In contrast, mixi introduced this capability only in 2009.

The data, reported in models 5.11 to 5.14 in the online appendix, show that these privacy lists were very important to helping Facebook begin to overcome the trade-off. As shown in figure 5.2, Facebook users who did not use privacy controls did indeed provide less content once the number of their friends crossed a certain threshold. In contrast, users who used friend lists and privacy controls continued to provide more content even as the number of their friends increased. Clearly, privacy controls allowed users to continue to post content even if their overall network size grew.

Of course, functionalities that seek to reduce these derivative costs may themselves generate new derivative costs. Consider, for example, what happens when one of your friends was made privy to your primary content, but another one was not. If the friend who saw the content mentions it in an offline conversation with the friend who did not see the content, the one who was left out of the original loop may conclude that his relationship with you is not as strong as he thought, which may lead him to reduce contact with you. The potential for such second-order derivative costs calls for additional functionalities that can limit the likelihood that they will occur.

Indeed, Facebook seems to have recognized this concern and as of this writing gives users who can see someone's content the ability to see who else can view that content (by hovering over a little icon next to every primary piece of content). Forewarned, viewers can limit their discussions of that content to those who were made privy to it. And with greater assurance that their content will not be leaked inappropriately, users will be more apt to post primary content. This way, for example, a high-school student can post a picture, making it visible only to his friends but not to his family. Now that his friends are aware that the original poster's family cannot see their interactions, they may feel freer to contribute their secondary content, which will in turn encourage the original poster to display more content in the future.

Search

Search interaction costs arise when it is hard for people to acquire information about their friends and acquaintances. Like all the other interaction costs, they arise due to economic and social factors. The economic ones include the difficulties of finding information about others when these others are not available to furnish the desired information.

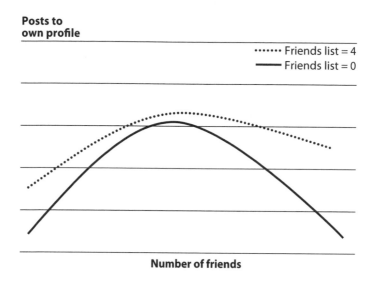

Figure 5.2. Privacy controls and posting content on Facebook

Social reasons arise out of the same norm that mandates that we interact with others in a way that benefits them. This overarching norm helps us understand why, for example, snooping on others is frowned on, and individuals who care about what others think about them will refrain from such behaviors (Goffman 1967).

Although this norm prevents many unnecessary interactions, it can also lead to social failures, particularly in situations where both parties would benefit, but the party asking for information does not know that the interaction will benefit the friend she wants to ask. Consider, for example, a situation in which you are concerned about your friend and want to ask him about how his relationship is going. Even though your friend may actually want to disclose some of the problems he is experiencing and seek your advice, you do not know that your friend is willing to do so. As a consequence, you might never ask for fear of coming across as too nosey and incurring search interaction costs. Your mistaken belief that your friend does not want to share a particular piece of information will lead to a social failure.

To lower these costs, "friend" solutions offer functionalities that allow people to view their friends' information. By allowing people to view the information without their friends having to be present, such functionalities address the economic causes of search costs. In addition, the functionality can address the social causes of search costs by allowing people to view that content without their friends' ever knowing that the content was consumed. This way, people can find what they are looking for without transgressing the norm and incurring concomitant search costs.

Both Facebook and mixi allowed users to search for and view content provided by others. The two sites approached search solutions differently, however. Facebook allowed users to browse friends' profiles without letting those friends know that their profile was visited. In contrast, on mixi, every visit to a friend's profile left an electronic footprint, which allowed that friend to see that his or her profile had been visited. In the language of our theory, Facebook alleviated both the economic and the social causes of search interaction costs, but mixi attended to only the economic ones, but left the social causes of search costs unchanged.

Those design choices had a significant effect on users' willingness to visit their friends' profile pages. To understand the full effect of those choices, I calculated the percentage of all clicks in my mixi dataset related to users viewing others' content. Subsequently, using public data on clicks on Facebook, I calculated the percentage of all clicks related to users viewing others' content there. The results show that almost 60 percent of all clicks on mixi were related to viewing others' content. In comparison, a full 80 percent of clicks on Facebook were related to viewing others' content. Furthermore, results indicate that almost 10 percent of all actions on mixi were related to users viewing the list of who viewed them, suggesting that users were clearly paying attention to who viewed their content. Clearly, therefore, the functionality informing users that others viewed their content reduced the extent to which those others were willing to view that content.

To gain a deeper understanding of how the footprint functionality affected users' viewing patterns on mixi, I estimated statistical regressions predicting the number of pieces of content a user would view as a function of the number of friends the user had and the user's characteristics. The results, reported in model 5.5 in the online appendix, revealed that mixi users with more online friends view more content, but every additional friend increased the amount of viewing by increasingly less. For example, on mixi, users with 50 friends viewed just about as much content as users who have 25 friends. It is easy to account for this finding once we consider that users usually start by establishing online relationships with close friends, and then every additional online friend is more likely to be an acquaintance. With these additional ties being acquaintances, users likely find it awkward to view these acquaintances' content, particularly when these acquaintances are informed about the visit.

I did find, however, that users who have a lot of online friends who are also friends with one another on mixi continue to view more content as the number of their online friends increases. This is probably because such users feel closer to their friends, and this perceived closeness makes it easier for users to view their friends' content even if these friends are informed of such visits. When the ties between friends do not exist, however, users feel that their online friends are less close to them, so it is more awkward to view their content on mixi.

Consider, too, what the research revealed about gender differences in search behaviors across the two sites. On mixi, it was predominantly women who looked at other women's content. In stark contrast, on Facebook, it was predominantly men who look at women's content. This difference can be easily understood if we go back to our discussion of offline norms of interaction between the two sexes, where we argued that men face relatively significant obstacles in acquiring information from women in the offline world. On mixi, it is difficult to view content from others without their knowing, in much the same way as it is in the offline world. For this reason, users who are least likely to engage in search behaviors in the offline world (i.e., men who want to find out more about women) are also least likely to engage in these behaviors online. In contrast, on Facebook, it is possible for users to view content from others without their knowing, thereby overcoming the social failure. As a consequence, users who are most likely to face normative constraints in the offline world, for example, men seeking to find and learn more about women, will be most likely to engage in search behaviors on the site.

What's more, men with more female friends on mixi during the observation period were no more likely to examine their content than men with just a few female friends. They would, however, examine more women's profiles when they had a lot of friends in common with these women (see models 5.5 to 5.7 in the online appendix). Thus, on mixi, where women can find out who visited them, men felt uncomfortable examining the content from the many women they know online, unless these women were fairly close to them (as proxied by the friends in common).

The final piece of evidence for this norm-based explanation comes from an analysis of users who checked to see who visited their profile. That analysis revealed that male mixi members were more likely to check who visited them than female mixi members (see model 5.8 in the online appendix). And, of all users who checked who visited them, men were more likely to visit the profiles of women friends who had looked at their profiles. This suggests that men viewed the list of who visited their profile with the hope that female friends visited them, which in turn would give them an excuse to visit those female friends.

Taken together, these results indicate that Facebook provided a very strong functionality that addressed both the economic and the social causes of search interaction costs. In contrast, mixi addressed only the economic causes, but left the social considerations largely unaddressed, and so the feature was used much less.

So why did mixi take this approach? After all, mixi could have replicated Facebook's approach and thereby attended to the social causes of search interaction costs. I hypothesize that the company chose this course to encourage its users to contribute more secondary content, as users felt more obligated to contribute content when they knew that their friends would be informed of the visit to their profile. This suggests that mixi was willing to provide a less powerful search functionality (one that addressed only the economic sources of interaction costs) to strengthen its display functionality.

It is not clear, however, whether it was necessary for mixi to do this. After all, mixi was focused on facilitating interactions between a small number of close friends who already had every incentive to contribute secondary content. Encouraging them to contribute even more content through the footprint feature was unlikely to generate much additional content.

Indeed, by all indications, mixi understood its strategic mistake and removed the footprint feature in the summer of 2012. My sense, though, is that the company took this action much too late—mixi should have recognized that by letting people know who visited their profile it was exposing itself to a huge threat from Facebook. Unfortunately, the company did not pay attention to this threat and continued to ignore the social causes of search interaction costs. Its lack of attention to these eventually caught up with mixi and cost the company its leading position in Japan.

Communication

Finally, we examine private communication costs that arise in the context of people we already know. As before, these arise for both economic and social reasons. The economic reasons underlying communication costs pertain to the fact that it is often time consuming to engage in private communication. Building social functionalities to alleviate these economic factors is fairly straightforward—emailing or instant messaging functionalities usually take good care of these, and both Facebook and mixi provided these for their users.

The social reasons underlying communication costs are related to the fact that it is often awkward to initiate interactions, particularly for acquaintances. Building social functionalities to alleviate these social factors is far from straightforward. As we already saw with OkCupid, email or other straightforward messaging functionalities are unlikely to achieve this goal. Instead, as we saw with eHarmony, it is necessary to restructure the interaction process to remove the social awkwardness of initiating an interaction. This can be done by structuring interactions through a series of questions and answers, or by providing a joint activity for people to engage in, which will in turn allow them to interact with each other. Neither Facebook nor mixi have provided any functionalities to alleviate these social causes of communication costs.

I do not have data on private interactions on Facebook to document the implications of these choices. I do, however, have these data for mixi. Not surprisingly, the results, reported in models 5.9 and 5.10 in the online appendix, show that mixi users with more friends were more likely to message others or receive a message. I also found that younger mixi users were more likely to send messages, but that older users were more likely to receive them. The results also indicate that users who displayed more pictures were less likely to send or receive private messages. This suggests that users who were perhaps too shy to display content publicly used private interaction channels to catch up with people they cared about on mixi.

Finally, I found that men were more likely to send messages and to receive them, suggesting that most private communication on mixi occurred between men. Why is there so little cross-gender communication? I believe this is probably caused by the fact that mixi did not attend to the social reasons underlying communication costs. This made it very awkward for men to send messages to women or for women to send messages to men for fear of such messaging being interpreted as a normative violation or an expression of romantic interest. Once again, we see how addressing the economic causes of communication costs allowed users to communicate freely. In contrast, we see how the failure to address the social causes of communication costs made it awkward for certain groups to communicate with each other. As a consequence, only those interactions that were relatively free of these normative costs were facilitated.

Conclusions

The objective of this chapter was to demonstrate that the same claims I put forward in chapter 2 apply to "friend" solutions. First, we saw that interaction costs differ quite a lot, both across people and across relationship types. This insight became particularly salient when we examined how various interaction costs differ in close personal relationships and in more distant acquaintance relationships. Second, we saw that social functionalities must attend to both the economic and the social causes of interaction costs. This was highlighted for us when we examined search functionalities offered by mixi and Facebook. Specifically, using mixi as an example, we see just how dangerous it is to provide functionalities that address the economic but not the social sources of interaction costs. Third, and relatedly, our comparison of the strategies of mixi and Facebook confirmed that social solutions need to reduce interaction costs related to breadth, display, search, and communication to be successful. In this case, our focus was on mixi's failure to provide powerful search functionality. This left a huge opening for Facebook to come in, with a better set of social functionalities, and become the leading social network in Japan.

Finally, our analysis underscored an important trade-off in providing "friend" solutions that arises between those offering narrow breadth and focusing on closest friends versus expansive ones that include both close friends and acquaintances. The two types of functionalities result in very different display behaviors. Specifically, a narrow breadth functionality encourages people to disclose more content and more personal content. In contrast, an expansive breadth functionality steers users toward displaying less personal and more generic content. But when breadth is too expansive, users reduce the amount of content they contribute. Despite these disadvantages, extensive breadth friend solutions are at a substantial advantage for growth in the user base, particularly by having existing users invite new users to join. This underscores an important trade-off between the two types of "friend" solutions: the narrow one will produce more display but will grow more slowly, the latter will result in fewer display behaviors but will attract more users quickly.

CHAPTER 6

"Meet" and "Friend" Solutions

LinkedIn and Friendster

Having examined the characteristics of platforms that entail only "meet" or "friend" solutions, we now turn to more complex platforms that feature both "meet" and "friend" solutions, using LinkedIn and Friendster as examples. To set the stage for considering dual-solution platforms, it helps to recall table 1.1 from chapter 1, reproduced here as table 6.1. The vertical dimension denotes all of the "meet" solutions we have studied, and examines differences between them. The horizontal dimension denotes the two "meet" solutions we studied.

Since LinkedIn went through a transformation in the summer of 2005, I will start by describing LinkedIn's breadth, display, search, and communication functionalities before the transformation, and then proceed to describe how these functionalities evolved. As I do this, I will focus on the complementarities that arise in combining "meet" and "friend" solutions in the same platform, and analyze how well LinkedIn exploited them. We will then examine how many of the same principles we will discover with LinkedIn apply to Friendster.

Breadth

There are substantial benefits to giving people the ability to interact with strangers and friends for reducing breadth interaction costs. As we discussed in chapter 3, platforms where people interact with strangers

Table 6.1. Strategic Trade-offs among Social Platforms

		"Friend" solution	
		Many friends	Few close friends
	Limited interaction with strangers	Facebook	mixi
"Meet" solution	Private interaction with few strangers	LinkedIn	eHarmony
	Private interaction with many strangers	Friendster	OkCupid
	Public interaction with many strangers	MySpace	Twitter

require significant advertising to reduce breadth costs. In contrast, platforms where people interact with friends do not need so much advertising, as users invite their friends to join. Thus, a platform that allows people to interact both with friends and with strangers can rely on users to invite their friends, and then leverage that growing user base to help strangers connect. By doing so, the platform can grow more cheaply than it would if it provided only a "meet" solution.

Indeed, LinkedIn's original launch strategy sought to benefit from this complementarity. LinkedIn's founders eschewed explicit advertising, and instead they invited their friends and asked them to start inviting others, both close friends and business acquaintances. At the same time, the company asked that users refrain from connecting to people they do not know.

Much to the founders' surprise, this strategy resulted in very slow growth. In its first month of operation, May 2003, just 6,000 users joined the site, and by month six, there were only 36,000 users. Users were also slow to connect to each other. At the time, the average LinkedIn user had 15 connections to others. Even after LinkedIn received significant media coverage, which increased registrations to 2 million users by the end of 2004, an average user had 20 connections to others. These numbers were particularly disappointing when compared to leading platforms of the time, such as Friendster, MySpace, or Facebook. Friendster started at the same time as LinkedIn and had 8 million users by the end of 2004, with the average user having slightly more than 100 connections. MySpace, which launched after LinkedIn, had 5 million users, and its users on average had 60 online friends. Facebook, which was still restricted to college users in 2004, had 1 million users at that point. Despite the network's limited size, the average Facebook user had almost 300 connections to others at that time.

There are at least two reasons why LinkedIn's users failed to invite many users or establish connections to the ones on the platform. First, recall that breadth interaction costs arise when people fail to reconnect with others when they mistakenly believe that those individuals no longer find them interesting. Those failures are salient in personal relationships, but they do not really apply in business relationships. For example, it would be embarrassing to extend an offer to rekindle a friendship, only to have one's advances rebuffed. In contrast, there would be little embarrassment in approaching someone and offering a business deal only to discover that the other party is not interested. For this reason, people did not feel as if they needed to connect to others on LinkedIn; they could simply reach out directly in the offline world.

Second, and relatedly, people connected to others on platforms like Friendster or Facebook to obtain additional information that they could not obtain otherwise. By connecting to someone on LinkedIn, however, users only found out where that other person went to school or where they worked—hardly the kind of information that is hard to gather elsewhere, nor the kind of information that would truly help establish a deeper connection with that person. So people were less motivated to join LinkedIn and establish connections to others. Indeed, my data from late 2005 seem to bear this out. Of all the people who set up profiles on LinkedIn and provided their names, only 40 percent of users provided any data regarding their education or employment history, and of those who did, only 10 percent managed to obtain any secondary content in the form of endorsements from others.

To get a sense of the magnitude of these numbers, consider Friendster, which at the time was the leading "friend" platform focused on personal relationships. As many as 75 percent of Friendster users provided school and employment information, even though the site had very little to do with professional networking. Presumably, the reason why more people provided their work and school information on Friendster than on LinkedIn is that Friendster asked for these data in the context of asking for other more personal data. In contrast, without the prompt to enter personal information first, LinkedIn users saw little reason to enter their work-related information on its own.

These considerations suggest that even though LinkedIn could have benefited from complementarities that arise from combining "meet" and "friend" solutions for breadth, the company failed to realize these benefits. This is because the company chose to tackle a relationship that was not subject to many breadth interaction costs, which meant that people were not motivated to invite and connect to others. This slowed LinkedIn's viral growth and undermined its ability to provide a breadth functionality for its "meet" solution.

Display

Just as there are unique benefits of combining "meet" and "friend" solutions for breadth, this combination also creates unique advantages for display functionalities. Specifically, "meet" solutions often find it hard to provide display functionalities in which people disclose truthful information about themselves. For example, people on dating sites often represent themselves as younger, taller, and skinnier than they are in reality. Similarly, people seeking employment online may embellish the extent of their achievements or blatantly lie about where they went to school or where they worked.

This is much harder to do on platforms where people are also interacting with their friends. For example, it is hard to claim publicly that one has graduated from a particular school or was employed somewhere when friends know that to be untrue and can easily see that information on the site. Even more subtly, a manager would have a hard time claiming that he "singlehandedly won a huge account" when in fact a team of people worked on the deal and all were instrumental in securing it. It is likely that the manager in question would be connected to many of those who worked on the deal, and that those other people would be offended if they saw that their contributions were not acknowledged. To avoid such embarrassment, the manager would be more likely to disclose accurate information and say that he "was part of a team that won a huge account."

To get a sense for how successful LinkedIn was at benefiting from this complementarity, I compared a group of people on LinkedIn who were also present on a stand-alone recruitment site. To do so, I purchased a recruiter subscription in mid-2005 from a site, where individuals simply posted equivalents of their CVs for recruiters to see, but were not given the option to be connected with any of their friends or acquaintances.

First, I executed a search for people on the recruitment site with broadly defined IT backgrounds in the San Francisco area (a segment of the labor force that, at the time, was overrepresented on LinkedIn, making up almost 12 percent of LinkedIn's membership). I took a random sample of roughly one thousand profiles from the resulting list of people matching my criteria on the recruitment site. I was not able to find each person on my list on both sites. I was, however, able to match just under 50 percent of the profiles I sought, resulting in approximately 485 matched profiles. And what I found was that a full 90 percent of these matched profiles included data on education and employment history on LinkedIn. For the 485 matched profiles, I examined job descriptions, responsibilities, and achievements people put on the recruitment site and LinkedIn. In 12 of the 485 profiles I found that individuals described their jobs, responsibilities, and achievements on the recruitment site in a way that clearly overstated what they claimed for the same jobs on LinkedIn. (In fact, I found the quotation about someone singlehandedly winning an account, as opposed to being a part of the team, in one of those twelve profiles on the recruitment site.) By comparison, I found that seven individuals described their jobs, responsibilities, and achievements on LinkedIn in a way that clearly overstated what they claimed for the same jobs on the recruitment site.

Clearly, LinkedIn was not at a huge competitive advantage in terms of truth disclosure over the stand-alone recruitment site at that point. Either most people were misrepresenting themselves equally on both sites, or most people were reporting the truth on the stand-alone recruitment site and as a consequence there was very little opportunity for them to report more truthfully on LinkedIn.

If anything, further analysis revealed that LinkedIn was probably at a disadvantage over the recruitment site with regard to the range of information available to viewers. For approximately 28 percent of matched profiles, users did not disclose certain jobs on LinkedIn but did so on the recruitment site, and in only 4 percent of cases was the reverse true. In a great majority of cases, people failed to report their early job experiences on LinkedIn (mostly the jobs they had held within the first five years after college graduation), but they did report these jobs on the recruitment site. The fact that users did not feel compelled to fill out their LinkedIn profile fully suggests that they did not believe that their online friends were expecting them to fill out their profile and/or they did not believe that their online friends were monitoring their profile carefully.

Although it is impossible to know exactly why that was the case, one plausible hypothesis is that, at that point, users on LinkedIn had very small networks, which meant that they did not really believe that a lot of people would be watching them, and also that they knew that the people who did watch them were not necessarily close friends who already possessed full information. As a result, these individuals did not feel compelled to display their information fully. Had LinkedIn been able to motivate individuals to build more connections to others on the site during that time, I would presume that the number of complete profiles would also have increased dramatically. Either way, once again, we see that LinkedIn did not benefit from the complementarities that could have arisen from the combination of "meet" and "friend" solutions in the same platform.

Search

To understand how LinkedIn stood to benefit from combining "meet" and "friend" solutions for search, consider search interaction costs when meeting strangers through friends. We already considered these costs in chapter 2 when we discussed broker-based means of establishing a new relationship brokered. To see these costs in practice, consider a situation in which someone wants to find and hire a vice president of marketing through friends. First, that individual would probably ask some of his or her friends if they know someone who could be a good vice president of marketing, and if one of those friends knew of an appropriate candidate, then the individual would ask for an introduction and a referral. If the friends did not know an appropriate candidate, the individual would then probably ask if they could ask *their* friends if *they* knew someone who might be a great vice president of marketing. As illustrated in figure 6.1, this process would continue until the right candidate was found. As documented by Granovetter (1974) and many others who followed (e.g., Fernandez, Castilla, and Moore 2000), many jobs are found this way, particularly through bridging ties that take us outside the realm of our closest friends (Burt 1982).

In reality, this process is fraught with search costs. Some of these costs are economic in nature. For example, the brokers may really want to help, but may completely misinterpret the requirements of the search, such that a search for a vice president of marketing turns out to be a search for a marketing manager. Or the brokers may have insufficient incentive to act. After all, they may not get any benefits for making the connection. Other costs may be more social. For example, the brokers may also be worried that if they refer someone for a job and something goes wrong, they will have to suffer the embarrassment of making an inappropriate recommendation.

To address these concerns LinkedIn allowed its users to search for others on the basis of keywords, employers, positions held, and current location, as long as these others were within four degrees of separation from the searcher. This functionality alleviated the economic underpinnings of search costs in that it ensured that the right search would occur, and it solved the incentive problems by enabling the person who would benefit most from the search to conduct the search. Furthermore, it addressed the social concerns about disappointing a friend or colleague by identifying someone who turns out to be a mismatch. After all, the person doing the search was also identifying the potential candidates—the friends only acted as intermediaries doing the introduction.

At first glance, the data I collected while interviewing LinkedIn executives back then suggest that this functionality created considerable appeal for LinkedIn members. For example, in April 2004, members ex-

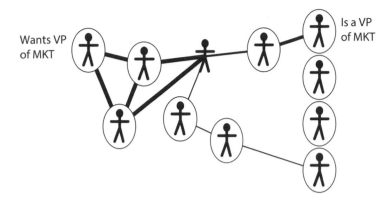

Figure 6.1. Finding strangers through friends

ecuted approximately 2 million searches per month. By mid-2005 that number had grown to 5 million per month, amounting to one search per month per member on average. Digging more deeply into these numbers, however, revealed a number of concerns about the power of this functionality. First, as many as 35 percent of LinkedIn users in early 2005 did not search for anyone; the median user executed a single search per month; the most active 10 percent of searchers executed more than 15 searches per month; and some users conducted as many as 600 searches. What's more, five million searches didn't equal visits to five million *profiles*. A search would merely reveal a list of individuals who matched the search criteria; it was then up to the searcher to click through to visit any given profile. LinkedIn managers estimated that only 15 percent of searches resulted in a profile being viewed, suggesting great opportunities for improvement. In fact, that statistic was one of the key reasons why LinkedIn's senior managers began considering one different way in which to help people search more effectively (the first option in the preface).

To understand why users were not inclined to view profiles after conducting a search, recall that an average user on LinkedIn had only 20 online friends. Now, take me as a representative user with 20 friend connections. Each of my friends is then connected to 20 people, but since I am one of these 20 people, this gives us a net of 19 people for every one of my friends. If we take the most optimistic scenario and assume that each of my friends is connected to 19 unique people, we obtain 380 two-step connections. If we repeat this calculation for three steps, we get 7,220 people, and at four steps we get 137,180 people. On a social platform of 5 million people, this amounts to 3 percent of the total number of people. Realistically, however, some of my friends will know people that some of my other friends know. So if we assume that each person connects me, say, to 12 unique people, then the number of connections I can get in four steps is reduced to 34,560, or just over 0.5 percent.

The small number of people users could access had important implications for the searches. Consider that most users looked for people matching fairly specific criteria, such as industry background, experience, or geography. Once they applied those criteria to an already restricted set of candidates, it is likely that the searches resulted in a very small number of candidates, or even no candidates at all. When that happened, the probability of a user clicking through and looking at a profile declined significantly, as the data show.

Once again, we see that even though LinkedIn could have potentially benefited from complementarities of combining "meet" and "friend" solutions for search, the company failed to realize them. This is because LinkedIn did not build proper breadth functionality for its "friend" solution, which undermined the efficacy of the search functionality. As we will see in the next section, LinkedIn's approach to breadth also affected its communication functionality.

Communication

To understand what kinds of complementarities arise with regard to communication functionalities when combining a "meet" and a "friend" solution, consider what typically happens on a stand-alone "meet" solution. If people can contact others directly, the most attractive people are overwhelmed with requests for contact to the point that they withdraw from a given social environment. When they withdraw, however, these people are also blocking themselves off from contacts who might actually offer them a mutually beneficial interaction. In lieu of withdrawing, people can ask their friends to act as filters to make sure that all of the requests are beneficial to the recipient. This creates a complementarity between a "meet" and a "friend" solution for a communication functionality.

LinkedIn sought to leverage this complementarity by allowing users to compose a message for someone who was not a direct connection, and then asking that the friend who was the first node linking the user and the final recipient to endorse it. The friend read the original email, and then could forward it the next person in the chain. The process could be repeated up to two times before the message would reach the recipient. Once the recipient obtained the message, the protocol was lifted; he or she could then contact the sender directly, via LinkedIn, regular email, or telephone.

Despite providing such a powerful messaging functionality, LinkedIn found that its members sent only 25,000 messages per month this way. It is possible that LinkedIn users did not send messages because they were not interested in others. That idea is hard to reconcile, however, with the fact that users executed five million searches every month, and followed up with at least 750,000 profile views. Clearly, LinkedIn members were interested in others; but with messaging rates amounting to at most 3 percent of all profile views or 0.5 percent of all searches, they were just not writing to other people. It is possible that users simply bypassed the LinkedIn system and asked their friends directly to make introductions to people they identified online. Indeed, consistent with this explanation, LinkedIn found that only a few messages, out of all messages sent, requested introductions to friends of friends or introductions to friends of friends of friends.

Most likely, however, LinkedIn's low messaging rates can be attributed to the small average size of each user's LinkedIn network, which implied that people could only find a small number of others when they conducted a search. As a consequence, it was unlikely that users were finding people who met their requirements, and so they were unlikely to send those individuals a message.

Once again, this discussion suggests that LinkedIn could have benefited from combining "meet" and "friend" solutions to create significant complementarities for communication functionalities. Unfortunately, the company failed to realize these complementarities, as it had not attended to the breadth of its "friend" solution.

LinkedIn Evolves

In 2005, LinkedIn's leaders realized that the combination of the "meet" and "friend" solutions was not achieving its goals. They reacted in two ways. First, they retained the existing broker approach, but limited the free referral system so that people could contact strangers only up to three degrees of separation. Second, they introduced a market way of meeting others and offered the ability to search for and contact anyone on the platform, with the purchase of a monthly subscription. Subscribing members were offered unlimited search opportunities, but they were limited to sending just a certain number of messages each month. By offering this new functionality, LinkedIn allowed recruiters to contact people in organizations and, potentially, offer them jobs. Indeed, recruiters quickly flocked to LinkedIn to take advantage of this functionality.

With a lot of people obtaining jobs this way, there existed a real threat that many people who were currently employed and were *not* looking for a job would abandon LinkedIn for fear of being incorrectly seen as looking for a job. And yet it did not happen. In fact, the reverse happened. As this book was going to print, LinkedIn had grown to 238 million members, with many of its members completing their profiles fully. As it turns out, a substantial part of LinkedIn's success can in fact be traced to a very different type of complementarity between a "meet" and "friend" solution. To understand this complementarity, we need to back up a little and examine social causes of display interaction costs in labor markets.

Display Interaction Costs in Labor Markets

To understand display interaction costs in labor markets, consider how an employee might go about looking for a better job than she currently has. First, she can quit her current job and start searching for a new one. Although this option gives her complete flexibility in her job search, it also saddles her with many costs. She will have to forego her salary while looking for the new job. What's more, potential employers may interpret her unemployed status as an adverse signal of quality, which will lead to her obtaining a worse job than she could get if she stayed employed throughout her search.

Second, she can look for a job while on the job. She can do that via a broker who would scour the job market on her behalf, thus allowing her to downplay the fact that she is looking for a new position. She could ask a friend to be her broker, but as we discussed earlier, taking that route has its own drawbacks; friends are often not sufficiently motivated to be effective brokers. She could also hire a professional broker, but since that is usually quite an expensive option, only a limited set of employees do so in practice. Third, she can also attend various tradeshows or conferences where she can make herself visible to others in the industry, while not explicitly appearing to seek new employment. That approach also has its limitations, however; as we discussed earlier, its reach is limited as compared to what a market solution would offer.

Finally, she can display information about herself, her skills, and her achievements broadly to the market, say, by joining an online recruitment platform. Although this option maximizes the chances of being found by another employer, it also creates significant costs. Suppose, for example, her boss is contemplating investing time to coach her, so she can be promoted, but sees that she has posted information about herself on such a site; that boss might believe that she is looking to leave the organization. As a consequence, he will not want to invest in coaching. Similarly, think of a subordinate who considers whether to put in extra effort for her, so that when she gets promoted, she takes the subordinate with her to the new position. If the subordinate sees evidence that she is looking outside of the company for another job, he will be unlikely to put in that extra effort.

This discussion suggests that the employee gains broadest exposure, and hence potentially best job opportunities, by joining the market, but she also incurs display interaction costs in that market. If she underestimates the benefits of the new job or overestimates the display interaction costs, she might refrain from using the market even though doing so would actually get her the best job.

The magnitude of this problem varies across different types of employees. Independent contributors or consultants can easily display information to the market and signal that they are looking for new opportunities while on the job. They are cheap to train and they usually supervise few others so there is very little costly disappointment when they leave or intend to leave. These costs increase dramatically, however, as we progress up the corporate ladder. Even someone who is a manager should not be seen as looking for a job; a director or a vice president even less so, not to mention someone at the chief level. Those people face the highest costs of going on the market publicly and thus are likely to refrain from doing so (Khurana 1998). For this reason, we will largely focus on the latter category of employees, and we will examine the concerns of one such prototypical "manager."

REDUCING DISPLAY INTERACTION COSTS IN LABOR MARKETS

Given that markets give the manager broadest exposure but are also subject to display interaction costs, the manager might seek to minimize these costs, particularly those related to looking for a job while on the job. To do so, the manager needs to display her information in a way that generates additional benefits for people in her organization during the time she still works there. To see why, consider that when the manager displays information about herself that leads her to a great job, she is essentially shortening the period during which her boss might realize the benefits from coaching, or the subordinate gets the benefits from the anticipated promotion. The expected benefits for these people decrease, and so do their investments in the manager.

But now suppose that the fact that the manager displays information about herself increases the value of the boss's or the subordinate's investments during the time that the manger still works at the company. For example, the manager's market activity generates a set of new deals that create additional benefits for the manager's bosses or subordinates. When that happens, both the manager's bosses and her subordinates know that the manager's act of displaying information about herself on the market will shorten the time during which they will benefit from their investments. But on the other hand, while the manager is still on the job, their returns will be higher. If the higher benefits offset the costs of shorter tenure, the bosses and the subordinates will continue their investments, and this will reduce the manager's costs of looking for a job while on the job.

This is where social relationships with friends and acquaintances become very important and potentially useful to the person seeking a new job. These acquaintances could be potential buyers, potential suppliers, or potential employees. Alternatively, they could act as brokers bringing referrals to buyers, suppliers, or employees. Either way, the existence of these friends and acquaintances gives the manager the ability to create benefits for her company, her boss, and her employees.

To realize these benefits, the manager needs to display some information about herself. If the manager wants her friends and acquaintances to find her and offer their services directly, the manager needs only to display just basic pieces of information about herself, such as where she works and what she does. But, if the manager wants her friends and acquaintances to act as brokers and refer other people to her that she can then leverage for organizational benefits (job hunt aside), she might need to provide additional information, such as her educational and work history and perhaps a list of some of her achievements. This makes it easier for her friends and acquaintances to show other people that the manager has had a very solid career and her achievements merit the referral. What will happen, at the same time, is that the manager will be seen by new potential employers, or by contacts that can lead to a new job.

Notice the parallels between this scenario and what happens on LinkedIn. Users display information about themselves, their educational and career history, as well as their achievements for their friends and acquaintances to see. This is the "friend" solution provided by LinkedIn. Others can then use this information to contact users through the acquaintances, in a way that benefits both the users and the acquaintances. This is the integration of the brokered "meet" and "friend" solutions offered by LinkedIn prior to 2005. Finally, by providing such extensive information about themselves, they can also be targeted by recruiters who can seek to offer them a job or at least a job interview. This is the integration of the market "meet" and "friend" solutions that LinkedIn introduced in 2005.

Notice the extensive complementarities between combining all three types of solutions in the same platforms. Specifically, the "friend" solution and the broker "meet" solution help LinkedIn users generate benefits for their companies, bosses, or subordinates. These benefits then give the users the ability to engage in a marketplace "meet" solution without jeopardizing their relationship with people in their organizations. Put differently, users can safely provide a lot of personal information about themselves on LinkedIn, which will increase the likelihood that recruiters will contact them. Current employers can be fully aware of the possibility that this might happen, but will not penalize employees for joining LinkedIn. This is because the same information can be used to benefit the firm through the users' relationships with others. These relationships make LinkedIn users more productive at their current jobs, and that in turn compensates the current employers for the higher likelihood that a LinkedIn user will move to a different job. Thus, the online networks that users establish on LinkedIn and the benefits they generate act as covers for those same users to display information on the market when it is illegitimate for them to be there.

EMPIRICAL EVIDENCE

Having established that there exist substantial benefits to adding "friend" solutions to marketplace "meet" solutions, consider the quantitative evidence that supports this view, using data from a research collection effort with a team of dedicated researchers in Poland. For this study, we selected a random sample of ten thousand U.S.-based profiles of LinkedIn users in September 2011 and monitored them until December 2012.

First, we took the current positions that the people held and coded them on the seniority scale, distinguishing between users holding C-level and vice president–level positions, those occupying director-level positions, those occupying manager-level positions, and those in independent contributor positions. We also included those who own their own company, or act as independent consultants, to that independent contributor category.

Then, every two weeks, we would inspect each profile and note if there were any changes to the users' education and job histories and summary blurbs, and whether the number of their LinkedIn connections changed. Finally, on the basis of the job history data, we kept track of when users changed jobs. As many as 785 people did, most of whom reported their job change on LinkedIn within a month of making the move. (LinkedIn did not allow people to enter anticipated dates of a job change).

The data revealed patterns consistent with the arguments above. First, we examined whether people are more likely to add more information about themselves publicly after they added more connections on LinkedIn, and how that relationship varies across people in different levels and types of positions. Using regression analysis, we found that people are more likely to add information to fill out their education history or their work history, or to add data to the blurb about themselves, after they increased the number of online relationships they had. Interestingly, the magnitude of this effect varied substantially with the position the user held. Users who occupied C-level and vice president–level positions and director- and manager-level positions were most likely to add information about themselves when they already had more relationships. This suggests that they felt that it was legitimate for them to display more information about themselves only when they had what they considered to be a critical mass of relationships. Users who occupied independent contributor positions, consultants, and those who owned their own businesses were much less sensitive to these concerns and felt freer to add information to their profiles regardless of how many connections they had or added. Clearly, they had little to lose by adding content to their profile.

In the second set of analyses, we examined the likelihood of users in our sample moving to a job at another company during the observation period. There are several ways in which those users could obtain a new job. For example, they could actively look for a new position, they could hire a professional broker to help them with the job search, or they could activate their offline connections to help them with a job search. In this vein, they could also use their connections on LinkedIn to secure the job. They could also be found by recruiters or hiring managers and then be offered and accept a job. LinkedIn is one of many ways in which they could have been found. Given our theory, we were highly interested in documenting that LinkedIn allows people to get jobs because they can now obtain higher visibility, but we were unable to ascertain how users got new jobs.

We were able to glean some insight into the effects of LinkedIn by comparing what filling out information in the profile did to the likelihood of job transition for people in different positions. As reported in models 6.1 to 6.4 in the online appendix, for people in independent contributor positions, there was a very weak relationship between how much of their profile they had recently added and the likelihood that they changed jobs during our observation period. This is presumably because these people have numerous options to find new jobs—whether or not their LinkedIn profile is filled out has little impact on their likelihood of being seen by a recruiter, as recruiters can spot these people on other platforms, such as Monster.

In contrast, the relationship between adding personal content on LinkedIn, such as changing one's headline or self-description on the profile, and the likelihood of changing jobs during observation period was very high for people occupying managerial and director-level positions. This is presumably because for people in these positions it is important to have their LinkedIn profile filled out, as it is very difficult to get information about these people on other platforms. Now that recruiters can see information about these people, they are more likely to obtain a job offer.

Finally, changing the headline or self-description on the profile had very little effect on the likelihood that someone holding a "chief" title (for example, chief marketing officer) would change jobs. This is presumably because these types of candidates are not recruited through LinkedIn, but through professional headhunting firms.

Although these data are consistent with the hypothesized mechanism, it is possible that people who filled out their profiles also ended up using LinkedIn to actively pursue job opportunities. To the extent that those in managerial positions succeed more at doing this than those in independent contributor positions, we would observe the results we do. Since we do not directly observe user behavior on LinkedIn, we cannot disprove this alternative explanation directly. We can provide some indirect evidence, however. Specifically, to the extent that such searches involve using the online network on LinkedIn, we would expect that users with larger online social network are more successful at such searches, and therefore more likely to get job offers. Indeed, models 6.1 to 6.4 in the online appendix attest to this—LinkedIn users with more online ties do get jobs at a higher rate. But the results also indicate that this effect is strongest for people in independent contributor, rather than managerial, roles. This suggests that people in managerial roles benefit less from active search through their online network, and the main benefit they obtain is through putting up their profile for others to see and waiting for offers to arrive.

LinkedIn's Strategy and Your Personal LinkedIn Experience

Armed with an understanding of LinkedIn's key advantage, we can examine more confidently the key strategic questions the company has been facing since rolling out this strategy. For example, LinkedIn has constantly faced the choice between improving its "meet" solution by giving recruiters better search tools and better ability to contact LinkedIn members, or improving its "friend" solution by giving members more tools to be more productive at work, such as giving people access to affinity groups? Although the company has constantly attended to both, it is fair to say that the "friend" solution has received more attention.

Our analysis makes it easy to understand why. Without a powerful "friend" solution, LinkedIn would quickly lose its cover, and would alienate those who do not want to be seen as looking for a job, leading to their departure. On the other hand, recruiters will still use LinkedIn even though it does not give them all of the functionalities they might want from a "meet" solution. After all, the next best option for companies wanting to hire people who are already employed but might be interested in a better job is to use brokers, and that is expensive. Thus, even a rudimentary "meet" solution, particularly if offered at a reasonable price, might be attractive. For this reason, LinkedIn has emphasized improving its "friend" solution.

Finally, I want to touch on your personal experience with LinkedIn, as I am sure some readers will find my interpretation of the company at odds with how they perceive it. Some of you might say: "Well, I am on LinkedIn, but I am not expecting to find a job there. In fact, I am not looking for a job at all. I only use LinkedIn to look up people's bios before a meeting and to scour my friends' networks to see who I should meet, and sometimes to look for people who can help me with my business needs." There are at least two reasons why this kind of comment is entirely consistent with my interpretation.

First, consider that even though you are not looking for a job, your boss or subordinates can never be sure if that is the case. For this reason, they try to infer your motives from your behaviors. If they saw you on a platform where people display information about themselves, and consequently get jobs, and there was no other reason why you would be there, they would quickly infer that you are looking for a job. So, if you were not looking for a job, and were intent on conveying that, you would quickly abandon the platform for fear of being falsely accused of looking for a job.

Second, your observation assumes that you are using LinkedIn to help you find others. Consider, however, that LinkedIn helps you be found by others, even though you are not explicitly looking for anyone. In fact, some of my own interviews with LinkedIn users revealed that many of them signed up for LinkedIn out of curiosity, then filled out their profile a little just so that it does not look empty, then filled out their profile more in preparation for a big conference where they expected to do a lot of business. Then, one day, they received a message from a recruiter offering them a job or a job interview. It is at that point that they discovered the unique power of LinkedIn. It is possible that this has not occurred to you, yet. But when it does, I hope it results in a wonderful job offer, with all of the attendant benefits such an offer can bring to you, whether or not you accept it. Updating your LinkedIn profile, and building many online relationships there, will maximize your chances of such an offer materializing.

Conclusions for LinkedIn

By studying LinkedIn, we gathered even more evidence in support of the four claims outlined in chapter 2. First, as before, we saw that interaction costs differ a lot both across people and across relationship types.

This became particularly salient when we understood that people in long-term employment relationships face significant display interaction costs that do not apply to people who are not employed. Second, we saw that social functionalities must attend both to the economic and the social causes of interaction costs. Indeed, most of LinkedIn's functionalities, with the exception of those related to breadth, did exactly that. Third, once again, we saw just how important it is for social solutions to reduce interaction costs related to breadth, display, search, and communication to be successful. This became particularly salient when we discussed the benefits of combining "meet" and "friend" solutions. Some of these benefits included being able to reduce breadth, display, and communication costs better than a stand-alone "meet" solution could. We found, however, that to realize these benefits, it is necessary to build complete social solutions, something that LinkedIn did not manage to do in the first couple of years of its existence.

In addition, we also gathered new insights when we discussed LinkedIn's evolution to a pay-to-contact-anyone regime. This analysis allowed us to see and understand the types of complementarities that arise when a marketplace "meet" solution is paired with a "friend" solution. The biggest benefit of combining the two arises with respect to display functionalities. This benefit is particularly powerful for people in exclusive relationships who face particular problems of displaying their information in marketplace settings without jeopardizing their relationship. The integration with the "friend" solution gives these people the excuse to display information about themselves to strangers, even though seemingly this information is targeted at friends.

Thus far, however, we talked little about strategic trade-offs with other types of platforms, for example, those that offer only "friend" solutions. To do that we examine user behaviors on another platform that combines a "meet" and a "friend" solution—Friendster—and provide further evidence that dual-purpose platforms enable people who are in relationships to go "on the market" under the guise of interacting with others. We will use these results to articulate strategic trade-offs entailed in combining "meet" and "friend" solutions.

Friendster

Friendster was founded in 2002 by Jonathan Abrams, a 32-year-old software engineer and self-described social butterfly. The original inspiration for the site came from Abrams's experiences with online dating sites. In an interview, he recalled: "I found the idea of chatting with random, anonymous strangers really creepy. I started thinking about a dating site that wasn't about dating. Something where I wasn't going to be cyberkitten307. That's not how we interact in the real world. In real life people meet each other through their friends."

To achieve his goal, Abrams set out to build a platform that combined interaction with friends and ability to meet others. He coded most of it himself and released it in March 2003, allowing anyone over the age of 18 to join. Within four months, one million members signed up for the site, and membership continued to grow at the rate of 25 percent per week. Soon after, the site began to experience performance problems—users had trouble accessing the website and logging in, and member profiles took a long time to load and were often incomplete. In large part, these issues were due to the site's complex inner workings—one of its most computationally intensive elements involved documenting the path connecting a viewer of a particular profile to the owner of that profile—information that Abrams insisted on showing.

Friendster started adding new servers, but this did not solve the problems. Then, the company tried setting the servers up differently. When that action also proved ineffective, Friendster focused on rewriting the computer code, and hired top engineers in Silicon Valley, some of whom had written textbooks on the computer languages required to power sites like Friendster. These efforts were also unsuccessful. Despite Friendster's subsequent investments, which included new memory and hard drive installations, the site did not function any faster.

These massive changes in the site infrastructure were accompanied by equally fast changes in its leadership. In April 2004, the board replaced Abrams with Tim Koogle as the interim CEO. Then, just a few months later, in July of that year, that position was given to Scott Sassa, a former president of NBC Entertainment. Neither had the skills to fix the technological issues marring Friendster. Sassa was put in a particularly difficult position when the vice president of engineering was asked to leave at the end of 2004, leaving the position vacant until early 2006. The turmoil continued into 2005, when Taek Kwon, a 31-year-old executive vice president of product and technology at Interactive Corp's CitySearch, took over the CEO position, only to be replaced by Kent Lindstrom, Friendster's longtime vice president of finance, who took the position of president in January 2006.

Lindstrom righted the boat and recruited a new vice president of engineering who fixed the problem rather quickly, paving the way for Friendster's growth. But by that time, both Facebook and MySpace were far ahead of Friendster in terms of the number of active users, frequency of visits, and the number of pages viewed per visit, at least in the United States. The site continued to be incredibly popular, however, in Southeast Asia, particularly in the Philippines and in Indonesia. That's probably because when Friendster was experiencing its technological problems, most of the Southeast Asian users accessed the Internet through a dial-up connection. With slow Internet access speed, Friendster seemed no different from other sites on the Internet, so Southeast Asian users continued using the site regardless.[1]

Fortunately for Friendster, as the speed of user access to the Internet in Southeast Asia increased, so did Friendster's speed, allowing the company to retain those users. And ultimately, the ability to hold on to that group of customers allowed the company's original investors to sell Friendster to MOL, a Malaysian e-commerce giant, in December 2009. In 2011, MOL completely changed Friendster's strategy, deleting all of its profile information and reinventing the site as an online gaming platform.

The arc of Friendster's history provides an interesting backdrop against which to analyze its breadth, display, search, and communication functionalities, and appraise those choices using data from 2007—a time when Friendster was a well-functioning site, with about a third of its traffic coming from the United States, a third from Southeast Asia, and a third from other parts of the world. As I describe these functionalities, I document their impact using data from the company that record every action taken by site users for three randomly chosen one-hour blocks in April 2007. My study took a random sample of 320,000 of these users (a quarter of them 20 years old or younger, 70 percent younger than 25, and 88 percent younger than 30). Then, I identified all people they became online friends with, viewed, or messaged, yielding an additional 904,000 target users. For each user, I gathered reported geographic location, age, sex, marital status, sexual orientation, profile information, who they were online friends with, and all online ties between these online friends. As always, all data were scrambled to protect user privacy.

Friendster's Breadth Functionalities

Right from its inception, Friendster encouraged people to connect with a broad set of friends and acquaintances, making it a fairly broad "friend" solution. Indeed, my data attest that Friendster users were keen to connect with others. In 2007, an average Friendster user had 250 online relationships, while the median one had 170. These numbers are comparable to Facebook's statistics in 2012. Only 5 percent had zero friends, only 10 percent had fewer than 10 friends, and only 20 percent had fewer than 50 friends.

As is the case with most "friend" platforms, Friendster did very little advertising to attract its users, instead relying on friends inviting their friends. When Friendster first launched, there were no competitive sites, so users almost insisted that their friends sign up, fill out their profiles, and upload their photos—a process that Abrams called "viral nagging." Indeed, the data seem to bear out the importance of this process. In 2007, every Friendster user invited 0.75 other user to join the network, with some users in the sample inviting in excess of 150 others.

Very quickly, the site also benefited from media attention, receiving extensive coverage on CNN, *Newsweek, Esquire, Vanity Fair, Rolling Stone*, the *New York Times*, the *Wall Street Journal, Wired*, and other media outlets. Subsequently, when the site gained notoriety overseas, and particularly in Southeast Asia, the media covered it broadly again. To get a sense of just how many people joined the site independently, I took a sample of 15,000 Friendster users who joined in the summer of 2007. After removing entity profiles, I found that 40 percent of people still did not have a single friend on the site after two weeks of being on the site, suggesting that 40 percent is the lower-bound estimate of people who joined the site without an invitation. Presumably, they joined the site having heard about it through the media or other nonfriend sources.

In addition to allowing people to interact with friends, Friendster also allowed users to interact with strangers. Indeed, within a year of the public release, the company lifted all restrictions on contact and allowed any user to see and message any other user. To protect themselves from unwanted overtures, users could restrict the visibility of their profiles and ability to contact to friends or friends of friends. My data indicate, however, that approximately 50 percent women, and 32 percent men, chose to do so, indicating that a lot of people on Friendster were quite open to being viewed by and contacted by strangers.

DISPLAY

Like most of the "friend" solutions we have studied so far, Friendster gave users the ability to populate their personal profiles specifying their age, hometown, current geographic location, schooling, and occupation, provide a list of their favorite books, movies, and TV shows, provide short descriptions of themselves, and upload pictures of themselves. Unlike Facebook, users could not easily write short status updates for their friends to see. They could, however, write posts on bulletin boards that could then be seen by their friends. Additionally, users could write testimonials on their friends' pages and ask their friends to contribute testimonials for them. Although users could not edit their friends' testimonials, they could approve them before they were posted on their profiles. Friendster also provided "meet" functionalities by allowing people to indicate their relationship status, their interest in finding dates, friends, or activity partners on the site, and also to provide a blurb regarding what kind of person they hoped to meet.

The data show that users were happy to display content for friends and strangers to see. For example, the median user in the sample posted 33 pictures, and 10 percent of users had more than 100 pictures on display. Only 6 percent did not have a single picture uploaded, and only 20 percent had fewer than eight. Further analysis revealed that women, younger people, and people who had the most online friends posted more pictures than other users. Declared intent of meeting others to become friends, dates, or activity partners had very little effect on the likelihood of posting pictures. Current relationship status did, however; people in relationships posted more pictures, and men in relationships were even more likely to do so than women in relationships. People who kept their profiles public were less likely to post more pictures, but this effect was much weaker for men, and completely disappeared for men in relationships. This suggests that, unlike other categories of users, men in relationships were apt to post their pictures and keep their profiles public for others to see.

Users were also quite prolific in providing testimonials for their friends. Although the median number of friend testimonials per user was two, 40 percent of users had more than 15 testimonials, and 25 percent had more than 60. Regression analysis again revealed more information. Women were more likely to receive and approve testimonials, as were older people, or people with more online friends. As before, declared intent of meeting others to become friends, dates, or activity partners had very little effect on likelihood of obtaining and approving posting pictures. Current relationship status did, however—people in relationships received and approved fewer testimonials. Furthermore, people who kept their profile public were less likely to receive and approve testimonials from others and this effect was slightly larger for men, particularly when they were in a relationship.

Taken together these results imply than men in relationships were more likely to post more content from themselves, while keeping their profiles public. They were actually less likely to obtain and approve content from others, however. Presumably, then, their behavior indicated that they were more intent than other users on shaping their image for others by posting more of their own content, and more cautious about having their image shaped by other people, by approving content posted by others on their profiles. We will return to these observations later.

SEARCH

Friendster gave users the ability to visit others' profiles. As was the case with mixi, users could inform their friends when they visited their profile. But unlike mixi, users could easily switch this function off. Friendster did not offer users the "newsfeed" function, thereby preventing users from seeing the most recent updates from their friends just as soon as they logged in. That restriction undermined the efficiency with which users could access new content from their friends, and further contributed to the eventual demise of the site. For our purposes, however, the lack of newsfeed is incredibly helpful because it allows us to understand what users were interested in without the influence of the platform itself.

Indeed, an analysis of Friendster weblogs revealed a number of interesting facts related to search activities. First, 79 percent of all clicks on the site were related to search activities. By comparison, all of the display activities amounted to 8 percent, while all of the breadth activities, including friend deletion, took another 8 percent, with the remaining 5 percent related to private activities and group communication.

The high percentage of search activities is largely consistent with what we saw when studying "meet" platforms, such as OkCupid in chapter 3, and "friend" platforms, such as Facebook or mixi in chapter 5. There also is a big difference between Friendster and these sites, however. On "meet" platforms, such as OkCupid, users mostly view content displayed by strangers, while on "friend" platforms, such as mixi or Facebook, users view mostly the content provided by their online friends. But on Friendster about 44 percent of search actions were directed at content belonging to online friends, while another 44 percent of search clicks were aimed at content belonging to people who were not online friends (see figure 6.2).[2] The remaining 12 percent of search activities were related to users viewing their own profiles (including to approve or reject a testimonial by a friend). These results seem to attest to the "meet" and "friend" nature of Friendster.

Another interesting finding pertained to user search patterns by sex. The largest category was men looking at female nonfriends (22 percent), followed by men looking at female friends (19 percent), as shown in table 6.2. In contrast to men, women looked largely at their own sex, with a focus on their female friends (17 percent); women also showed relatively little interest in women and men they did not know (9 percent and 7 percent, respectively). Overall, therefore, women received more than two-thirds of all profile and picture views because both men and women looked at them.

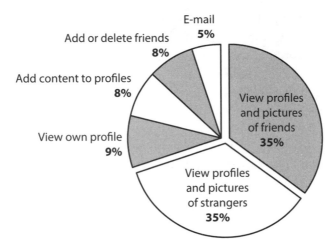

Figure 6.2. Distribution of activities on Friendster

Table 6.2. Who Is Looking at Whom on Friendster

	Profiles and pictures of men		Profiles and pictures of women	
	Friends	Nonfriends	Friends	Nonfriends
Male viewers	8%	8%	19%	22%
Female viewers	10%	7%	17%	9%

To get better insight into these search patterns, I took the two largest categories—men looking at women with whom they were *not* online friends, and men looking at women with whom they *were* online friends—and used regression analysis (reported in models 7.1 to 7.4 in the online appendix) to try to identify the distinction between men who had a tendency to engage in one type of behavior versus another.

As it turned out, men who declared themselves as single were more likely to view profiles of female friends, but less likely to view profiles of female nonfriends. For men in relationships, the reverse was true—

they were more likely to look at female nonfriends. The results also indicated that as single men acquired more online friends, they were even more likely to view profiles of female online friends, and even less likely to view profiles of female online nonfriends. Again, the opposite was true for men in relationships. For those men, an increase in the number of online friends made it even less likely that they would view female online friends, and more likely that they would view online female nonfriends.

These results are consistent with my earlier argument that the integration of "meet" and "friend" solutions generates a cover for people in relationships to go on the market without looking like they are on the market. In LinkedIn's case, people in exclusive employment relationships used the cover most. In Friendster's case, men in exclusive romantic relationships used the integration of the two products to look at women they did not know and thus bypass a situation that would be normatively inappropriate in the offline world. Not only did these men in relationships engage in these activities, but consistent with the predictions of the theory, they also built a number of online relationships with others to build a cover for their presence on the site. Presumably, the existence of some of these ties benefited these men's partners, such that even if these partners had doubts as to why the men spent so much time on Friendster, the men could always justify their presence on the site by pointing to the number of connections they had and the benefits these connections generated for their partners.

To understand these results more deeply, I further distinguished between men who were married and those who were in a relationship, but were not married, and found that the results described earlier applied more to unmarried men in relationships. That is most likely because married men are more likely to have gone through the process of assessing a number of partners to find one they feel is best for them, and so they are less likely to want to look for a new one. In contrast, men in relationships, but not married, are likely in the process of looking for that best partner. For them the pronounced need to look for new partners, combined with the restrictions on such contact in the offline world, attracts them to online social networks to look at and contact female nonfriends.

COMMUNICATION

Which Friendster users were most likely to send messages to their on-line friends, and which were most likely to send messages to strangers on the site? As reported in models 7.5 and 7.6 in the online appendix, regression analysis revealed that single people and women in relationships were more likely to message their friends and less likely to message people with whom they are not friends, particularly if they had a lot of online friends. In contrast, men in relationships were less likely to message their friends and more likely to message people with whom they were not friends, particularly if they had a lot of online friends. These results for private interaction mirror those for search, suggesting that men in relationships not only viewed the content provided by women they did not know, but also messaged these women.

CONCLUSION

The foregoing analysis of Friendster provides further evidence for the claim that providing a "meet" and a "friend" solution on the same platform will attract people in relationships who will use it to meet new people under the guise of interacting with their friends. In the context of the labor market, most people would consider such behavior ethically acceptable, and few would insist that an individual give up his or her current job before seeking a new one. I think most of us would find it ethically repugnant, however, that people would use the cover of a "friend" solution to seek new romantic relationships while the current partner is unaware that the individual is looking for a new relationship. It is easy to see why. In labor markets, the employer gets his compensation when he finds a new employee. In the context of personal relationships, it is impossible to compensate someone for the heartbreak and the disappointment of a cheating partner.

These conclusions warn us about the ethical perils of combining "meet" and "friend" solutions in the same platform. They also underscore the stark difference between the intent for a platform and its actual use. Abrams wanted to build a product that helped people date through friends, but he always had single people in mind. My interviews with executives at Friendster revealed that no one there ever intended to build a product that would serve as a cover for people in relationships who were looking to find a new partner. And yet, accidentally, Friendster ended up building a product that was used for that purpose, simply by allowing people to connect with friends and interact with strangers.

In fact, Friendster was not the only site to fall into this trap. In the first three and a half years of its existence, Facebook accidentally offered a "meet" solution by allowing people to search among strangers using a number of criteria, including age and marital status, and interact with them through private messages (previously available at http://www.facebook.com/s.php), and this functionality was used extensively to search and interact with strangers in ways that were not all that different from the way people used Friendster. Concerned about the long-term consequences of such behavior, Facebook curtailed the ability to look at strangers in the summer of 2007. This restriction would have certainly resulted in a reduction of page views if it had not been for the fact that the company released its Facebook Platform around the same time, which generated tremendous amount of enthusiasm from its users and ensured that Facebook users continued to be engaged. To this day, however, Facebook provides only very poor tools to search for strangers, emphasizing searching for friends.

The foregoing argument allows us to understand the strategic trade-off between platforms that offer "friend" solutions, such as Facebook, and those that combine "meet" and "friend" solutions, such as LinkedIn. Specifically, for many years, industry observers expected that Facebook was going to replace LinkedIn and become a single platform for personal and business relationships. This has never happened, however, and our analysis helps reveal why. For Facebook to replace LinkedIn, it would have to introduce a "meet" solution complete with the ability to search for strangers and interact with them. If that happened, users in relationships would use the platform to reach out to strangers, most likely of the opposite sex. As a result, the "friend" solution would suffer because many people in relationships did engage in unethical behaviors. To avoid this, Facebook never reintroduced the ability to interact with strangers, thereby allowing LinkedIn to operate without a competitive incursion.

CHAPTER 7

"Meet" and "Friend" Solution

MySpace

MySpace is the last platform we'll examine in the first part of this book. Here is the essential background: Chris DeWolfe and Tom Anderson founded the site in 2003 in Los Angeles. The two had already started an Internet marketing business that sold lists of email addresses to other companies for direct marketing. But when that company was acquired by eUniverse in 2002, DeWolfe and Anderson sought a new venture, eventually developing MySpace, which became publicly available in January 2004.

Within the first twenty months of its launch, MySpace had acquired 20 million members. During that period of growth, in mid-2005, De-Wolfe and Anderson sold it to NewsCorp for $580 million. MySpace subsequently continued its growth, reaching 90 million members by July 2006 and becoming, at that point, the most visited site in the United States. The platform's growth continued until mid-2007, and then its usage started to decline, albeit quite slowly. Even in mid-2010, MySpace platform attracted more than 100 million users every month, and by early 2012, still more than 24 million people showed up every month; that's 70 percent of LinkedIn's traffic. Regardless, the decline led Fox (a U.S. subsidiary of NewsCorp) to sell the company to Specific Media and Justin Timberlake for $35 million in mid-2011. In January 2013, the company released a brand new version of the site, and then proceeded to delete almost all of the content from the original site. The new site version failed to attract new users, but the site continues to operate.

Right from its inception, MySpace also combined "meet" and "friend" solutions. However, unlike Friendster, where interactions with strangers were largely private, MySpace encouraged its users to publicly interact with people they did not know. Because of these public interactions with strangers, MySpace could not sustain the cover that allows users to go on the market and meet new people while maintaining a plausible excuse that they are not. Instead, the competitive advantage of MySpace lay in facilitating interactions with strangers while friends are watching. As we will discuss in this chapter, this functionality helped people to communicate information to their friends in ways they would not be able to do in the offline world.

To show this empirically, I collected data on more than 20,000 randomly chosen profiles of users in the United States (excluding bands and entities) who logged in at least once during June 2009. For each user, I identified all other users who publicly interacted with them (e.g., by leaving them a comment), yielding a sample of more than 170,000 additional users. For all of these users, I collected self-reported demographic data, the date and time when they last logged in, as well as their profile content, and tracked them until the end of the summer.

Breadth

When MySpace first launched, it was similar to Facebook or Friendster in that users connected to people they knew in the offline world. MySpace differed from those two platforms, however, in that users could also connect to and publicly interact with many people they did not know in the offline world. MySpace facilitated those interactions in at least three ways. First, any member could view any other user's profile and send that user a message. Second, establishing a relationship did not give people access to any additional information about each other. Both online friends and strangers saw the same profile information. This meant that MySpace users could easily build online relationships with people they did not know in the offline world, as doing so did not really change much about the way they interacted with each other. MySpace subsequently changed its policy and allowed people to make certain content visible only to their online friends. At that point, however, many MySpace users had already established online relationships both with people they knew and people they did not know in the offline world, so the change in policy had a somewhat limited effect on user behavior.

Third, MySpace was unique among other platforms set up during that time in that it allowed entities to set up their own profiles and connect to people. Bands in particular took up this functionality, becoming friends with their fans, posting their lyrics, and announcing new releases and gig or tour dates. By March 2006, there were more than 660,000 bands on MySpace, and fifteen months later that number had grown to more than two million. The company estimated that between 60 percent and 70 percent of MySpace users had music on their page or engaged with music every time they logged on. MySpace quickly added targeted functionality for bands, allowing them to upload up to four songs for free (songs that could then be streamed by users), and to even sell their own merchandise through the site. One MySpace executive recalled:

> We started to promote bands that used MySpace to build their own community of followers. And at the same time we went top-down. We debuted a Nine Inch Nails album, then we worked with artists who were really attuned to this stuff, such as will.i.am, and Rivers Cuomo from Weezer, and all the Black-Eyed Peas. But then came My Chemical Romance, or Fall-Out Boy, both of which leveraged our platform to start from zero and go to platinum in two years. MySpace also had impact on smaller bands. For example, one of many bands I met said: "We're out from Ohio, but then we got 500 fans on MySpace, and they were all from some place in Texas . . . so we went there to play our music."

The band and entity pages were important to breadth because users did not use the entity pages solely for the purpose of interacting with bands, but also to socialize with other fans online. Users did not know many of these other fans in the offline world. But because adding someone as a friend on MySpace did not reveal much new information about either party, many, but not all, of such interactions on entity pages led to subsequent formation of online relationships between MySpace users; there was little risk in doing so. With time, many of these online relationships transitioned into offline interactions.

Some readers might wonder why people are interested in forming online relationships with people they do not know on the same platform where they also interact with their friends. The answer to this question goes to the core of understanding the competitive advantage of platforms like MySpace over other platforms that offer only a "friend" solution or a public "meet" solution. To understand this advantage, it's useful to consider the types of people who might find the public "meet" solution particularly useful, and then examine the people who seem partial to the combination of public "meet" and broad "friend."

To understand the kinds of people who might find the public "meet" solution helpful, recall that in chapter 2 we discussed a number of reasons why people may find it hard to form offline relationships and as a consequence may seek to establish them online. For example, people who live in rural areas may find it harder to form new offline relationships because there are fewer people to choose from close to where they live. Also, high-school students, who usually have very little control in the offline world over whom they can interact with, may wish to go online to find new people who suit them better than the people with whom they have regular contact in school or in their communities.

Indeed, the data attest to the popularity of MySpace with younger people and those in the rural areas. Half of all the users under the age of 50 in the sample (which was split pretty evenly between men and women) were 21 years old or younger. Thirty percent were between the ages of 22 and 30. And the remaining 20 percent were between 30 and 50 years old.

We can also test whether people in rural areas found MySpace attractive by taking advantage of the fact that MySpace encouraged users to pinpoint their location fairly precisely. For example, from my data, I could tell whether a user was in Brandon, Florida (which is 13 miles from Tampa, Florida with a population of slightly more than 100,000 people), or in Plant City, Florida (23 miles from Tampa, with a population of slightly less than 35,000 people), or in Polk City, Florida (45 miles from Tampa, with a population of slightly more than 1,500 people). Armed with the data, I took every location listed by MySpace users and consulted the U.S. Census to find out the population of that location. I then multiplied that number by the Internet penetration in the state of the location to calculate the expected number of Internet users in that location.[1] I divided that number by the number of all expected Internet users across all locations I had, which gave me the percentage of expected users in each location. I then compared that number to the percentage of MySpace users in my sample hailing from that location. If the percentage of MySpace users was lower than the percentage of Internet users in that location, I presumed that users in that location did not find MySpace attractive. In contrast, if the percentage of MySpace users in that location was larger than the percentage of Internet users in that location, then users in that location found MySpace very attractive.

I used these data to create a heat map of United States, available through a link on the book's website: http://press.princeton.edu /titles/10190.html. I encourage readers to examine the map in detail, where red and yellow shading tells us that Louisville, Tampa, and Dayton, had almost twice as many MySpace users as we would expect on the basis of Internet users alone. Cities such Austin, Bronx (New York), Columbus, and Denver (with green shading) had MySpace users proportional to the Internet-user population. In contrast, large cities, such as Chicago, New York, San Francisco, and Washington, DC, (with blue shading) had only half the MySpace users we would expect on the basis of the Internet-user population in these cities.

The preponderance of MySpace users in smaller rather than larger towns and cities becomes even more salient when we examine even more rural areas on the map. There you can see a number of yellow and red dots in various rural areas in both the Midwest and the South. These appear because I found clusters of between four and 10 users hailing from a very small location (whereas I had expected to find no more than one or two). Of course, not all rural areas showed up as overrepresented, but that's because with a sample of 20,000 MySpace users, the likelihood that we would pick up all of the small rural areas would have been slim. (I suspect that with a bigger sample we would have seen greater representation of these rural areas.) Even with the sample we have, however, it is intriguing that MySpace was very popular in places like Greenfield, Ohio, or Peebles, Ohio, with populations of slightly more than four thousand and one thousand, respectively.

To confirm the claim that MySpace is particularly attractive in rural areas, I took the ratio of MySpace users to Internet users and aggregated it to a three-digit ZIP code group (e.g., users from all ZIP codes starting with 900 were treated as a single observation). Subsequently, I regressed this ratio against a number of variables. Consistent with expectations, I found that areas with smaller population density did indeed generate more logins than expected given the number of Internet users. I also found that areas with lower GDP per capita generated more logins, as did areas with higher proportions of young people. All of these findings were consistent with the claim that people in rural areas and younger people have a greater need to meet new people, which may explain why they are drawn to platforms like MySpace.

One caveat is that it is possible that people in rural areas are attracted to all social platforms, regardless of whether they provide "meet" or "friend" solutions. Unfortunately, as I suggested earlier, we cannot pinpoint the exact locations of Facebook and Friendster users, making direct comparisons very hard. I did, however, undertake a comparative analysis of where MySpace and Facebook users hailed from at the state level. Although it is harder to make these assessments at the state rather than location level, regression results do show that the states where users prefer MySpace over Facebook are characterized by lower population density, lower average income, and a higher proportion of younger people, providing additional evidence that it is the "meet" component of MySpace that makes the platform preferable in these locations. For a quick visual representation, see figure 7.1.

Having understood the appeal of the public "meet" solution that MySpace offered, consider the costs and benefits of combining it with a "friend" solution, especially as the combination applies to the users' proclivity to display content for friends and strangers to see.

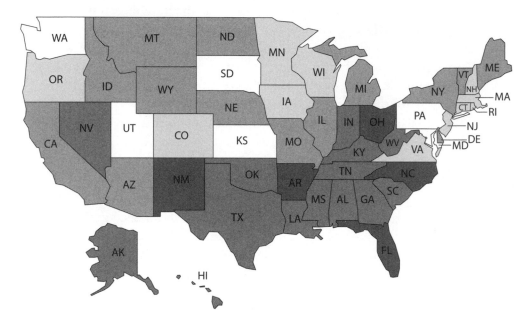

Figure 7.1. MySpace users across U.S. states. Darker colors represent states where MySpace was preferred by users.

Display

MySpace allowed users to display personal information about themselves together with their pictures. The platform, through an unintended programming loophole, also gave users complete control over their profile pages, allowing them to change backgrounds, fonts, and colors, and to add content from other websites. As a result, an entire ecosystem of websites quickly emerged, offering MySpace users a huge variety of backgrounds and pictures they could bring into their "space." With time, users were also able to decorate their profiles with videos, and with boxes that featured some of the games they played online. They could also add music, which would come on just as soon as someone visited their page. Although such flexibility fulfilled members' need to express themselves to others, it offended some older visitors who complained about sensory overload.

The importance of self-representation was not lost on MySpace executives. One of them noted in an interview with me:

You know who a 14-year-old is when you walk into their bedroom, and you see if they have a Mac or a PC, Nike or Puma, or what color their walls are and what books are on their shelves, and what music do they listen to. A MySpace page isn't really that different. That's how we used to express it to advertisers. The idea of self-expression is something that I think very much has been who we are and why we're so different than other social networks. There are a lot of people in the world that don't feel the need to self-express on the Internet. In a way, maybe MySpace isn't for everyone.

Despite being known for expression through pictures and other profile decorations, MySpace also became an important place for people to express themselves through blogs. Given how many people MySpace attracted in its heyday, many of its users blogged frequently, as they were assured of an audience. Indeed, by some estimates, more than 500,000 blog posts were contributed to MySpace every day in 2007, on topics ranging from personal matters to cooking, current affairs, and politics.

Even though MySpace gave users so many different ways to express themselves, however, my research shows that users were less likely to post personal content on MySpace than on some of the sites we've already discussed. For example, the median user on MySpace had fourteen pictures, which is less than half of what the median user had on Friendster, and less than 20 percent of what the median user had on Facebook. Similarly, 60 percent of users in the MySpace sample did not contribute even a single blog entry. These simple statistics suggest that the average user of MySpace did not want to share his or her private information broadly, presumably because they knew that the content would be seen both by people they did and they did not know offline. Put differently, the combination of public interaction "meet" and "friend" solutions together reduced the amount of content people contributed about themselves. In many ways, this is no different from what we saw on Twitter, where the presence of public interaction reduces people's willingness to display content.

On the other hand, my analyses showed that more than 20 percent of MySpace users posted more than 100 pictures, which is twice the percentage that we saw on Friendster and in line with what we saw on

Facebook. Similarly, even though only 40 percent of MySpace users in my sample had a blog, the median user had roughly 14 posts of average length of 272 words, suggesting substantial engagement. These results imply that although, on average, users were likely to post less content, a large number of deeply engaged users were quite happy to post much more content on MySpace than they would on other platforms.

To understand who those people were and why they chose to put so much content on a platform that displayed it both to friends and strangers, Andreea Gorbatai and I interviewed a number of MySpace users in 2008. During the interviews, a number of themes emerged regarding how and why people used MySpace. One type of story in particular came up again and again as users described why they chose to display certain types of content on MySpace. The following quotation from an 18-year-old high-school student in western Massachusetts illustrates the insight most succinctly:

> You know . . . everyone thinks I am a jock. . . . I mean, I am, but I also have a brain. I really like jazz, blues, that kind of stuff. Yes, I know, I know . . . (*laughs*) But my friends don't listen to this kind of stuff, and we are all tight with each other, and if I told them, I think they would tease me a lot. . . . Anyway, I posted some blogs about this stuff and I connected to some [of these] bands on MySpace, and was chatting with a lot of their fans. . . . You know, I never met them before, and I am MySpace friends with some of them, but not all. . . . [M]ost they live like 600 miles away and they are much older than me usually. . . . So we would go and read each other's stuff, leave notes for each other on the blog, stuff like that. Someone must have stumbled upon my blog. That's not hard, coz we all spend way too much time snooping around people's profiles. (*laughs*) . . . And I did get real flak for that from my friends. . . . Some of them thought I was showing off with all this jazz stuff, but I guess some of them went on the profiles of some of these people and saw I was for real. . . . I said to them: "Hey, no one asked you to look," and so they stopped and it's all good now.

There are three important elements to this user's story. First, this user, like many others, was having a hard time reaching out to people in the offline world with whom he wanted to interact. In his case, the problem was that he was in high school in a relatively rural area, and did not have a car he could use, which made it hard for him to interact with people outside his primary place of residence. Second, he wanted to establish and maintain a coherent and comprehensive identity; he wanted his friends to know about his interest in jazz and blues, despite his also being a jock. Third, he found it difficult to convey those interests to them directly. This particular student was concerned about being mocked by his peers for violating normative expectations of being a jock, but in other interviews, MySpace users expressed fears that disclosing certain parts of their identity would fundamentally undermine their relationship with others (e.g., when coming out as gay). They also expressed concern about being seen as boastful or different from typical. In some cases, users said they would have a hard time, in the offline world, expressing their interests to their friends in a way that was comprehensible to them.

Within the context of these "friend" display interaction costs, it is relatively clear how a platform like MySpace alleviated them. MySpace allowed users to publicly interact with strangers online and at the same time make those interactions visible to their friends. The users did not force their friends to observe these interactions. They merely put them out there for their friends to see, which, as the jock's comment indicates, they knew they would. The friends could then examine these interactions at will and decide whether or when to approach the users and discuss what they had learned. It is interesting to note that those subsequent offline interactions could still be quite uncomfortable: the jock in our example still described being teased after some of his friends saw his interactions with online strangers. Having said that, he was able to minimize the teasing by pointing out to his friends that they too undertook a minor social transgression by stalking his profile—something that he would not be able to do in the offline world if he simply announced to his friends that he was interested in jazz and blues. As a consequence, the teasing quickly subsided and his new interest was integrated into this social identity.

Taken together, this analysis shows us two different views of MySpace. On the one hand, for the average user who wants to communicate information to their friends, and is completely capable of doing so, the combination of a "meet" and "friend" solution generates negative effects on display. Such a user will produce less content because he or she knows that it will be shared both with friends and strangers. On the other hand, for a smaller class of users who want to communicate certain information to their friends, but do not feel that they can do so easily, the combination of the two products generates positive effects on display. Such users will be happy to display more content, under the guise of posting it for the strangers, while hoping that friends will see it and discover parts of their identities that would otherwise be unknown to them.

Although it is difficult to identify people who will have the hardest time communicating their true identities to people they know, existing sociological theory provides some clues (Burt 2001). Specifically, Burt suggested that when people have friends who do not know each other, they are free to represent themselves differently to different people. In this case, they also have full latitude in narrating their social interactions in the way that suits their identity. In contrast, people who have many friends who are friends with each other will find it difficult to assert their own identity. When someone's friends all know each other, they are likely to discuss the characteristics of that person, and reach a consensus on what this person is like and what his or her characteristics are. It will also be impossible for the individual to assert that he or she interacts with someone in a very particular way, as such claims will be quickly verified and corrected. As a consequence, individuals in such dense networks will find that their identity is determined for them socially, which may or may not be consistent with how the person sees himself or herself. Rather aptly, Burt (2001) calls this phenomenon character assassination.

Having a network in which all friends know one another does not always mean that individuals are unable to express their identity to others. After all, it is possible that people chose such a network exactly because it supports and reinforces the identity they chose for themselves. When people are thrown into a dense network with fairly little control over it, however, the problem can become quite acute and people may have real problems expressing themselves freely to others. One prominent example when this happens is high school—there we have very little control over the people we interact with, and the network of people we know is very dense. Other examples abound, however. For example, individuals in rural areas are more likely to find themselves embedded in networks in which they had little control over whom they interact with, and these networks are likely to be dense. If that is indeed the case, we would expect that people embedded in those dense networks, particularly when they are of high-school age or live in rural areas, might find MySpace particularly useful to communicate their true identities to people they know by way of interacting with strangers.

My analysis of MySpace indeed shows that users in rural areas post more pictures and more blogs. Furthermore, consistent with expectations, I find that users who have friends who are friends with each other tend to post more photographs and more blogs, and this effect is particularly strong for users who live in rural areas. Taken together, the results suggest that although on average MySpace users posted less personal content, there was a group of highly committed people, particularly characterized by dense social relationships in rural areas, for whom the display characteristics of the platform were very attractive, and those users contributed a lot of content.

We can get further confirmation of this claim by examining secondary content on MySpace in the form of users' comments on other people's profiles and blogs. Initially, everyone was allowed to comment on others' content, regardless of whether they were online friends. (Eventually MySpace allowed users to prevent strangers from commenting on their profiles or their blogs, but this was not the default option.) And, in many instances, when MySpace users received comments from strangers, they reciprocated, either by commenting on the stranger's comment or by going to his or her profile and leaving a comment there. Viewed this way, MySpace was akin to Twitter, in that people could send a public message to others, receive a reply, and have third parties witness this interaction.

Consistent with our earlier analysis, users embedded in large and dense networks in rural areas should have the greatest need to engage in public interactions with strangers that their friends can see and, hence, should be most likely to engage in these behaviors. To test this prediction, I used the data to examine what kinds of users received and retained comments on their profiles or blogs from people with whom they are not friends offline.

As reported in model 8.1 in the online appendix, the results confirm this prediction. On average, online friend density had very little effect on the likelihood of obtaining public entries from other users who were not online friends. When I divided users into those living in rural areas and metropolitan areas, however, I found significant differences. Specifically, people who lived in metropolitan areas and had friends who were connected to each other were much less likely to obtain comments from people they did not know online than people who had friends who were *not* connected to each other. In contrast, people who lived in rural areas and had friends who were connected to each other were much *more* likely to obtain comments from people they did not know online than people who had friends who were *not* connected to each other.

To get a more robust picture of interaction, I repeated the same analysis for people of different ages, as reported in models 8.2 and 8.3 in the online appendix. I found that for people 18 years of age or younger, both friend density and rural location increased the likelihood that they would publicly interact with strangers. For people 18 years of age or older, however, the effects disappear, suggesting that the effect is related to being unable to choose friends in the first place, and being stuck with an externally given identity. All of these results highlight the unique value proposition of MySpace for people embedded in dense networks over which they had fairly little influence, as is the case for people in high school or those who live in rural areas. For them, the ability to interact publicly with strangers enables them to project their identities in ways that would be hard to do in the offline world.

Search and Communication

MySpace also gave its users the ability to view profiles of others without their explicit permission. Like Facebook, MySpace did not inform users when their profile was visited. MySpace did, however, feature a counter attached to every photo posted, showing everyone how many times this particular photo was viewed (without showing who viewed it). Furthermore, on the "meet" side, MySpace provided users with an extensive set of tools to search for strangers, through the "browse people" function. Users could easily search using sex, age, relationship status, whom the users were looking for, and location and obtain a list of people matching these criteria. It was equally simple to search for and locate bands and other entities. Finally, like all other "meet" and "friend" platforms, MySpace provided functionalities to communicate privately through private messages.

Given that I have no data from MySpace to measure the amount of search and communication activity during the study period, I cannot clearly identify what kinds of users searched for others, viewed others' profiles, or messaged them. Such data would be incredibly interesting, as they would provide us with additional evidence that people in dense networks in rural areas are most likely to search for others and communicate with them privately. Without these data, we have to rely on results from the previous section, where we showed that people in dense networks in rural areas end up publicly interacting with others they do not know, suggesting that these people also engaged in search behaviors. Sadly, given that the original site data were deleted, it will be quite difficult for future researchers to access such data.

Conclusions

This description of MySpace's strategic choices, accompanied by the data, allows us to understand how the company attracted so many users so quickly, and then proceeded to lose a great majority of them to Facebook, and yet retained a substantial proportion of committed users before being sold and restarted.

When MySpace first launched, Friendster was experiencing significant technological problems that prevented the platform from scaling up, thereby opening a window of opportunity for another service to step in and fill the demand. MySpace did exactly that and allowed people to connect to people they knew. At the same time, it allowed users to expose their information to strangers and meet them directly or through various activities such as band fan groups—something that Friendster did not offer—giving MySpace another strength that fueled its rapid growth.

MySpace faced a penalty, however, for combining the public "meet" solution with a "friend" solution in that users on average disclosed less information than they would on a platform with a standalone "friend" solution. This left an opening for a platform with a "friend" solution only to step in and allow users to share more information to a smaller set of people whom they actually knew. Facebook did exactly this and drew users who cared about disclosing more information to friends away from MySpace. Additional privacy functionalities and the third-party developer platform, offered by Facebook but not by MySpace, only served to accelerate this exodus. Poor public relations and negative coverage in the media further reduced MySpace's appeal.

At the same time, however, the combination of "meet" solution with "friend" solution continued to generate significant benefits for a fairly large group of people—those in rural areas and especially those in dense social networks in those areas. For those people, the ability to interact with strangers, and the ability to do so while friends were observing, was invaluable and they chose to stay on MySpace even as other users decided to move to Facebook. Of course, as more and more of their friends moved to Facebook, the utility of MySpace as a place to interact with strangers and friends declined, eventually leading to the platform's demise. Still, even with the massive exodus from MySpace, many of its core users still found the site incredibly useful.

More abstractly, this analysis has provided additional evidence in support of the four claims from chapter 2 that have guided this book. First, we saw that people do indeed differ in the kinds of interaction costs they face. This was highlighted for us when we focused on a sub-section of people who face extensive display interaction costs with their friends. Second, we saw that social functionalities need to address both the economic and the social causes of interaction costs. Specifically, it is only through the simultaneous attention to both types of causes that MySpace was able to alleviate display interaction costs for a set of its users. Although we saw less evidence here that social solutions need to reduce interaction costs related to breadth, display, search, and communication, the discussion articulated a very important strategic trade-off. Specifically, we saw that on the one hand, the integration of a public "meet" solution with a "friend" solution helps a fairly narrow set of users reduce their display interaction costs. On the other hand, for a broad set of users, this combination increases these display interaction costs knowing that strangers will be watching. This leads to a trade-off between platforms that simply offer a "friend" solution with those that offer both a public "meet" and a "friend" solution. Specifically, platforms offering just "friend" solutions will refrain from adding public "meet" solutions for fear of undermining the efficacy of the "friend" solution for a substantial proportion of its users. At the same time, platforms offering public "meet" and "friend" solutions will refrain from removing either of the components so as not to alienate those who actually need to display information to friends under the guise of showing it to strangers.

Next Steps

At this point in the book, you should have a great understanding of what it takes to build a successful social platform. First, you need to identify various interaction costs that generate social failures for a particular segment of the population. Second, you need to build functionalities that address the economic and social causes of these interaction costs. Third, you have to ensure that these functionalities address breadth, display, search, and communication costs, or else you run the risk of not building a complete social solution. Finally, you have to ensure that you do not provide too many solutions, or you run the risk of exposing yourself to the adverse effects of strategic trade-offs illustrated in table 1.1. For example, if you want to build a platform that helps people communicate with their friends and acquaintances, you should refrain from providing functionalities that facilitate public interactions, as doing so will undermine the efficacy of the "friend" solution.

Mastering these insights allows us to understand why some social platforms perform better than others. It also helps us build new social platforms more effectively. This foresight is very important for entrepreneurs who are building brand new social platforms, as well as for large and established companies seeking to incorporate social platforms into their strategy. After all, as we have seen over and over, designers of these social platforms may think they are building a particular type of platform, but the outcome of their work is often very different. For example, LinkedIn's founders sought to help people meet strangers through friends, but in the end they actually helped people display information when it was normatively inappropriate for them to do so. Similarly, Friendster's founder sought to alleviate failures related to dating for single people, and instead the platform ended up being used most by people in relationships. MySpace, which sought to provide unrestricted contact for everyone, ended up appealing only to those who were interested in conveying information to their friends by displaying it to strangers. With the aid of the framework we now have at our disposal, most of these surprises could have been avoided.

With this in mind, we now turn to apply this framework to understand how large existing companies can incorporate social platforms into their strategies. The next chapter sketches out the general framework, and the remaining chapters serve to illustrate it.

CHAPTER 8

Social Strategies

With this chapter, we shift our focus from understanding how to build a well-functioning social platform to understanding how a firm that produces economic goods can benefit from such platforms. To do that, I will introduce a framework that I developed by applying the insights in the first part of the book to the experiences of more than sixty companies that have tried to leverage online social platforms for economic gain. These companies span a wide spectrum of industries, from manufacturing through consumer-packaged goods to services and consumer finance. I have also employed the framework in a number of paid and unpaid consulting opportunities; my experiences in that realm are reflected here as well. Those engagements both tested the framework's underlying concepts and helped me refine a process through which companies can implement it with ease.

What My Research Revealed, in Broad Strokes

As I began my research, it quickly became clear that there are two major ways in which companies have tried to leverage social platforms for their own strategic benefit. In the first instance, observing that millions of people connect to friends and strangers on social platforms, some companies have chosen to enter the fray in a similar way, by trying to build relationships with people online as if those people were their friends. That approach has often entailed setting up a corporate page on Facebook, getting people to "Like" it, and then broadcasting messages to those fans with the expectation of receiving a response (in the form of either feedback or increased sales). Companies have also undertaken the same set of activities on Twitter—establishing an account, getting people to follow the firm, and hoping that those people will respond in kind.

Such strategies have allowed firms to engage in an activity that's very familiar to them: broadcasting content to customers. And for many, the approach has generated incredible engagement in terms of the number of likes or followers, the number of responses, or the number of times corporate messages are forwarded to others. For example, by mid-2013 Target had slightly less than 22 million fans on Facebook, Wal-Mart had 30 million, while Converse and Starbucks had about 35 million each. Disney had more than 44 million, and Coca-Cola had gathered more than 69 million fans, 800 thousand of whom reportedly liked the Coca-Cola page or posted a status update on that page; liked, shared, or commented on a Coca-Cola post; mentioned Coca-Cola or its page in their own post; tagged Coca-Cola in a photo; shared or liked a Coca-Cola-related deal; or wrote a product recommendation.

Indeed, many firms began to compete with each other over who can have most Facebook fans or Twitter followers. Fueled by the desire to increase these numbers, many of those responsible for social engagement online reached out to key decision makers in the company to try to obtain an ever-larger budget for such efforts. Invariably, however, they are met with the same question: "How much do all of these social efforts contribute to our bottom line?"

And that's where, for many companies, the frenzy grinds to a halt. In rare cases, it is possible to answer that question with specifics and document some connection to profits. More often than not, however, the answer is something along the lines of: "Well, we cannot really demonstrate that any of these actions actually translate into dollars and cents." That answer usually stops budget increases in their tracks; soon after, social efforts become just another box to check in the company's marketing manual.

In the second instance, companies have behaved very differently. These organizations have eschewed broadcasting messages to customers, instead focusing on connecting customers to each other, subsequently linking those customers' actions to increased profitability.

To see this approach in action, consider eBay's Group Gifts app, launched in late 2010 and designed to help people pool funds to buy gifts for friends. To buy a group gift, a person goes on eBay's Group Gifts site, and names a recipient, either by typing the name in directly or by picking the name from the list of his or her Facebook friends. eBay then offers a set of general gifts, or allows the organizer to give the application the right to collect the recipient's Facebook "likes," which are then used to recommend a gift. Thus, if the intended recipient has indicated on Facebook that he likes the Beatles or Apple, Group Gifts then recommends Apple brand gifts, or items related to the Beatles. The organizer then decides on a gift, determines her own monetary contribution, and issues invitations to other contributors by posting an "invitation to contribute" on her Facebook profile. This invitation contains a link taking users directly to the appropriate gift page to contribute additional money. Once enough money has been collected, eBay sends the gift, along with the list of all contributors and short notes from them, to the recipient.

This application generated three types of immediate benefits for eBay. First, the average price of Group Gift goods was reportedly five times higher than the average eBay sale. Second, a third of those who participated in a group gift sign up for a PayPal account. Finally, another third returned to visit eBay within a month with the intent to purchase other items. Importantly, eBay obtained all of these benefits *without having to pay additional customer acquisition costs*. These results suggest that eBay's foray into leveraging the social Internet for profit reveals a replicable strategy that benefits both the company and the consumer and can be succinctly summarized as:

(1) eBay increases its profitability
(2) by allowing people to strengthen their friendships through gifts
(3) when they ask their friends to buy from eBay

Consider the key features of this strategy. First, the social engagement eBay facilitates is *directly related to strategic goals of the company—*

increased sales or lower cost. The direct connection to strategic goals allows the company to realize immediate benefits that made it easy to justify future investments into using social channels to power the company's strategy. It also stands in marked contrast to the firms pursuing the first approach, which sought to engage with customers in the hope that the "likes" they received on Facebook or retweets they got on Twitter would translate into sales or lower costs (which they rarely did).

Second, with this approach, eBay is not trying to become friends with its customers with the intent of broadcasting messages to them. Instead, it *seeks to help people establish interactions with each other that they would otherwise have a hard time entering into*. As one participant in a Group Gift transaction said in an interview: "If it wasn't for the eBay update from my friend that I saw on Facebook, I don't think I would ever know that we were buying a gift for [name of the person], and I don't think anyone would think to ask me for money to chip in, but I saw this and chipped in, and just the other day I got a thank you note. . . . I think it will make it easier for us to stay in touch." Viewed this way, eBay actually offers a "friend" solution, which allows people to overcome interaction costs related to the awkwardness of asking acquaintances for money.

Third, and perhaps most important, *the two benefits co-occur and are tightly integrated*. This is critical to the broad acceptance and long-term success of any such efforts. Take the *co-occurrence* of benefits. It is fairly easy to imagine a scenario in which a firm asks its customers to tell their friends about a particular product in exchange for giving these people monetary benefits. Although such a scheme will probably benefit the company, it will also probably undermine many of the social relationships that people have, thereby limiting the scope of people willing to engage in such behaviors.

The tight *integration* of social and economic benefits is equally important—users can obtain the social benefits only if they undertake actions that clearly benefit the firm. Specifically, to be able to overcome social failures, users need to post a status update on Facebook, which then also advertises eBay to their friends, which then allows the company to acquire new customers without having to pay for it. It is fairly easy to imagine scenarios in which the firm provides a social solution for users, but the users do not need to create benefits for the firm to obtain the social solution. When that happens, users will gain social benefits but the economic returns to the firm will be mediocre.

Digital Strategies vs. Social Strategies

To help us distinguish between the two approaches that most firms take and eBay's approach, I call the first a *digital strategy*, and the latter a *social strategy*. I hypothesize that well-designed *social* strategies are likely to get more engagement than *digital* strategies because the former leverage what people naturally do on social platforms—interact with others in ways they would find hard to do in the offline world or on other social platforms. At the same time, social strategies also benefit companies in that they can ask people for whom they solved social failure to undertake jobs for the company for free—jobs that the company would otherwise have to do on its own and pay for. Such strategies therefore translate into concrete outcomes that affect both the top or the bottom line.

Clearly, social strategies are much more complicated than digital strategies in that the former require that firms grasp both unmet *economic* and *social* needs of customers, and act to meet both needs at the same time. Addressing economic needs is straightforward. Companies have centuries of marketing history to draw on to perfect their understanding of customers' economic needs (as they relate to security, shelter, nourishment, clothing, education, or entertainment) and help them determine how best to provide solutions. In contrast, most organizations know very little about social interaction costs and customers' unmet social needs. Even less is known about how to meet those needs effectively. As a consequence, most companies to date have found it very difficult to identify the particular social failure they might be best suited to address and match it with an appropriate social solution that also layers in an interdependent economic solution.

That's why the primary goal of this part of the book is to help readers construct a social strategy that jointly addresses unmet economic and social needs. Half the work needed to reach that goal is already done. After all, the first part of the book has already identified many social failures and discussed some of the most effective ways to go about solving them. The remainder of the work comes in understanding how to make a social solution part of a process that helps commercial organizations become more successful.

The fact that social strategies are inherently more complex than digital strategies makes them much more risky to implement. For a digital strategy, all that a firm needs to do is port its marketing or customer acquisition efforts to the social platform and execute the same kinds of tasks that it has been doing before. No major changes in the business model are required, which minimizes any risk of failure. In contrast, social strategies require that the firm change at least one part of its value chain and hand control over that part to its customers or suppliers. Although this approach results in a higher willingness to pay or cost savings, it also means that the firm no longer directly controls the process. For example, the company can no longer pay money to ensure that customer acquisition happens; now it has to hope that its customers will do customer acquisition.

The inherent riskiness of social strategies leads me to the second major goal of this part of the book—to help readers develop a process that maximizes the chances that they will succeed. To do that, I devote the rest of this chapter to explaining the ideas underlying the concept of social strategy. Then, in chapters 9 through 12, I exemplify the four types of social strategies by examining social strategies of various companies. Then in chapter 13, I propose a method for developing social strategies in large and established companies. This process entails developing a set of integrated options, applying a series of strategy tests to eliminate or refine some of these options, and then picking one of them to implement. I will illustrate this process using a real-life, albeit disguised, example from a credit card company and an undisguised example from the *Harvard Business Review*.

The Elements of a Successful Social Strategy

What does a successful social strategy entail? To answer that question, think back to eBay's social strategy, which had at least three distinct but integrated elements: (1) it articulated how it improved the company's existing business strategy, (2) it explained how it will alleviate social failures, and (3) it specified the kinds of jobs people needed to undertake to solve these failures and at the same time benefit eBay's business. When we generalize eBay's approach, we obtain the following framework:

(1) A viable social strategy seeks to increase a company's profitability
(2) by improving interactions between people
(3) if they undertake a set of corporate functions for free

To understand how to develop a strategy that fits the framework, it is necessary to dive more deeply into each of its three parts. We'll start with the business impact, as described in (1).

Business Impact

With regard to increasing profits, or business impact, there are two major choices to consider—one strategic, the other tactical. The strategic choice is related to the well-known and widely accepted theory that firms can essentially pursue two types of successful strategies (Porter 1996). First, a firm can embrace a *differentiated* strategy, whereby it incurs a higher cost to deliver its products, but then it also compels, in its customer base, a higher willingness to pay for these products. When this strategy is successful, the increase in willingness to pay is higher than the cost, allowing the firm to survive any price wars effectively and benefit from higher profit margins. Second, a firm can adopt a *low-cost* strategy, whereby it incurs a lower cost to deliver its products, which results in a lower willingness to pay for these products. When this strategy is successful, the decline in willingness to pay is much lower than the cost savings, also allowing the firm to survive price wars effectively and benefit from higher profit margins.

Social strategies build on top of existing business strategies and allow firms to attain greater advantage than they would be able to achieve otherwise. Thus, social strategies will come in two distinct flavors. A *differentiated social strategy* will help a firm increase its customers' willingness to pay without a commensurate increase in cost. A *low-cost social strategy* can help a firm reduce its costs without a commensurate decline in its customers' willingness to pay.

Once the firm decides on the nature of its social strategy, it then faces a tactical choice whether to apply this strategy companywide or just to individual functions. A companywide strategy will pertain to the entire organization and entail an integrated set of decisions that span the gamut from sourcing inputs, transforming the inputs into outputs, marketing, distributing and selling, and providing after-sales support. For this type of strategy to be successful over the long term, companies must ensure that all of the choices they make reinforce one another. Otherwise, other organizations will quickly replicate the approach and eradicate the firm's competitive advantage. A functional strategy will, by contrast, be limited to a particular function, for example, operations strategy or marketing strategy. Functional strategies help firms implement the companywide strategy, but on their own they are insufficient to insure that the company remains competitive in the long run. Given the complexity of developing a strategy for the entire enterprise, however, firms often start with developing a number of functional social strategies, and only then seek to embark on a companywide social strategy.

Social Solution

In developing a social solution for the social strategy, a firm also faces a strategic as well as a tactical decision. The strategic choice is whether to offer a "meet" solution or a "friend" solution, as described in the first part of the book. There is no logical reason to believe that one of these two types of social solution is better suited to either a differentiated or a low-cost social strategy, suggesting that four types of social strategies (shown in table 8.1) are equally viable: a low-cost social strategy with a "friend" solution; a low-cost social strategy with a "meet" solution; a differentiated social strategy with a "friend" solution; and a differentiated social strategy with a "meet" solution. To illustrate the differences between these strategies, consider a few concrete examples, which we will consider at greater length later in the book.

THE LOW-COST "FRIEND" STRATEGY

To see an example of a strategy that reduces costs while providing a "friend" solution, consider a typical computer game development com-

Table 8.1. Types of Social Strategies

		Social solution	
		"Meet"	"Friend"
Strategy impact	Higher willingness to pay	American Express	Nike
	Lower costs	Yelp	Zynga

pany, which not only needs to incur costs to develop its games but also needs to market them to ensure sales. Such a company's advertising expenditures can be substantial, in some cases reaching 40 percent of the game revenue.

One possible social strategy entails having the firm substantially reduce its advertising expenditure and make up for that reduction by having the people who own or play the game reach out to their friends to ask them to start playing. Such forms of new customer acquisitions will probably be less effective than, say, targeted advertising, thereby lowering the average willingness to pay. This lower willingness to pay, however, will be offset by even lower costs of customer acquisition, resulting in a successful low-cost social strategy. To encourage users to invite their friends to play, the game could promise them the ability to reconnect with friends in ways that would be difficult for them to do in the offline world. As long as the act of inviting a friend also unambiguously helps people reconnect with others, the strategy will benefit both the firm and the individuals. In fact, Zynga, an online social gaming company, adopted substantial parts of this strategy, which for a certain amount of time allowed it to dramatically reduce customer acquisition and retention costs as compared to nonsocial competitors. Thus, Zynga's social strategy could be described as:

(1) Zynga's social strategy seeks to reduce user acquisition and retention costs
(2) by allowing users to reconnect with their friends
(3) if they ask their friends to join the game

In chapter 9, we will examine how successful Zynga was in implementing this strategy.

THE LOW-COST "MEET" STRATEGY

To see an example of a low-cost "meet" strategy, consider Yelp, an online company that provides professional opinions written by a cadre of professional reviewers of establishments across the country. This company makes money by charging those establishments for presence on the site and by charging advertisers for promotional materials that site visitors see when they look for a particular establishment. It saves the expenditures associated with writing the reviews by having an army of volunteers write the reviews instead. Even though such user-generated reviews may potentially generate lower willingness to pay (because some people will not trust reviews written by volunteers), the decline in cost will far outweigh these willingness-to-pay losses, making this a successful low-cost social strategy. To encourage volunteers to write, the company could promise them the ability to meet prolific volunteer contributors if and only if they themselves contribute content. To the extent that people care about meeting others who love to review various establishments, but find it difficult to meet these people in the offline world, they may be willing to provide the reviews. As we will discuss in chapter 10, Yelp's strategy can then be described as:

(1) Yelp's social strategy seeks to reduce the cost of acquiring inputs
(2) by allowing volunteer reviewers to meet other reviewers in the offline world
(3) if they contribute establishment reviews for free

THE DIFFERENTIATED "MEET" STRATEGY

To see how a firm can develop a social strategy that increases the willingness to pay for its products while providing a "meet" solution, consider a fairly nonsocial solution offered by financial institutions—a credit card. Credit card issuers are fiercely competitive because customers have very little preference for one card over another. Thus, just about every issuer offers free cards, and those that offer cards that cost money tend to offer additional perks and benefits, such as miles, cash-back options or lower interest rates for people who carry balances from month to month, which eat into those companies' profitability.

One possible social strategy is for the credit card issuer to allow its cardholders to meet other cardholders as long as they hold the card, or incur a minimum expenditure on the card. Although the willingness to pay created this way may be lower than, say, giving people direct monetary rewards for using their card, the cost to provide these benefits is much lower, resulting in a successful differentiated social strategy.

At first glance, this scheme might seem far-fetched. After all, why would credit card users have interest in meeting other credit card users? Recall, though, that certain credit cards may be aimed at classes of people who may in fact wish to meet one another. For example, owners of small businesses may wish to connect with other owners of small businesses, and a credit card targeted at small businesses may be a great tool to employ in helping them to identify each other. American Express, which we cover in chapter 11, adopted this strategy, allowing it to increase the willingness to pay for its small business credit card as compared to nonsocial competitors. This social strategy can be described as:

(1) American Express seeks to increase the willingness to pay for one of its cards
(2) by allowing cardholders to meet other cardholders
(3) when they are willing to hold and use that credit card

The Differentiated "Friend" Strategy

The final strategy type allows a firm to increase willingness to pay by providing a friend solution. We are already familiar with this strategy; this is exactly what eBay did. By allowing people to reconnect with other friends through gifts, eBay was able to increase its customers' willingness to pay, in terms of both the absolute ticket price and the average expenditure per person who contributed to the group gift. eBay's approach can be described as follows:

(1) eBay's social strategy seeks to increase willingness to pay
(2) by allowing people to strengthen their friendships through gifts
(3) when they ask their friends to buy from eBay

In chapter 12 we will review similar differentiated "friend" strategies in the context of Nike.

Tasks

This part of the strategy statement pertains to articulating the tasks that the company expects people to undertake for free. These actions can pertain to any part of the value chain—they can entail providing inputs, or free labor for production, free marketing, sales, or after-sales support. The actions can also be related to corporate tasks, for example, helping firms recruit others.

There is no limit to the kinds of tasks people can perform for a firm for free. To help us classify these actions, it is easiest to rely on our familiar framework that entails breadth, display, search, and communication actions. Specifically, breadth actions involve people joining a particular type of community in "meet" solutions, or inviting their friends to join in "friend" solutions. The tasks in the American Express example cited earlier fall squarely into this category, as the company is asking people to be in the specific community of credit card holders. Display actions ask that individuals provide certain content—personal or otherwise—for strangers or friends to see. In the Yelp example, reviewers were asked to provide restaurant reviews to strangers, while on eBay users posted status updates for their friends to see. Search actions ask that individuals engage in acts of discovery about others. For example, in the eBay example discussed earlier, users were asked to discover their friends' preferences to buy them an appropriate gift. Finally, communication pertains to all actions that lead users to interact with others directly. For example, many of Zynga functionalities pertained to communication with friends.

Although the nature of the task depends on where in the value chain it will occur, it is important to remember that the task must simultaneously improve the company's profitability while allowing the individual to improve his or her social interactions. As noted earlier, without such tight integration between the benefits for customer and company, a social strategy is bound to fail. Specifically, when the task merely solves the social failure but does not benefit the company, individuals will undertake the task, but it will not have any effect on corporate performance. In contrast, when the task benefits the company but does not help the individuals, they will simply refuse to undertake the job, resulting in no profit increases for the company. Getting this alignment to work is perhaps one of the most difficult parts of designing a workable social strategy.

Choosing to Go It Alone or to Use an Existing Social Platform

Throughout the process of developing a social strategy, it's important to consider the benefits and risks of implementing that strategy independent of the existing social platforms or integrating certain activities with them.

Consider the ways in which many existing social platforms offer points of integration for traditional firms. For example, since 2007, Facebook has given third-party companies a set of tools that allow them to access user data from Facebook and contribute content to users' profiles, both with explicit permission by the users. In some cases, integration with existing social platforms is critical to the success of the strategy. For example, eBay's Group Gift application we discussed earlier relied on integration with Facebook to discover the preferences of the gift recipient to recommend the right gift, and to post status updates to the gift organizer's profile for his or her friends to see. The ability to post on the gift organizer's page was critical to eBay; without it, eBay could not acquire new users at low marginal cost.

In other cases, integration with existing social platforms is nice to have but not critical. For example, Nike has built its own social platform, which has attracted more than five million runners who use it to track their progress, discover new running routes, meet other runners, and interact with their existing friends. Although Nike integrated this platform with Facebook, allowing users to import their friend list to

Nike's platform and post status updates documenting their running achievements, neither functionality was critical to the Nike platform's success.

Sometimes, integration with existing social platforms is contraindicated. For example, a site that encourages users to meet others afflicted with a particular type of mental or physical condition may wish to refrain from integration with general-purpose social platforms to protect their members' privacy or to prevent accidental leakage of information from the specialized site to a more general site, such as Facebook.

Next Steps

In the next chapters, we will examine in depth several companies that employ various types of social strategies. We will begin this analysis with recent start-ups that critically rely on social strategies for their survival. The relatively small size of these companies and relative simplicity of their business models will allow us to identify some of the critical mechanisms underlying social strategies and quantify benefits with data. Then, we'll turn to larger, more established, and more complicated companies. These analyses reveal how firms can combine various social strategies at the level of a function to a corporate-level social strategy. They also help illustrate some of the critical processes firms go through to develop their social strategies and the organizational conditions that facilitate these processes.

CHAPTER 9

Social Strategy at Zynga

I n this chapter we will focus on a low-cost "friend" strategy in the context of a set of social gaming companies. Specifically, we draw on qualitative data describing Zynga's strategy and combine them with quantitative insights from publicly available industrywide surveys undertaken by Information Solutions Group, and user behavior data from one of Zynga's competitors (the competitor elected to remain anonymous). Zynga chose not to provide any quantitative data for this book.

Zynga's Background

Casual social games were first developed by companies in Asia in the mid-2000s. These games eschewed a focus on destroying enemies in favor of encouraging players to build, develop, and cooperate. They featured simple rules and graphics and asked that users engage in familiar tasks, such as gardening, cooking, or socializing. Zynga, a U.S.-based start-up, brought these games to the U.S. online market when it began developing them in 2007. The company's first big breakthrough came in June 2009, when it released its first fully fleshed Flash game: FarmVille.

The mechanics of the game were fairly straightforward. Users accessed the game by logging into Facebook, and then choosing to play the game through the Facebook platform. At this point, their demographic characteristics as well as the composition of their Facebook online network was sent over to the game. To start, users were given a small amount of virtual currency, which they could use to plant virtual flower or vegetable seeds on a virtual plot. They would then wait for the plants to grow, at which point they would harvest and "sell" them. Users needed to come back to the game frequently, as unharvested crops would wither away. With virtual revenues from the harvest, users could buy more seeds or animals, expand the size of their farm, or invest in virtual machinery, buildings, or decorations. Although the game never ended, users progressed through various levels, which gave them abilities to invest in new crops, buy new types of animals, or continue to expand their farms.

The game became an instant hit, amassing ten million installations within days of being released. Within a month, FarmVille had more than 5 million users who played the game at least once a day; a month later, that number was 15 million. Zynga continuously analyzed which game features were most interesting to users and refined the game accordingly, releasing upgraded versions of FarmVille as often as twice a week. These evolved versions often included "seasonal" items, including Thanksgiving items in late November, or holiday decorations in December. These changes in part contributed to the game's continued success, allowing FarmVille to reach 80 million daily players by February 2010 (roughly 20 percent of Facebook users at the time). Many of these users were very committed to the game, decorating their farms extensively and then taking screenshots to share with others.

Encouraged by FarmVille's success, Zynga began building a series of similar games in different contexts. These included CityVille, released in December 2010, where users played to build a "city of their dreams"; FrontierVille, released in June 2010, where users farmed and crafted virtual items to build a Western outpost; CastleVille, released in November 2011, where users farmed and crafted virtual items to build a magical castle; and ChefVille, released in August 2012, where users managed their virtual restaurant. Zynga also released or marketed a number of other titles, such as a competitive game called Empires and Allies, released in June 2011, and a hidden objects game called Hidden Chronicles, released in January 2012, and a host of other games, such as Words with Friends. At that point, Zynga had amassed more than

230 million users (almost one-third of Facebook's members) from 166 countries who played at least one Zynga game at least once a month. More than 60 million of them played at least one Zynga game at least once per day.

Despite differences between the games, they were all based on the same premise. They all presented players with goals and obstacles to achieving them, and then gave them an opportunity to overcome these obstacles by engaging in online interactions with their friends. These interactions were fairly standardized and entailed sending requests for help or offers of help. Research has found that these standardized interactions did actually translate into offline interactions. For example, two surveys by Information Solutions Group, each of which covered more than a thousand users in the United States and the United Kingdom found that 25 percent of players connected or reconnected with others they knew as a result of their participation. Of those who claimed to reconnect with others, 22 percent reported that the game is their only way of interacting with those others, 23 percent said the game is their primary way of interacting, and 42 percent stated that interacting through the game now comprises only a small percentage of their overall interaction with those others. If these numbers are representative of the overall population of social game players, a single game with 10 million users could help 1.05 million people (10 million * 25% * 42%) establish better social relationships in the offline world.

The foregoing description suggests that social games play a dual function. On the one hand, they provide entertainment value for the players. On the other hand, they provide social platforms for people to reconnect with their friends. Clearly, these games are not as effective at reconnecting people as a typical social platform like those we studied in the first part of the book. Still, facilitating a million new reconnections by a single game is nothing to sneeze at. To understand how these games create friend reconnections, though not at the level of a typical "friend" solution, we use our familiar breadth, search, display, and communication functionality framework. (Doing so will also allow us to articulate the various jobs that social game players are required to do on the companies' behalf.)

Breadth

Social games were able to facilitate social interactions for so many of its players because they attracted a wide breadth of people who came to play these games. Some of the quotes collected through the Information Solutions Group surveys help animate the point. For example, one interviewee claimed: "I found one of my old school friends who was my best friend, and the games have helped us build up a new friendship," while another one said: "It has been almost 40 years since I was in high school, and a broken relationship from school was left unresolved. I actually looked up this person's name, found him, reconnected, and started playing FarmVille on a regular basis with him. The game smoothed the way for us to resolve and reconnect as friends after all these years."

To understand just how broad the coverage these games achieved was, I analyzed the Information Solutions Group U.S. survey, and found that the distribution of player characteristics did indeed mirror the distribution of those characteristics in the overall U.S. population across a number of salient dimensions. Specifically, the survey found that 55 percent of players were female, which was in line with the percentage of social platform users who are female. The average player age hovered around 40, with approximately 20 percent of players in their thirties, another 20 percent in their forties, and another 20 percent in their fifties. Again, this roughly mirrors the U.S. social platform population. More than 40 percent of players had an associate degree or more education, which was in line with the percentage of U.S. adult users of social media. Next, almost 45 percent of social game players claimed their household income exceeded $50,000 a year—and the same percentage of American households reported this level of income. Finally, the percentages of players who were single, had no children, were married with children at home, and were married with children away were also consistent with the underlying U.S. population.

The only marked difference, in fact, between those playing online social games and the overall Internet-user population was in the geographic distribution of players. These were distributed fairly uniformly across the country, except there were 25 percent more social game players in the Southeastern United States and 25 percent fewer online game players in Texas and the rest of the South than we would expect on the basis on Internet users in those parts of the country.

Not only were the social game players roughly representative of the Internet-user population overall, but also, they were very committed to gaming. More than half of all social game players had been playing for more than a year and social games took up 40 percent of the total time they spent playing games. Sixty-five percent played at least once a day, and a half of those daily players actually played multiple times a day. Slightly more than 55 percent played more than a half hour a day, and more than 30 percent played more than an hour a day. Indeed, roughly half of the time social gamers spent on social networks was related to playing social games. Taken together, these data suggest that social games as a category do indeed reduce breadth interaction costs. Not only do they proportionally draw from all sectors of the online society, but also they involve people deeply, giving everyone an opportunity to strengthen their "friend" interactions.

To understand whether the games provide narrow or wide breadth functionality, I turned to data from a social gaming company, which administered a survey to six hundred of its game players. The survey revealed that 54 percent of those people played with their families, 59 percent played with close friends, and 71 percent played with acquaintances and colleagues. Roughly 20 percent of people played with people they had never met, suggesting that some social games also have a "meet" component. Similar surveys by the Information Solutions Group (covering Zynga games and other social games as well) yielded equivalent results.

To get a better sense of how many different people players interact with, I relied on data from one of Zynga's competitors—a social gaming company with a set of games equivalent to Zynga's suite of Ville games. I found that on average, players of those games were "neighbors" with roughly thirty-five other players. This suggests that social games provide relatively narrow breadth functionalities. Having said that, the data showed that the number of "neighbors" was linearly related to how advanced the player was in the game, suggesting that users did not lose interest in connecting to others as they progressed through the game. Instead, it provided a continuous vehicle for players to build increasingly more, and thus broader, relationships with others as they continued to play the game.

These findings allow us to understand how social games, like those offered by Zynga, were able to facilitate reconnections between so many friends. The sheer number of people who played these games combined with proportional representation of the underlying population meant that just about everyone who wanted to reconnect with a friend or an acquaintance could actually find one. At the same time, these results inform us why these social games are not as effective at reconnections as some of the social platforms we studied in the first part of the book. Specifically, the relatively narrow set of people with whom the user played these games limited the potential for reconnections with others.

Display

Online social games provide two different display functionalities. The first set pertains to displaying virtual buildings or decorations inside the game environments. Unlike typical social platforms, these display functionalities do not allow players to share personal data. The virtual achievements in the game could still be used to initiate interactions, however. In the words of one of the players I interviewed: "I have had people message me on Facebook to say, wow, your farm is really beautiful . . . and then we would chat a bit about what's going on in life. . . . I know this might be a little bit lame to say this, but you know, it did motivate me to decorate more and get the compliments."

The second set of display functionalities entail giving social games permission to post status updates on players' Facebook timelines for these players' friends to see. These status updates would document players' achievements in their games; issue requests for help in the games; and offer help in the games for others. Facebook users could provide such help or use the help offers by simply clicking on the link included in those status updates. Although some players did not even realize that they were posting these status updates (some games posted them automatically once they got user permission), other players used these updates to convey information to their friends. A younger male player said: "I am not going to post on Facebook that I had a bad day, but I will post that I need something in a game, and make some comment on that post, and my friends will see it and they know what I mean, and then someone will email me." Another one claimed: "I know that some people do not like when people ask for help in FarmVille on Facebook, but to me this is an indication that you are playing the game and an invitation to connect with you. I will usually click on those and start connecting."

To get a sense how much users engaged in those display behaviors, I used data from Zynga's competitor and divided all of its user activities into those that are necessary to progress in the game, such as planting or harvesting, and those that are related to display inside the game, such as decorating, expanding, or building, or achieving goals, and then display activities outside the game on Facebook. Not surprisingly, the activities required to progress in the game dwarfed all of the other display activities by a factor of twelve. Within the class of display activities, however, decorating led the way, followed by expanding, with status updates being the least frequent activity. In fact, further analysis revealed that on average only 10 percent of players posted such status updates.

It is not difficult to understand why so few players posted status updates on their Facebook timelines. These updates were very standardized and conveyed very little personal content. As a consequence, they provided very little direct utility to their friends who would see such updates. Players who posted such status updates often received negative feedback from their friends. Some of these friends went as far as to join a Facebook group called "I do not care about your cows or your tractors," referencing the fact that many of the status updates generated by social games on behalf of players pertained to various virtual farm animals and machinery.

Indeed, players seemed to be acutely aware that the status updates provided little value to the recipients and sought to compensate for this. Data I have indicate that as many as 50 percent of the status updates initiated as a result of an online social game were offers of help— for example, a user found a particular item that he could not use, but he chose to share it with others. What's more, of those updates, a great majority pertained to special "collector" items that could only be obtained from friends, indicating that users were being particularly thoughtful about when their friends were likely to benefit from their status updates. In contrast, requests for help accounted for less than 15 percent of the status updates. Players were also very unlikely to post updates that boasted of their achievements in the game. These results hold, even when we control for the frequency with which users are given opportunities to post the various types of status updates.

To the extent that these results apply to Zynga's games, they allow us to understand how display functionalities on Zynga's games allowed players to reconnect with friends. As evidenced by the qualitative comments, both types of content could be used as an excuse to initiate interactions between friends. At the same time, the data I furnished help us understand why display functionalities further contributed to the limited impact of social games on the rate of reconnection between friends. Most of the display functionalities conveyed little personal content, and in the case of game-related status updates on Facebook, the display functionalities actually had the potential to increase, rather than reduce, interaction costs. For this reason, few users actually wanted to post them, limiting the opportunities for reconnection. This is not to say that such status updates could not have reduced display interaction costs. For them to do so, however, social games would have to ensure that people were able to post something that provides a clear benefit to the poster's friends. We will return to this shortcoming of social games when we examine its business implications.

SEARCH

Online social games also offered certain search functionalities. For example, players could become virtual neighbors with their friends who played the game, and then visit their virtual environments. Many friends, in turn, valued these visits, viewing them as opportunities to show off what they had created. As I suggested in the previous section, such visits could then turn into interactions between friends and acquaintances.

To gain a better understanding of how much this search functionality was used, I asked the online social gaming company to share data on visiting behaviors. The results indicated that, on average, players each visited roughly 1.5 friends per day if they played the game that day. Further analyses, however, revealed that the average hides substantial variation across players—as many as 70 percent did not visit any of their friends' virtual environments. Those who did visit on average visited only 10 percent of their virtual neighbors. Both the average number of visits and the percentage of players who viewed more than one profile were orders of magnitude smaller than the number of comparable actions we saw on platforms like Facebook or mixi.

There are at least a couple of hypotheses that could explain why people engaged in so few search behaviors. First, it is possible that visits to other people's virtual environment are inherently nonsocial and are instead motivated solely or primarily by the prospect of obtaining rewards by visiting friends. To test this hypothesis, the social gaming company ran a set of experiments in which it manipulated the need to visit friends to obtain rewards from the game. Surprisingly, the experiment showed that even two weeks after the manipulation (a very long time in the social gaming world) users did not significantly change the frequency at which they visited friends. This suggests that, on average, economic incentives have little to do with the frequency of visits.

Another hypothesis to explain the relatively low level of search activity has social underpinnings. The ability to visit a friend's virtual environment and help them proceed in the game more quickly can serve as a great excuse to reconnect with a friend. Once the reconnection happens, however, and the two friends start interacting with each other, it's possible that the incentive to go and check out and help them in the game diminishes. After all, the information revealed by visiting someone's farm or city reveals very little interesting personal information that is hard to find out in the offline world and could be used to improve interactions with that person even further.

Data from the online gaming company are more consistent with this hypothesis. Users who joined the game recently are much more apt to visit virtual environments of their online friends than veteran users are. Furthermore, when asked in a survey about the kinds of features they really appreciate about the game, it is the users who joined the game recently who put the ability to visit others' virtual environments at the top of their list. In stark contrast, users who have already established a large number of "neighbor" relationships in the game tend to visit others' virtual environments less frequently. In fact, when asked in a survey about the kinds of features they really dislike about the game, these users name visiting others as one of the top features they *dislike* about the game. Presumably at this point, the users have fulfilled any social needs they may have had, and now visiting friends becomes a chore needed to advance in the game without an obvious social benefit.

To the extent that these data apply to Zynga's games, they help us understand that the company's online social games reduce some search interaction costs. These reductions are particularly powerful for people who are new to the game—some of whom use this functionality to reestablish contact with others. As soon as contact is reestablished, however, the value of the solution becomes rather thin, particularly as the search functionalities result in little direct insight into the private lives of others.

COMMUNICATION

Most of the functionalities related to communication in social games entailed sending requests for and offers of help sent through the game's internal messaging system or through Facebook's notification system. Users had a strong incentive to send these, because certain tasks in the game could only be achieved by sending help requests to friends and having them approve it, or by relying on friends to offer help. Most of these interactions were standardized and did not allow users to convey any personal information or ask questions about others. Despite its standardized nature, this way of communication still allowed users to interact with their friends. One player put it this way: "For me, Farm-Ville has become a very easy way to network with my friends. . . . You know, I can send a gift to someone who is my Facebook friend but I don't know too well. It's easy and noncommittal. If they want, they can send me a gift back. So then I can go on their farm and clean it up a little for them, and they can do the same for me, so then I can send them a little thank you message. . . . [S]ometimes this leads to an IM chat or an email exchange on Facebook. Once I even got invited to a real party by this friend who I only sort of knew." Some games also allowed users to send messages to each other and users took advantage of them. For example, one player, interviewed by the Information Solutions Group, said: "I have not seen my sister in years. She plays Fish World, and invited me to play. I leave her messages by Fish Mail."

Although I do not have data on messaging use, I do have data on requests for and offers of help. These data indicate that only one in eight people who played a game on a given day asked for or offered help. This percentage is fairly low compared to player participation in other actions in the game. For example, when a game explicitly asked users to invite some of their friends to join the game, roughly 20 percent complied.

To better understand why users may prefer not to interact with friends in online game environments, I separated those data into asking for help and offering help and compared the two. Results indicate that users were much more likely—by a factor of four—to offer help than to ask for help. Additional data revealed some aversion to asking friends for help, even if withholding a request meant not completing a goal in the game. Specifically, by the company estimates, anywhere between 10 and 30 percent of users who started a particular task, but then were forced to ask friends for help to complete it, failed to do so. And ultimately, more than 80 percent of those players abandoned the game altogether.

With those facts in mind, I inquired further into the process of interacting with others by sending them a gift. The data indicate that slightly less than a third of those who sent gifts received something in return for that gift within 30 days of sending it (for comparison, on an average dating site, where there is presumably often much more social risk attached to interaction, at least 20 percent of messages receive at least one reply). This number is surprisingly low given that online social games typically prompt users to accept all requests for help and reciprocate all gifts when they sign into the game (though they can bypass the prompt). This suggests that although some reciprocity is at work here, it is not as strong as we would expect between friends.

To the extent that these findings apply to Zynga, they allow us to understand how communication functionalities of Zynga's social games were able to facilitate reconnections between friends, but their effect on facilitating interaction is smaller than what we saw on other social platforms. This is probably because the standardized forms of interaction—offers of help or requests for assistance in the game—convey little personal information to others, making people somewhat reticent to engage in such behaviors even if they need to do so to get ahead in the game faster. The data also suggest that users are more reticent to engage in communication behaviors than in display or search behaviors. To a certain extent, that's not surprising—we already saw in the first part of the book that users engage in display and search activities more than communication activities on almost every social platform. Even here, however, players seem to be acutely aware of norms of social interaction and prefer to initiate interactions by providing, rather than requesting, help.

SUMMARY

Our analysis of the breadth, display, search, and communication functionalities provides a very consistent view of social games, like those offered by Zynga. On the one hand, each of these functionalities gives players the ability to reconnect with others. On the other hand, each of these functionalities offers only a limited reduction in interaction costs, implying that only a limited set of players will be able to use these games to interact with others. Perhaps the biggest limitation of these games is that they allow users to convey only limited personal content as compared to what is available on other "friend" platforms. This should alert us to the importance of helping people display, search for, and communicate around truly personal content. For example, these games could conceive of a way to encourage people to display, say, their hidden talents or athletic achievements, both of which are hard to find out in the offline world and on Facebook. Without those, it's hard to generate reconnections between friends.

Social Tasks

Having understood how online social games facilitate various types of social activities, we turn to evaluate whether they help game developers improve their competitive advantage. Most of the games I studied chose to emphasize tasks to reduce customer acquisition and retention costs.

Consider, for example, display functionalities—social games could have settled for simply letting people decorate their virtual environments to express who they were. Instead, they added specific display functionalities that required people to advertise the game to others on Facebook.

In the previous section, we already saw that people did not wish to engage in such behaviors because they did not think the behaviors benefited their friends. But perhaps, despite their low frequency, these postings were actually very effective in acquiring new players? To test this, I used the data from the online gaming company to establish various customer acquisition and retention metrics. The data showed that users needed to post on average 500 status updates before the company gained one new user for free. There was broad variation in this number—status updates related to sharing gifts with others received the most clicks, and roughly 200 of such updates were needed to result in one new user. Requests for help stood at roughly 400 updates per new users, while almost 2,000 generic updates advertising user's success in the game were needed to get someone to play a game. Regardless of the variation, however, these numbers suggest that the display functionalities had fairly limited impact on reducing customer acquisition costs.

To the extent that these numbers apply to Zynga, they have clear implications for our understanding of the first part of Zynga's social strategy, which can be summarized as follows:

(1) Zynga's social strategy seeks to reduce user *acquisition* costs
(2) by allowing users to reconnect with their friends
(3) if they ask their friends to join the game

Even though Zynga was in the position to use its players to reduce its customer acquisition costs, it *did not successfully execute this strategy*, because individuals did not engage in sufficient number of display activities to engage their friends, and even if they did, friends did not respond. One of the key reasons why this was the case was that these display behaviors conveyed very little benefit to the viewers. After all, few users found it worthwhile to click on the link to obtain a virtual cow. This is not to say that social games could not have given players such benefits. But to do that, they would have to offer users greater visibility into the personal lives of others.

Next, consider search and communication functionalities that allowed players to visit others and send them gifts or request for gifts. These functionalities had the strongest effect on encouraging players to stay in the game, thereby potentially reducing customer retention costs. Earlier in the chapter I documented that only a small proportion of players actually engaged in such behaviors. Data indicate, however, that the search functionalities, such as visiting and receiving visits from friends, and communication functionalities, such as receiving gifts from them, had a much more powerful impact on users. In the most extreme case, players who obtain visits from all of their "neighbors" and receive gifts from them have almost zero probability of abandoning the game. More realistically, those who receive a visit and a gift from at least from three of their friends when they play the game are 50 percent less likely to abandon it than those who do not receive at least that number of visits.

To the extent that these numbers apply to Zynga, they have clear implications for our understanding of the second part of Zynga's social strategy, which can be summarized as follows:

(1) Zynga's social strategy seeks to reduce user *retention* costs
(2) by allowing users to reconnect with their friends
(3) if they ask their friends to join the game

Here, we see that Zynga was in the position to use its players to reduce its retention costs, and the company did a much better job of executing this strategy. Although players were not very likely to engage in search and communication behaviors, when they did, they had a substantial effect on retention. Our earlier reasoning allows us to understand why. People who had already played these social games and were invested in them appreciated visits and gifts from friends, as these allowed them to go more quickly through the game. By the same token, those players who did not receive visits or gifts found it difficult to proceed in the game, and were more likely to leave. Of course, social games could have done a much better job of encouraging their players to engage in the search and communication behaviors. But at least the level of search and communication activity they managed to elicit had significant effects.

Impact on Business Outcomes

Zynga sought to engage its players in customer acquisition, but failed to give them sufficient social incentive to do so. To understand the economic implications of this failure, consider the underlying business model. Most of these games were free to play; gaming companies rely on users buying in-game currency as the main source of their revenue. Users were offered virtually currency packs, costing between $2 and $100, and could pay for them using their credit cards, PayPal accounts, or mobile phone accounts. Alternatively, users could go to their local convenience store and buy a scratch card that would allow them to enter the code into, say, a Zynga game to obtain the currency. Finally, users could obtain a certain amount of that special currency by signing up for Disney Channel or Netflix.

This in-game currency allowed players to advance through the game more quickly without having to acquire neighbors, display content to them, search, or communicate with them. It could also be used to purchase decorative items in the game. By the end of 2011, Zynga had around seven million customers, each spending on average more than $100 per year on a product that had no marginal cost, allowing the company to book around $740 million in revenues in the first nine months of 2011 alone. Even though an average paying user spent more than $100 per year, the company could not afford to spend that much to acquire players, as only 2 to 6 percent of players were actually paying customers. With conversion rates like this, the company could pay between $2 to $6 per player, which did not leave it much wiggle room if it wanted to invest in advertising online or offline. Most Internet businesses have found that they need to spend at least $20 in advertising before they acquire a customer, with some paying as much as $100.

Put differently, with economics like this, it was critical for social games to acquire customers as cheaply as possible, get them to buy the in-game currency, retain them for as long as possible, and encourage them to invite as many others as possible to join. For example, if every player that a company obtained through advertising brought at least one other player with him for free, an online social game would be able to pay $4 to $12 to acquire that player in the first place. If every player brought two more for free, the payment could reach between $6 and $18. Clearly, the rate at which players invite others to join a game has fundamental implications for the businesses' long-term prospects.[1]

To see how these dynamics play out in reality, I asked Zynga's competitor to share data on the composition of users and where they came from. These data revealed substantial variation across different games. On one end of the spectrum, the company developed games for which it had to acquire more than 60 percent of players through advertising. At the other end, there were games for which the company only had to invest to acquire 20 percent of its players, getting the remaining 80 percent for free. At first glance, these numbers are reassuring, suggesting that for the best-performing games, one paid user could have brought in as many as four unpaid users. That might be taken to mean that many of the display tasks I described in the previous section, as rare as they were, did indeed have a fundamental impact on social games' business.

Deeper analyses revealed, however, that not all of the "free" users were actually acquired through the social tasks. Indeed, only about a third of those users were acquired through those tasks (between 10 and 25 percent of all game players). The remaining two-thirds of "free" users (between 20 and 50 percent of all game players) joined the game on their own, by typing the name of the game in the search bar on the social platform, or by being sent to the game as a cross-promotion from other games created by the developer.

Given that two-thirds of "free" players joined on their own rather than through social actions, I decided to probe this category further and consider two competing interpretations. First, it is possible that players saw a number of status updates and requests from existing players, researched the game, and then decided to start playing by typing the name of the game, rather than clicking on a status update. If this were the case, given the data, we would severely underestimate the effects of social actions on the acquisition of new players. Second, it is possible that players were exposed to a lot of advertising, but they chose not to click on it, instead researching the game more and deciding to join it independently. If this were the case, we would severely underestimate the effects of advertising on customer acquisition in that the players coded as "free" actually joined as a result of advertising.

It is very difficult to establish empirically the strength of these two effects. The company did, however, undertake a number of experiments that can help us get a sense of their relative power. Specifically, the company manipulated the amount of its advertising spend and the frequency with which it encouraged users to post status updates in certain geographic markets. The experiments showed that increasing advertising spend almost instantaneously increased the number of "free" players who started playing the game without an invitation from an existing user. At the same time, exposing users to an equivalent increase in the number of status updates they see from others also increased the number of "free" players who started playing the game without an invitation from an existing user, but did so to a lesser extent. That increase was about four times lower. This suggests that most of the "free" traffic is probably attributable to unobserved effects of advertising rather than social actions. If that is the case, then the earlier finding that between 10 to 25 percent of players were acquired through social action represents a fairly accurate estimate.

There are at least two ways of interpreting this estimate. On the one hand, they attest to the power of social strategies. Put simply, between one in ten and one in four customers brought one customer in for free, allowing the games to save between 10 and 25 percent of their customer acquisition costs. If we assume that a high-quality game spends $50 million on advertising to bring in customers, then these savings can add up to anywhere from $5 million to more than $12 million—a sizable sum indeed.

The other interpretation is less favorable, suggesting that the social strategies of online social games may be insufficiently powerful to sustain their economic viability. Online social games, including Zynga, find themselves in a difficult situation in that their low expected lifetime value of a customer requires them to acquire customers inexpensively. When advertising on the largest distribution platform, Facebook, was cheap, they were able to acquire customers at very low cost. Even if only every fourth customer brought in a new one for free, the customer acquisition strategy was still profitable. As more advertisers flocked to Facebook, however, and the price of advertising there increased, so too did the cost of acquiring paid players. As a result, many online social games, Zynga included, found that it was not economically viable to pay the going advertising rates; they were generating negative returns. That's why many of these social games enjoyed early fast ascendance and subsequent economic difficulties.

Conclusions

The foregoing discussion provided us some insight into the original success of online social games and the subsequent problems that led to concerns about the industry's long-term viability. But it also gave us some general lessons related to what makes for a good social strategy, as discussed in the previous chapter.

First, in order to have a functioning social strategy, it is necessary to build a social solution. But to build a successful social solution, we need to identify a powerful set of social failures and then provide social functionalities that address them. Social games sought to tackle failures related to reestablishing contact with acquaintances. The solutions they provided, however, were not powerful in that they did not allow users to display or search for personal information, or give them direct interaction functionalities. These choices reduced the ability of social games to help people reconnect, although, as evidenced by the data, some people succeeded. It is my hope that this point will stick with readers: Simply getting people involved in a seemingly social activity, such as gaming, or calling a game "social" will not generate new interactions. To facilitate and encourage such interactions, social strategists have to think through explicit solutions to breadth, display, search, and communication functionalities.

This point becomes particularly relevant when we consider the social "jobs" that a company needs users to perform to implement its social strategy and contribute to its business strategy in a meaningful way. In principle, the jobs used by social games were sound; they called on users to get their friends involved in the game, thereby potentially reducing customer acquisition and retention costs. As discussed, however, these actions were not directly related to users' establishing better relationships. Only a limited set of people felt that they would connect with their friends better if they posted a status update on behalf of Zynga, or if they visit someone's virtual city. As a consequence, a limited set of users would post such updates or respond to them. Put differently, social games used social dynamics to achieve business goals. These social dynamics, however, were actually not all that social, in that they did little to solve underlying social failures, leading few players to engage in them, and thereby undermining their effect on business goals.

Separately, the business problems experienced by online social games underscore that social strategy alone is unlikely to help a social gaming company reach or sustain profitability. Firms still need to have a solid business strategy, and only then can they add social strategies to make the business strategies more powerful. This was very apparently in the case of many social games, which did not have a long-term business strategy for customer acquisition. Instead, they relied on a temporarily suppressed price for advertising to do so. When the market price became more realistic, the value of this strategy dissipated and there was very little that the social solution offered by social games could do to help.

That final point has important implications for existing companies that seek to introduce and implement a social strategy. At first glance, this description of online social games could be taken to mean that social strategies yield limited success. Nothing could be further from the truth—recall that online social games managed to reduce customer acquisition cost anywhere between 10 and 25 percent. If we assume that this level of customer acquisition savings represents an upper bound on how much firms can save by employing a social strategy, then a firm that spends hundreds of millions of dollars in advertising can expect to save tens of millions of dollars by employing social strategies! I hope that the insights in this chapter will encourage existing companies to adopt social strategies, but to do so in a way that truly solves social failures and connects those solutions to improving their existing business strategies.

CHAPTER 10

Social Strategy at Yelp

To illustrate a low-cost "meet" social strategy, we will examine Yelp, a U.S.-based website that boasts more than twenty-seven million reviews of businesses—such as restaurants, shops and beauty salons—that are written by a cadre of volunteers. I documented this strategy through qualitative analysis of Yelp's choices and interview data with Yelp contributors. In addition, I relied on quantitative data on the contribution patterns of almost 8,000 volunteer reviewers between 2004 and 2012 in the Boston area that I collected online. To obtain a baseline, I collected the contribution patterns of almost 20,000 volunteers posting on TripAdvisor, a site that gathers reviews of hotels, bed and breakfasts, and rental homes, over a similar time period. Finally, some comparisons in this chapter will be made on the basis of a dataset documenting all contributions to Wikipedia between 2004 and 2009.

Background

Yelp was founded in mid-2004 as a site that allowed users to get information about the services they sought in a particular location from a designated set of friends. Users provided the type of service they wanted, and the emails of the friends they wanted recommendations from, and then Yelp would send those friends an email message with the request. Yelp would then compile responses and send them to the original inquirer.

This version of the platform proved unsuccessful, and by early 2005, Yelp had changed its approach to soliciting reviews. Anyone could post a review of a local establishment to the site in any format they liked. Yelp explicitly forbade business owners, their employees, and their friends from reviewing their own or competitor establishments, however, and did not allow them to offer incentives for writing reviews. Businesses were also forbidden to badger reviewers via Yelp's mail system, and initially, they were also not allowed to respond to negative reviews on the site.

Most reviewers recounted their personal experiences in light prose, describing the food, service, ambiance, and even the attractiveness of the wait staff. And although the company did not edit reviews for spelling, grammar, or accuracy, the reviews were largely of high quality and the site quickly gained popularity. Initially available only for San Francisco establishments, Yelp soon expanded to Boston, Chicago, New York, Los Angeles, and Seattle. By the end of 2006, the company had expanded to an additional six cities in the United States, and by the end of the following year, it had entered fourteen more, including two in Canada. Expansion continued apace both in the United States and overseas, as Yelp entered the United Kingdom, Australia, and twelve European countries. And by March 2012, Yelp was active in forty-nine U.S. markets and thirty-three markets abroad. That month the company also started trading on the New York Stock Exchange, with market value of just under $1.5 billion.

At that point, more than 27 million reviews had been posted, up from 4 million by the end of 2008, and 1 million in mid-2007. In 2012, shopping establishments comprised 23 percent of all reviews, followed by restaurants at 22 percent, and home and local services, beauty and fitness, and arts and entertainment at 10, 9, and 7 percent, respectively. Other categories (auto, nightlife, travel and hotel, and other) comprised the rest.

To help visitors access the reviews, Yelp showcased a number of different establishments and reviews and created extensive search functionalities, which led users to various businesses' webpages on Yelp. Each of these pages featured an establishment's address and telephone number, a Google map, a link to its own website, and information on hours of operation, price range, credit card acceptance, Wi-Fi availability, reservations, parking, dress code, and suitability for children. The page also showed the number of Yelp reviews, the average rating the establishment had received, and the name and photo of the Yelp reviewer who first reviewed it. Following this information, Yelp displayed reviews, each prominently displaying its author's name and photo, which readers could click to access the reviewer's profile. An algorithm that reportedly incorporated factors such as newness, frequency of reviews by the contributor, and reader ratings ordered establishment reviews, but readers could always re-sort the reviews as they wished. Readers could also rate every review as cool, useful, or funny by simply clicking an appropriate button under the review. Additionally, each venue's page offered links to the pages of other enterprises viewed by prior visitors, and a selection of user-generated lists on which the focal establishment appeared. Each page could also include a sponsored search result or a piece of advertising.

In June 2006, Yelp had only 1 million unique visitors a month, but a year later it already had 4 million such visitors, by the end of 2008 that number had grown to 20 million, and by mid-2013 it had reached 108 million.

Yelp's Social Solution

Clearly, the site was successful, and a significant proportion of its success lay in its ability to source content in a unique fashion. Interestingly, Yelp first experimented with paying $1 per review, particularly when entering new cities. The company quickly found, however, that those reviews were often very poorly written, and so it pulled back hard on that approach, using it only in the first couple of weeks of entering a new market to ensure the availability of a very basic level of content.

Then the company focused on developing an "Elite Squad" program in those locales. This program allowed certain Yelp contributors to get to know one another through offline gatherings, such as wine events, cocktail parties, costume parties, or art events. The parties were organized by local Yelp community managers, whose job was also to encourage volunteer reviewers by commenting on their reviews, and start message-board discussions.

Initially, Yelp invited contributors who had not written much yet, but seemed to know the newest bars and restaurants and were very likely to share this information with others, to become Elite Squad members. Subsequently, the company evolved the program and started inviting those who contributed a lot of reviews across a broad variety of establishments, and wrote useful, personal reviews. Contributors could also apply to be granted Elite status, but only members who were 21 and over, revealed their real names, and posted photos of themselves on their profiles stood a chance to be admitted. Business owners and those affiliated with local businesses were excluded. The Elite Squad designation was granted only for a period of one year. To maintain their status, contributors had to continue providing content to Yelp.

Yelp contributors gave these parties high marks. Some Elite Yelpers favored the parties because of the easygoing nature of the interactions there. "It's a group of people who find unique, cool places to go, and they share it with each other. . . . It's really like a bunch of friends," commented one Elite Yelper. Others, including one 23-year-old female Yelper in Portland, Oregon, attended Elite parties to find dates. Having attended college out of state and then returned to work for an online business, she found that she knew few people in her hometown. "I'm not about to do online dating," she said, "but a network for meeting friends sounded good." At one Elite party she met a reviewer whose writing she admired. "He came on the scene a few months ago, and he's hilarious," she said. "I really wanted to meet this guy." Most parties were extensively photographed, and the pictures were posted on Flickr (http://www.flickr.com/photos/yelp). By October 2013, more than 416 thousand pictures had been posted. The company did not reveal the total number of Elites, but many estimated this number to be in the low thousands.

Interestingly, the idea to launch the Elite Squad and to host parties was completely serendipitous. As Jeremy Stoppelman, the CEO and the cofounder of Yelp, explained:

We had at the time one marketing person who was like, "Maybe we should meet some of our users that are addicted Yelpers now. . . .

They're in San Francisco; we're in San Francisco, it can't be that hard to meet up." . . . We had this first meeting; it was this really social bunch that came out and met up with us for drinks . . . and we're like, "Wow, this is really interesting." [The meetings] sort of spun out of that. We did our major event [at] Armani Café. It was really successful. People had a great time. . . . So it just seemed like, "Hey this really fits and makes a ton of sense, so let's just keep doing it." And so we kept doing it, and it got bigger and bigger and now [we're] a little notorious for it.

EFFECT OF YELP'S SOCIAL SOLUTION

This brief description of Yelp suggests that the company developed a "meet" solution, in which writing becomes the activity that subsequently allows people to meet. The success of this social solution depends on whether there exists a class of people who would like to meet a set of strangers for friends or dates, and have an appreciation of good food or other high-quality area businesses and the ability to write about their experiences. As evidenced by some of the interview comments, there are at least some people who are interested in meeting such strangers but are unable to do so in the offline world. For them, Yelp provides a social solution to their needs. There, for example, instead of paying a dating site a fixed sum of money, contributors are willing to incur the cost of writing reviews to make themselves known to strangers and subsequently meet them. Such an arrangement not only benefits the writers but also helps Yelp because it means more substance on the site—a sign of a solid social strategy.

Indeed, it is tempting to attribute Yelp's success to this strategy. After all, the company was able to solicit more reviews and attract more visitors than many of its competitors, such as Chowhound, which also relied on user-generated content, but did not offer social rewards to those who generated content. Yelp was also more successful in terms of the number of reviews and visitors it attracted than CitySearch, which provided professionally written reviews of local establishments.

On the other hand, it is easy to furnish a number of examples of successful user-generated content sites that do not offer social rewards.

For example, TripAdvisor, which gathers user-generated online reviews of hotels, bed and breakfasts, and vacation rentals, had more than 75 million reviews on 3.4 million establishments across the globe thirteen years after it was founded. Yet, at no point in its history did it offer an explicitly defined "meet" solution to elicit contributions. Similarly, Wikipedia, the largest online encyclopedia, has been widely considered to be the most successful user-generated content site, but it does not provide explicit social rewards to users for their contributions. Both of these examples imply that people will contribute content for free even if they are not remunerated with the ability to meet strangers. This suggests that it is not necessary to add a social solution to create a successful user-generated content platform, begging the question of what benefits Yelp obtained by adding its "meet" solution.

To answer this question, consider first a nonsocial platform in which individuals write just because they obtain personal satisfaction from doing so. If these individuals differ in how much motivation they have and how quickly it goes away after they have written reviews, only the most committed will stay, while others will leave the site. In such circumstances, the overall rate of new contributions will decline. Furthermore, contributions will become very concentrated in this committed group, and these top contributors will account for a very large proportion of the content. To the extent that these top contributors write the same kinds of content, or contribute similar types of points of view, the variety of contributions will decline, too.

Now consider the possibility that some contributors obtain additional value when readers mark their reviews as funny, cool, or useful or when they are chosen to be in an "Elite Squad" and, as such, get to interact with others. These rewards will make it less likely that they will leave and more likely that they will contribute more content, either because they will want to qualify to be in the Elite program or, once they are in the Elite program, because they will want to maintain it. Furthermore, if contributors who value the social rewards most are *not* the same ones who have the highest intrinsic motivation to write, we will see a broader set of contributors staying active on the site. This means that contributions will be less concentrated, and the top contributors will account for a smaller proportion of the overall content written.

To the extent that now more different contributors generate content, it is likely that the variety of contributions will increase, too. Or, in the language of this book, a company seeking to obtain contributions from others should be able to obtain more content, and have it less concentrated in the hands of few contributors, if it offers a social solution in return. The next two sections examine whether that hypothesis is actually the case.

BREADTH

Consider first the nature of breadth solutions offered by Yelp. The company did not explicitly advertise its social solution, instead relying on providing solutions to those who were already attracted to writing and reviewing. According to company data, the great majority of reviewers were college graduates (for comparison, about 30 percent of the U.S. adult population has graduated from college). Approximately 20 percent of the reviewers had postgraduate degrees, at least double the percentage of postgraduate degree holders in the general population. Reviewers' ages also skewed differently than the general population: even though 41 percent reviewers were between the ages of 25 and 54, which is exactly the percentage in the whole population, slightly more than 42 percent of reviewers, as compared to 33 percent in the population, were between 18 and 34 years old. Clearly, limited advertising limited the breadth of Yelp's social solution.

Once users started contributing to Yelp, the data show substantial bifurcation of their engagement. On the one hand, for the period studied, approximately 45 percent of contributors did not have any Yelp friends, suggesting that almost one-half of Yelp contributors did not care much about its social benefits. On the other hand, 25 percent of contributors had more than five Yelp friends, 15 percent had more than ten, and 5 percent had more than thirty-five Yelp friends, suggesting that a sizable subpopulation of contributors used Yelp to establish online relationships with others.

Users were also fairly well represented in the Elite program, with 14 percent of the reviewers in my dataset achieving Elite status for at least one year between 2004 and 2012. Of those who did, half held the status for a year or two, and 12 percent held it for five years or more. Despite members of the Elite program comprising a small proportion of the underlying reviewer population, almost 40 percent of reviews were written by members when they held Elite status. Overall, these data suggest that Yelp's social solution did not provide significant breadth. People who did get attracted to it, however, seemed to be fairly well engaged.

DISPLAY

Yelp's main display solution pertained to the ability to write reviews. To help reviewers show off their ability, Yelp generated automatic profiles for each reviewer. These included a chronological list of the contributor's reviews, a list of establishment lists compiled by the reviewer, and a compilation of compliments the reviewer had received for his or her reviews. The profile also listed the contributor's Yelp friends and events the contributor planned to attend. One user praised the profiles as invaluable for deciphering a review: "Member profiles are a cool yet efficient way to determine if a reviewer's interests match mine, and thus whether I should trust their opinions." Another one said: "Once you get into the community, you start going from profile to profile to get to know others, much in the same way you would do on Facebook."

To better understand the significance of how frequently different contributors posted reviews, I examined what proportion of Yelp reviews were posted by its top contributors and compared these numbers to TripAdvisor and Wikipedia. This analysis, illustrated in figure 10.1, revealed that contributions to Yelp were more equally distributed across contributors than was the case on other sites where users contribute review content. For example, the top 10 percent of contributors to TripAdvisor generated 58 percent of reviews, but on Yelp they wrote only 50 percent of them. And on Wikipedia, the top 10 percent of contributors generated more than 90 percent of edits to the encyclopedia. In the same vein, the top 20 percent of contributors to TripAdvisor wrote 75 percent of reviews, but the equivalent number was 68 percent for Yelp. On Wikipedia, the top 20 percent of contributors accounted for 95 percent of the site's content. This pattern continued all the way down the scale to the least prolific contributors, those who generated only one review. Even there, the distinction between Yelp and TripAdvisor was quite pronounced. On Yelp only 30 percent of contributors wrote one review and stopped, while the comparable number for TripAdvisor was 45 percent.

Although these numbers indicate that Yelp was more effective at facilitating more repeat contributions from a broader set of writers, they do not confirm that the Elite program was responsible for compelling individuals to write more. To examine what might cause certain individuals to write more (or less), consider how many reviews per year various *types* of reviewers posted between 2004 and 2012. My analysis of Yelp data shows that contributors with more Yelp friends wrote more reviews. Furthermore, reviewers who received more feedback that their reviews were funny or useful were also more likely to contribute them in the future (although those who received feedback that their reviews were cool were actually less likely to write them!).

Most important for our purposes, Elite members wrote more reviews than nonelite members did, although the explicit effect of Elite status was not too large and amounted to less than one review per year. This last result is subject to a number of interpretations. On the one hand, I could have overestimated the effect of becoming an Elite—after all, Elites are chosen because they like to write and that may be all that the difference between Elite posting numbers and non-Elite posting numbers reflects. On the other hand, I could have underestimated the effect of becoming an Elite—after all, those who want to become Elite members may be writing as many reviews as those who are already Elites, thus minimizing the difference between the two classes. To check those possibilities, I reran my analyses and focused only on the reviewers who became Elites and studied their behavior before and after being selected. That analysis revealed that Elites produced as many as *five* more reviews per year than they did before they were selected. This result suggests that the Elite program was indeed contributing to how much users were producing in terms of reviews.

Finally, I tested whether Elite status made contributors stay longer than those who contributed similar amounts of content but did not have Elite status. The empirical results show that reviewers who wrote more reviews in total were *less* likely to continue writing, implying that reviewers burn out as they write more. Results show, however, that this

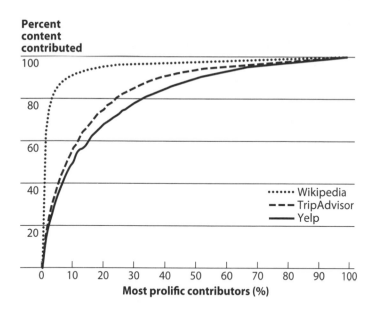

Figure 10.1. Distribution of contributions to Yelp, TripAdvisor, and Wikipedia

effect was substantially reduced in the years that contributors held Elite status. In other words, when a contributor wrote a lot of reviews and was recognized as an Elite member, he or she was less likely to drop out than someone who had already received that designation. This finding attests to the importance of Elite designation as a contributor retention device. And taken together, these findings attest to the power of the social solution developed by Yelp.

Tasks

Armed with an understanding of the nature of Yelp's social solution, we can evaluate whether the tasks required to meet others also helped Yelp with its business goals. Even cursory analysis reveals tight alignment on at least two dimensions. First, it would be very hard to meet someone through the platform without contributing content. Suppose, for example, that one reviewer reached out to another through the internal messaging system suggesting that the two start talking or perhaps meet.

In deciding whether to respond to this message, the recipient would be almost bound to go to the sender's profile to learn more about the sender. Unless the sender had contributed substantial content in the form of reviews, it is unlikely that the recipient would ever return the message. Viewed this way, those who want to be successful at using Yelp as a mechanism to meet others need to contribute content, which in turn benefits Yelp.

The same goes for the Elite Squad. The only way to join the Elite Squad and be able to meet others easily through offline parties was to write reviews. Put differently, without helping Yelp by contributing additional reviews, the site will not help individuals connect to others. Again, the same task benefits individuals with their social goals and the company with its business goals.

Business Effects

But here's the issue: Despite its powerful social strategy to source free reviews, Yelp has had many problems generating revenue and profit. Only in 2011, seven years after it launched, was the company able to generate more than $83 million in revenue, up from $48 million the year before. One of the key reasons Yelp made relatively little in revenue to that point was that it took a long time to settle on a business model. It started with a pay-per-call system, whereby Yelp would get paid if a customer called the business and mentioned Yelp. When that model generated little revenue, the company moved to pay-per-visit program, which sought to charge establishments every time someone visited their Yelp pages. That model also proved disappointing, and finally Yelp settled on giving businesses the ability to place sponsored search results.

Under this model (the one in play as I write this), if a reader searched for, say, a Thai restaurant in Boston, a sponsored listing would appear on top of the search results. Establishments could also place banner ads on competitors' pages. For example, a reader who was reading reviews for a restaurant might see a sponsored listing for another restaurant nearby. Clicking on that link would take the reader to the rival restaurant's Yelp page.

By the end of 2011, such advertising accounted for 70–80 percent of Yelp's revenues. The remainder came from the sponsorship program, introduced in 2008, which for a monthly fee allowed businesses to update the information on its Yelp page, post photos and updates, highlight a single review, track how many readers visited its Yelp page and contact Yelp reviewers directly. Sponsorship did not allow businesses to remove bad reviews, however, and did not give them priority treatment when they complained that a competitor wrote a review. By the end of 2011, Yelp had an average of 17,500 active local business accounts.

Even though Yelp finally settled on a revenue model that worked, many observers believed that it limited Yelp's growth potential. Some said that the model was limited because Yelp was focused on restaurants, which have limited resources to advertise. Others pointed out that only average restaurants would advertise, while those with very good or very poor reviews would have very little incentive to do so. Perhaps the most damning indictment of Yelp lay on the cost side, however, as the company needed to continue to invest in a huge sales force to generate additional revenues. Indeed, thus far, all efforts to increase revenue have resulted in deeper losses (e.g., the company lost $16.7 million in 2011 versus $9.6 million in 2010), calling into question the sustainability of Yelp's business model. As I wrote this book, it was still unclear whether the company would become profitable.

Yelp's inability to create sustained profits has important implications for our understanding of social strategy. There is very little doubt that the social solution that Yelp developed allowed it to source a number of reviews for free, leading to substantial savings. The high quality of these reviews allowed Yelp to attract numerous readers, which then made the site more attractive to advertisers. Since the strategy was never designed to attract advertisers, however, its pull was not strong enough, and as a consequence it never solved Yelp's most pressing and important problem—the ability to source paying customers cheaply. Without solving this problem, the company was not able to turn a profit. Put differently, even though Yelp built a social solution and connected social actions to certain business goals, achieving those goals does not have enough of an impact on profitability.

Conclusions

What can Yelp's experience, when compared with Zynga's, reveal about social strategy? First, a comparison shows us that firms can lower their costs not only by reconnecting people to their friends, as was the case with Zynga, but also by introducing them to strangers, as was the case with Yelp. Furthermore, it illustrates that low-cost social strategies are not limited to reducing customer acquisition costs, as was the case with Zynga, but can also entail decreasing the costs of acquiring inputs, as was the case with Yelp.

Second, the comparison suggests a way in which to develop the kinds of social solutions that are necessary for social strategies to succeed. Both companies emphasized activities as a way of helping people establish better relationships—in the case of Zynga it was a game, in the case of Yelp it was a writing activity. Zynga's display and search solutions conveyed little personal information, however, and its communication solutions did not lead to direct interactions. In contrast, Yelp's display and search solutions were quite personal in that they allowed people to express what they thought and others to find out about it. Furthermore, the Elite Squad parties gave certain Yelp users a straightforward way to interact with each other. These choices allowed Yelp to build a more powerful social solution.

Third, the comparison highlights the importance of picking social tasks that simultaneously improve social interactions and contribute to the business strategy. Zynga chose a number of tasks related to breadth, display, search, and communication, all of which benefited the company. Although players could engage in these tasks to interact with others, they did not necessarily have to do so, as they could simply just message the friends they saw playing the game. This implies that the tasks that benefited the company were only weakly aligned with improved interactions. In contrast, Yelp emphasized display solutions, but aligned the social and business benefits much better. Specifically, writing reviews was the only way in which people actually could make themselves known to others and qualify for the Elite Squad program to meet others. This tight alignment helped Yelp encourage people to contribute the content it valued.

Fourth, the comparison underscores the implications of the way in which a company links its social strategy to its business strategy. Zynga's choices were clearly linked to its business strategy and helped the company reduce its biggest cost driver—customer acquisition. This was not the case with Yelp—the company's social strategy allowed it to source reviews cheaply, but it did not solve the company's biggest cost driver, which also happened to be customer acquisition. As a consequence, the company was not able to reach profitability.

Taken together these considerations help us understand just how important it is to master all three parts of a social strategy. Successful social strategies *require* that firms (1) build powerful social solutions that (2) allow people to undertake corporate tasks for free with (3) high impact on business outcomes. Zynga chose the tasks with high impact on business outcomes, but it fell short on aligning the tasks to social benefits, which reduced the power of its social solution, which in turn undermined the long-term efficacy of its social strategy. In contrast, Yelp developed a strong "meet" solution with tasks that clearly benefited the people and the business. These tasks did *not* tackle the most fundamental task the company was facing, however, which in turn undermined the long-term efficacy of its social strategy. In the next chapters, we will play close attention to the interplay of these three factors.

CHAPTER 11

Social Strategy at American Express

In the previous two chapters, we examined how start-ups have used social strategies to gain competitive advantage over organizations that do not have social strategies. This chapter examines how large and established firms integrate social strategies into their overall business strategy to improve competitive advantage. The chapter will review the two types of social strategies we reviewed so far, and introduce a new one—creating a higher willingness to pay, while helping people meet—using American Express as an example.

Background

American Express's history dates back to about 1850, when it was in the business of transporting goods, currency, and other valuables around the United States. Thirty years later, the company started to issue money orders and traveler's checks, competing with the banks it had previously serviced. And in the 1950s, American Express entered the charge card market, rolling out its premium Gold Card in 1966. Roughly twenty years later, the company introduced its first credit card, which allowed members to carry a balance. And by 2011, its extensive lineup of cards included the Blue Card, the Platinum Card, the Centurion Card, a set of corporate cards, and a small-business card (offered under the OPEN brand), as well as a Serve charge card. According to J. D. Powers, American Express in 2011 enjoyed the highest satisfaction rating of all credit card issuers, thanks to high levels of service, advocacy in case of disputes with merchants, and an attractive loyalty program that gave members rewards on the basis of their expenditures.

American Express competed with Visa and MasterCard as well as Discover in a reasonably saturated market, with about 70 percent of adult U.S. residents holding at least one credit card. The industry as a whole has been growing at a 12 percent annual clip since 1999, but the competition between companies has been fierce; the average credit card holder used 3.5 cards. American Express sought to differentiate itself from its key competitors, Visa and MasterCard, on at least three dimensions.

First, the company focused on a more affluent segment of the U.S. population as well as on corporate clients. This choice limited the number of potential customers American Express could serve. Indeed, the company had only 44 million U.S. customers, as compared to Master-Card's 98 million and Visa's 111 million. The smaller customer pool, however, was more than offset by higher customer expenditures, which stood at $13,832 per American Express customer per year, as compared to $4,292 for an average Visa customer, and $3,458 for an average Mas-terCard customer. With these expenditure levels, American Express accounted for approximately 25 percent of the total dollar volume of credit card transactions in the United States, the highest of any card issuer.

Second, American Express charged retailers up to 3 percent of purchase value on every transaction, while Visa and MasterCard charged only 2 percent. The company used these higher merchant fees in part to offer higher levels of customer service and more generous rewards for spending money with American Express cards. The higher fees limited the number of retailers that accepted the card; those that did not benefit from the higher purchasing power of American Express card members were less likely to accept it.

Finally, American Express issued its own cards to customers, maintained merchant relationships, and settled funds between customers and merchants. In contrast, its main competitors, Visa and MasterCard, tackled only settlements between banks, ceding the card-issuing function and merchant management to banks and other financial institutions, like Chase or Bank of America. Because these banks already held commercial relationships with individuals and merchants, it was relatively cheap for them to cross-sell a credit card product. In contrast, American Express had to build these relationships anew, engaging in costly direct marketing and merchant development. As a consequence, American Express spent more than $300 to acquire a new customer, whereas competitors spent less than half of that number. In return for these investments, however, American Express had the ability to view actual transactions between merchants and cardholders, which gave the company the ability to assist both parties in making expenditure decisions. Visa and MasterCard merely saw aggregate expenditures, without being able to match them to individual customers or retailers.

These strategic choices generated a unique revenue mix (as compared to the mix generated by a typical credit card issuer). Almost 55 percent of American Express's revenue came from merchant fees; the industry standard was 45 percent. Interest on outstanding account balances comprised roughly 25 percent of American Express's revenue, as compared to roughly 50 percent for the industry. The remaining 20 percent of American Express revenue consisted of fees from card members, merchants, and partners, for cards, travel, and other commissions; the industry average for these types of fees was about 5 percent of overall revenue.

The company's positioning served it well. Between the end of 2001 and the end of 2011, American Express's valuation increased from $36 billion to $50 billion, its margins increased from 6 percent in 2001 to 15 percent in 2011, and revenue grew by more than 15 percent to $27.8 billion earned from 91 million active credit cards.

Nonetheless, during that same time period, new entrants to the market had begun to challenge the company's business model. These companies, which included PayPal and Google, either built their own payment systems or sought to integrate payments into digital wallets they wanted to offer. And so, to address these looming challenges, American Express CEO Kenneth Chenault had also begun to take action to ensure that the company would remain ahead of these developments. Among other things, American Express established its Enterprise Growth unit, acquired Revolution Money (a payments platform designed to facilitate person-to-person financial transactions, now branded as Serve), and launched and ultimately integrated digital and social initiatives in advertising, media relations, customer service, and employee recruitment (many of the details of these initiatives are described later).

Digital Strategy

American Express started its digital strategy by setting up its website. With time, the site allowed users to look up their transactions and balances and to pay their bills online. Around the mid-2000s the company started to use its digital assets to engage with its customers for marketing purposes. For example, in 2006, the company began preparations to launch Members Project, a philanthropic effort. Built as part of the American Express website, Members Project asked card members to contribute ideas for social entrepreneurship, which were then voted on by other card members. The first Members Project culminated in 2007, when American Express awarded two million dollars to UNICEF to implement the card members' first winning idea—a venture aimed at providing clean drinking water to children in developing nations. UNICEF used the money to further its efforts toward that goal in four African countries. American Express repeated Members Project in 2008, and again in 2010.

In 2008, the company made an explicit decision to start porting its digital strategy to social platforms. Before it did so, however, it launched an eight-month pilot study to "listen" to all the conversations going on about its brand on various social platforms. Led by Leslie Berland, who ultimately became a senior vice president for digital partnerships, this project revealed that most of the conversations, particularly on Twitter, were largely positive, with users saying: "Oh my gosh, I just got my Gold Card! I have arrived!" or "Just redeemed my Amex points for a vacation!" Only a small percentage of comments were negative—and Berland and her team realized that many of those complaints could be easily resolved if the company could communicate with the affected individuals directly.

Consequently, in the fall of 2008, the company decided to launch a Twitter handle (@AskAmex) to handle service-oriented issues. The account was staffed with a small team of dedicated customer service representatives with extensive experience of corresponding with customers over email. For the first time in its history, the representatives were able to use their actual photos online and they could respond any way they saw fit. This allowed for the interactions with American Express on Twitter to be very realistic and consistent with the rest of the Twitter experience.

American Express monitored the account's use, with an eye to finding out if Twitter service would prove to be a preferable way for customers to interact with the company on service-related matters. But over the next two years, although the account did garner a small following, its introduction resulted in no noticeable decrease in service calls in other channels. As a result, the company considered the Twitter service channel as a "nice to have," but made no plans to scale it up.

Shortly after American Express launched its service-oriented Twitter account, however, the company also rolled out a generalized Twitter account (@AmericanExpress) as well as a series of Facebook pages. Although initially there was no explicit strategy for using these accounts, the company quickly started using them to promote various specials, for example, double point offers, and events it was organizing, such as a closed Bon Jovi concert. These types of announcements gained significant traction with American Express followers, allowing the company, for example, to fill up a thousand-seat concert hall in a matter of hours. American Express also found Twitter very helpful in the aftermath of the Haiti earthquake of January 2011, when the company used Twitter to announce that it was waiving fees for nonprofit organizations serving Haiti. The post was subsequently picked up by all the news outlets on Twitter, which generated more publicity for American Express than for its competitors (companies that also waived fees for those organizations, but announced their actions through more traditional channels).

Even though both Facebook and Twitter allowed American Express to communicate with some of its cardholders cheaply and effectively, interviews with company executives in 2011 revealed that few initially had believed that such communication would result in real differences to profit. When American Express began using digital channels to advertise its social strategy efforts, however, the executives soon realized that the company's investments in the former became critical to the success of the latter. With this in mind, we turn to the company's social strategy.

Building Social Strategy

Although American Express's digital strategy projects mainly sought to connect the company to its customers, and did little to connect customers to one another, the company noticed that many of its members were connecting to each other anyway, through the content that the company provided. Indeed, internal research revealed that card members were very interested to connect with similar others around shared interests and projects. This finding energized the company to begin testing areas where member communities might be particularly valuable. For example, as one executive recalled: "We knew that American Express card members were 90 percent more likely to travel frequently and abroad than non-card-members were. At that time, there were—and there still are—tons of different travel communities. We did a lot of additional research, and found that card members actually trusted the advice of card members more than that of other people. So, for example, if you had a Platinum Card, you cared what another Platinum Card member said and where they were going, even if you didn't know that card member."

Acting on this insight, the company launched Members Know, a travel community within the American Express website, which allowed members to share travel tips with each other, and view data on the most popular travel locations, hotels, and restaurants among fellow card members. The site also had content areas managed by the editors of *Travel + Leisure* magazine, a company-owned travel publication. The site generated a substantial amount of traffic and facilitated many interactions between card members, some of which, importantly, had the potential to translate into business benefits. For example, it was conceivable that card members were more likely to continue paying for their card to continue to access the Members Know community. They were also presumably more prone to use their American Express card in locations discovered through Members Know.

The existence of these social and economic benefits distinguished the Members Know project from the Members Project, discussed in the previous section. The Members Project did not allow for any interactions between card members, thereby limiting its ability to solve social failures; neither did it offer a direct path toward improved profitability for Amex. In contrast, Members Know at least offered a mechanism for facilitating interactions that would not otherwise happen, and connected this functionality to lower retention costs. Admittedly, neither the social benefit nor the economic benefits were substantial. But at least they got the company on the path of thinking about facilitating social interactions in a way that helps improve profitability.

OPEN Forum

The broad member engagement on the Members Know project led American Express to incorporate similar principles and products into its OPEN Forum initiative, an extension of American Express's OPEN credit card unit targeting small business owners. In 2007, the company had launched a website—openforum.com—to help it share content from its offline conferences, which brought together small business owners to discuss the issues they were facing. Following the financial crisis of 2008, American Express relaunched the site, focusing on helping small business owners survive in the tumultuous economy. Then, in 2009, OPEN Forum relaunched again, this time with two major branded features. The first was Idea Hub, which displayed content from thought leaders in the form of articles, blog posts, interviews, and videos in seven core areas: innovation, lifestyle, managing, marketing, money, technology, and the world. The content was targeted directly at small business owners looking for practical advice. To deliver this content well, American Express partnered with Federated Media to find high-profile dedicated writers, many of whom also wrote about their association with OPEN Forum in other channels. Although all content was produced specifically for OPEN Forum, it was available to everyone on the Internet regardless of whether they had an American Express OPEN card.

The second feature was the Connectodex, which allowed American Express OPEN card members to establish an online profile of themselves and their business, and list their business needs, as well the various types of services they could offer. Only other OPEN card members could search through these profiles, and when they found someone they wanted to contact, they could do so. The introduction of this service was not coincidental—it was tightly related to what American Express had learned in earlier iterations of the Forum. As one American Express executive said to me: "We knew that small business owners were looking for connections.... And what we started to see in 2007 and 2008 in this blog was that people were connecting to each other through the content we published. That was the 'Aha!' moment, and the insight to relaunch in 2009 with a much [bigger] connections piece to the experience, as well as retaining what we had started to become known for, which was this great authentic unique content."

Connectodex proved to be a very useful tool for many small businesses. One of the key reasons small businesses were attracted to the feature, as compared to more general sites such as LinkedIn, was that OPEN gave them some assurance that the companies they were interacting with were legitimate and solvent businesses. One American Express senior manager summarized this benefit by describing the following example: "One OPEN Forum member, Jon Paley, started a marketing firm called The Vault. He'd doubled his number of employees; he needed to expand his office space and he needed a designer. Paley felt he could do business with companies in Connectodex, because he felt they were trustworthy, had credentials, since they had already been vetted to obtain an OPEN card. Once he started using the features on OPEN Forum, he quickly found a designer for his space."

This new iteration of OPEN Forum quickly garnered a lot of traction. By the end of 2009, the site had received more than 15.5 million visits, and by summer 2010, it had more than one million unique visitors per month—more than three times its total from the year before. By that time, more than eleven thousand small businesses had set up their profiles in the Connectodex. The site also received a number of accolades for its site design, including the 2009 Web Award for Outstanding Achievement in Web Development and a 2010 Silver Effie Award. By spring 2011, OPEN Forum's Twitter handle had over 25,000 followers, over seven times more than it had two years prior. A year and a half later that number increased six-fold to more than 150,000 followers. Furthermore, research undertaken by the company showed that OPEN cardholders who also use Forum have much higher net promoter scores—a gauge of their likelihood to recommend the card—than cardholders who do not use Forum. With these numbers, there was very little doubt at American Express that the social and digital strategies underpinning OPEN Forum have resulted in substantial economic returns for the card, in terms of both customer acquisition and customer retention.

At this point, it may help to pause and compare OPEN Forum to the Members Know project, both as it relates to solving social failures and improving American Express's competitive advantage. Even the most cursory analysis indicates that OPEN Forum solves more important social failures than Members Know does. After all, inability to interact with someone who can actually help my company survive or generate more business is a more powerful social failure than not being able to talk with someone who can tell me where I should go and travel or eat. And there are many more substitutes for the latter than there are for the former. Similarly, OPEN Forum's social solutions had the potential to contribute to American Express's profitability more than Members Know. After all, few card members are more likely to stay simply because the company is offering Members Know. In contrast, the ability to connect to many similar business people will make them substantially more likely to stay, thereby saving the company retention costs.

The progress in American Express's social strategy becomes particularly salient when we illustrate it on a two-dimensional graph, with the ability to solve social failures forming one axis, and contribution to profitability being the other (as shown in figure 11.1). Although Members Project sits in the bottom right-hand corner, with low impact on solving social failures and limited effect on competitive advantage, the Members Know represents an improvement on both dimensions. OPEN Forum represents yet another substantial improvement for the company's social strategy. Next we turn to examine the Link, Like, Love program, which represents a substantial advancement both in terms of solving social failures and having a substantial impact on American Express's business outcomes.

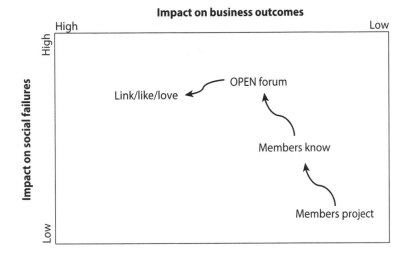

Figure 11.1. Evolution of American Express's social strategies

THE POWERFUL ENGINE UNDERLYING THE SOCIAL STRATEGY

Even though American Express started by developing "meet" social strategies, with time it started to devote more resources to implementing "friend" social strategies. Underlying these strategies was an Application Programming Interface, called a Smart Offer engine, which American Express developed in early 2010s, under the leadership of Ed Gilligan, the company's vice chairman and head of the Global Consumer and Small Business Card Issuing, Network, and Merchant businesses. The engine tapped into the company's core capabilities and consisted of four components: (1) a merchant database with detailed information on every merchant in the American Express network, including their locations in latitude and longitude; (2) a smart-offer repository, which allowed merchants to present targeted offers to card members (e.g., get $10 off when you spend $50 or more); (3) a couponless fulfillment program, which analyzed transaction flows and could trigger a statement credit automatically if offer conditions were met (e.g., the customer spent more than $50); and (4) a system that could send real-time notifications from American Express.

The Smart Offer engine provided a way to leverage and strengthen the core of American Express's competitive advantage and could not be easily replicated by Visa or MasterCard. Neither of these credit card networks had direct visibility into individual transactions, which prevented them from building a similar set of functionalities. Issuing banks also could not replicate the functionality fully in that they could offer it only to the subsegment of retailers they serviced and cards they issued, and not to all Visa or MasterCard cardholders. Given its potential, the Smart Offer engine team aggressively sought creative ways to put it to work.

SMALL BUSINESS SATURDAY

The first opportunity to use this engine to power a social strategy arose in early November 2010, when a small group of American Express employees came up with the idea of Small Business Saturday, a shopping holiday to encourage card members to patronize small local brick-and-mortar businesses. To be held on the Saturday after Thanksgiving, one of the busiest shopping days of the year, the holiday was designed as a counterpoint to Black Friday, whose focus is big retail stores, and Cyber Monday, which encourages customers to shop online. The first Small Business Saturday was to take place on November 27, 2010, just three weeks after the initiative was conceived. To meet this extremely ambitious goal, Gilligan assembled a small team from various units across the company, including Leslie Berland, and gave it a significant level of autonomy.

The team developed a fairly straightforward program, which offered card members a $25 statement credit if they spent at least $25 at a small business on November 27th using their American Express card. To receive this credit, card members had to register their card before shopping. Subsequently, when American Express's Smart Offer engine detected that the card member had paid $25 at a small business with the enrolled American Express card on Small Business Saturday, it would promptly issue a $25 credit to the card member's statement.

Fully knowing that it would be very expensive to advertise the program in such a short period of time, the team decided to leverage a basic Facebook social distribution channel (such as we've seen in the chapters on eBay and Zynga). Specifically, every time card members enrolled their cards in the program, they would be asked to "like" the Small Business Saturday Facebook Page and share a status update with their friends inviting them to enroll their cards, too. The exact number of shares is unknown, but we do know that more than 250,000 card members opted to shop at small businesses that day, and more than 1.2 million Facebook users "liked" the page, with one in three Americans being aware of the program, suggesting extraordinary levels of engagement in a very short time period. Although American Express also advertised the program through other channels, its internal research later revealed that levels of program awareness and likelihood to enroll were higher when a card member learned about Small Business Saturday through Facebook than through all other channels.

FOURSQUARE INTEGRATION

Thrilled at the success of Small Business Saturday, Gilligan sought to continue integrating the Smart Offer engine into the company's social strategy as quickly as possible. To that end, he brought together a group of employees involved in digital efforts across the company for an all-day meeting. The goal was for people who would not otherwise cross paths to collaborate on new ways to advance the American Express brand through social platforms. Gilligan reflected: "We had all these people at the ground level of the company who are constantly on Facebook and Twitter, and so they are full of great ideas of how we can leverage these platforms to help our strategy. But they are not senior enough to get their ideas heard. So when I called the all-day meeting, I asked these people to join—and some of them were two or three levels down—to get them talking to each other to develop new ideas."

Berland and Luke Gebb, a vice president at the company, both attended the meeting and began discussing possible uses for the Smart Offer engine. They quickly decided to merge the engine with foursquare, a location-based social platform that had more than seven million users at the time and allowed people to "check in" to locations using smartphone apps. Often, these check-ins unlocked special offers, such as a buy-one-get-one-free deal at an ice cream shop, or 50 percent off a massage at a spa.

The foursquare functionality was quite successful, but it was also relatively difficult to use. As one observer noted: "You go into the four-square app, you see a special nearby, you go in, there's a promo code or a coupon that appears on your phone, and you have to show it to the cashier. And 80 percent of the time, the cashier has no idea what you're talking about because it's a big chain. They haven't been trained, and it's awkward and clunky. Sometimes the customer doesn't even want to do it. You don't want to show your phone and ask, 'Can I have my extra scoop of ice cream?' " But both Berland and Gebb believed that the Smart Offer engine could substantially improve on the foursquare experience. Starting in December 2010, they worked with foursquare toward the goal of releasing an integration between the American Express Smart Offer engine and foursquare at the South by Southwest Interactive Festival in March 2011 in Austin, Texas. The festival was a major technology conference that had previously served as a launching pad for hot tech start-ups such as Twitter and even foursquare itself.

They met their goal. Developed at record speed and launched on time, the integration offered a "Spend $5, Get $5" check-in deal with 50 merchants in Austin. To obtain these $5, users first had to link their American Express card to their foursquare accounts. Subsequently, when the user checked in to a particular location, American Express would check if there was a deal offered at that location. If there was, the user simply pressed a button within the foursquare app to load the deal to the card. To claim the offer, the user did not have to show any coupons or codes. All that was required was that the user paid with the enrolled American Express card, at which point the foursquare application alerted the user that the terms of the deal were fulfilled, and a few days later the user would obtain $5 back as a credit on the statement. No information about the card member was given to foursquare during the process; neither did foursquare receive any money from the integration.

LINK, LIKE, LOVE AND TWITTER INTEGRATIONS

Four months after South by Southwest, American Express released its Link, Like, Love application on Facebook. Link, Like, Love shared many similarities with the foursquare integration (as well as with the Small

Business Saturday initiative): Users first linked their American Express cards with their Facebook accounts; they would then receive offers that they could load onto their cards; and then once they fulfilled the terms of the offer, their American Express account was credited automatically.

Amex introduced three major enhancements with Link, Like, Love over the foursquare integration, however. First, the company secured a broader set of retail partners, which included Dunkin' Donuts, H&M, BestBuy, Sheraton, and Neiman Marcus, among others. Second, the application used various Facebook data, such as users' "likes," to prioritize among the expanded menu of offers. Finally, the application asked that users share the offer with their Facebook friends by posting it on their timelines as soon as they added it to their cards.

Initially, the company toyed with the idea of letting users opt in to having their transactions trigger a status update; for instance, a purchase might result in a status update that read "Just ate at Dunkin' Donuts." But conversations with customers revealed no interest in that functionality, so the status update only reported having obtained a deal in the first place.

The results of this integration with Facebook were impressive. A large percentage of users who loaded offers onto their cards also shared them with their friends on Facebook. Card member interviews revealed that they were happy to do so, as they wanted their friends to participate in such offers, and were further encouraged to do so by the numerous "likes" that such posts generated. American Express executives were also very happy with the initiative, as the status updates generated numerous click-throughs, which subsequently led to increased card usage and numerous new card applications.

Encouraged by the powerful business results generated when people shared offers with others, American Express continued to experiment with other social platforms that offered those functionalities. To that end, in the spring of 2012, the company released an integration that asked users to sync their American Express cards with Twitter. American Express would then tweet out various offers, which users could load onto their cards by composing a tweet with an appropriate hashtag. For example, users wishing to claim an offer to get $10 back after spending $20 at U.S. Open concessions, would compose any tweet they wanted adding #AmexTennis. This tweet would then become highly visible to the user's followers, who could simply retweet it to load the offer onto their card (assuming their account was connected too). After the tweet, the user would obtain an automatic @ reply from the American Express account, confirming enrollment.

This integration yielded even higher financial rewards for American Express than its previous ventures, for at least two reasons. First, this integration more tightly integrated the act of loading the offer with the process of advertising it to others. Second, the tweet advertising American Express was potentially visible to everyone on Twitter, resulting in much broader reach.

Now that we have examined the integrations of the Smart Offer engine with various social platforms, it's useful to pause and evaluate each one against the yardstick of contributing meaningful social solutions and improving the company's competitive advantage. For simplicity of exposition, however, I will focus on the Link, Like, Love integration and compare it with the OPEN Forum—our front-runner in terms of social solution and impact on profitability. At this point, we lack precise measurement tools to compare the magnitude of social solutions. We can still undertake qualitative comparisons, however.

The functionalities provided by OPEN Forum pertain only to a small set of card members who run small businesses. These functionalities solve important social failures, however. In contrast, functionalities provided by the Link, Like, Love program pertain to a broad set of card members, but solve only a fairly shallow social failure. Thus, there is no reason to believe that one of these solutions is definitely better than the other and hence we will consider Link, Like, Love to be at least as good as OPEN Forum.

Nonetheless, the Link, Like, Love project has a much bigger potential to affect American Express's profitability than OPEN Forum, and to do so in a way that cannot be easily matched by other issuing banks, such as Chase or Bank of America. To see this we could simply examine the acquisition cost via Link, Like, Love and compare it to the typical $300 cost required to acquire a new card through traditional channels. It is actually much more instructive, however, to delve into the economics of Link, Like, Love and identify assumptions that we would have to believe are true in order for the company to acquire new customers at a much lower cost.

Consider, for example, what would have to be true for American Express to acquire new cardholders at a 20 percent lower cost than other channels—namely at $240 per card. Now, take the most conservative scenario and assume that American Express funds all of the Link, Like, Love discounts, where an average discount costs the company $20. At this rate, American Express needs to acquire at least one customer out of 12 people who loaded and redeem the offer for the cost to be $240. If we assume that every person who actually redeems the offer also posts one status update, then these 12 redemptions generate 12 Facebook status updates. Since an average Facebook user in the United States has 250 friends, and an average post is seen only by 16 percent of friends, these 12 updates generate 480 impressions. If one out of these 480 impressions (or 0.20 percent) leads to a new card, then American Express can achieve its goal of saving 20 percent on customer acquisition costs.

To gauge how realistic it is to expect that American Express will enjoy that 0.20 percent conversion rate, it is useful to compare it to other rates on Facebook. For example, simple banner advertising on Facebook yields a 0.05 percent click-through rate (the number of times users click on an advertisement divided by the number of displays). Since not all clicks result in a sale or a new-customer acquisition, the conversion rate is lower than 0.05 percent. Similarly, social advertising on Facebook, which is similar to banner advertising, but includes a short blurb in forming users which ones of their friends like the advertised product, obtains roughly a 0.20 percent click-through rate. Again, since not all people who click on an ad subsequently convert, the conversion rate is lower than that. These considerations imply that the status updates generated by the Link, Like, Love program would have to perform much better than existing Facebook benchmarks for the company to save 20 percent on customer acquisition costs. It is possible that American Express can reach these goals, but since doing so means beating Facebook benchmarks, it may be difficult.

Having said that, it's important to note that we reached this conclusion by assuming that American Express funds all of the discounts. In reality, that's not the case; many merchants are willing to take on that funding. If merchants fund half of these discounts, the conversion rate that American Express needs in order to achieve a 20 percent reduction in customer acquisition costs becomes only 0.10 percent, which sounds much more realistic. In the most extreme case, if merchants fund *all* of the discounts, American Express benefits regardless of the rate at which card members' friends click on the Facebook posts and sign up for new cards. In that case, American Express would acquire each new customer on the back of retailers' investments.

The extent to which retailers will fund these offers will depend on the kinds of returns they obtain from such offers. Although the exact economics of such offers will vary depending on the merchant, we can at least compare the economics of a similar offer given to American Express card members and to cardholders of a competitive issuer, such as Bank of America or Chase. The economics of these offers critically depends on their ability to get customers in the door and then get them to purchase items that generate more profit than the cost of the offer—or get them to return to the merchant and purchase more items later. Doing so is easier if individuals are already wealthier and therefore more willing to spend more money. And that's where American Express is at an advantage over all other card issuers—its card members are substantially richer than those holding competing cards, suggesting that merchants are more likely to see return on their investment into attracting American Express cardholders as compared to other card issuers. For this reason, they are more likely to fund offers through American Express, implying that the company will be able to run a project like Link, Like, Love without having to fund many offers as compared to competitive issuers. As a consequence, American Express will be able to acquire new card members more cheaply than competitors would if they chose to roll out a program like Link, Like, Love.

Taken together, this discussion suggests that Link, Like, Love can substantially reduce the costs of acquiring new card members. It becomes a very lucrative proposition only if merchants cover a substantial portion of Link, Like, Love offers, however. Merchants will do so if they expect customers to spend substantial amount of money—an action that American Express is very well positioned to deliver on. In fact, it is much better positioned to do so than competitors are, suggesting that a program like Link, Like, Love will have a much bigger impact on reducing acquisition costs with American Express than it would if undertaken by competitors.

GoSocial

Given the importance of merchant-funded offers to the success of the Link, Like, Love program and its Twitter instantiation, American Express soon started to develop strategies to get more merchants on board. To that end, American Express released a new program in August 2011, called GoSocial, which was a self-serve platform allowing merchants to sign up and distribute American Express deals via its social channels. To start offering deals, merchants would simply enter their merchant username and password, and then create the couponless offers that American Express would then include in its foursquare, Facebook, and Twitter integrations. American Express provided immediate feedback to participating merchants, including the number of redeemed offers, the average purchase value, and the total amount of sales.

Although GoSocial is still small in scope, it foreshadows a set of important changes in American Express's strategy, which Gilligan summarized for us in 2012 as follows:

> We care as much about adding value to merchants as we do about the cardmembers. We want to change the conversation with merchants so they see American Express not just as a form of payment, but as a marketing partner that helps them grow their business. To do that, we have to scale what we're doing to bring this to life. In the future, I believe, millions of cardmembers will have synced their cards to our offers, and we'll be marketing with hundreds of thousands of merchants where we can give them information that says, "Here's what you spent and here is the number of customers who came back a week later, three months later, six months later. Let's continue to fine-tune your marketing to improve your business results."

These comments signal a fundamental shift in American Express's strategy. Whereas in the past, the company's success was attached to efficient settling of funds for transactions that were arranged by others, now the company is moving toward using its proprietary data to facilitate transactions and then settle the funds. The introduction of the Smart Offer engine was at the core of that experience, with the GoSocial platform allowing the company to scale it up efficiently. This change appears strategically sound in that Visa and MasterCard cannot match it easily. Similarly, because American Express is the largest card issuer in the United States, as of this writing, competing issuing banks cannot offer the same number of card members to merchants, giving the company an advantage. The integration of this system with social strategy has allowed the company to leverage it to acquire new members in a way that no competitor can match.

Overall, GoSocial increases the number of merchants participating in the Link, Like, Love program, therefore allowing more cardholders to share more offers with their friends on Facebook. As a consequence, the impact of GoSocial on social solutions should be even higher than the original iteration of Link, Like, Love. At the same time, this improvement in the number of merchants participating also generates higher returns for American Express than the original Link, Like, Love program did.

Conclusions

The foregoing description of American Express's forays into social strategy allowed us to review the two types of low-cost social strategies, but also allowed us to introduce a new type—high willingness-to-pay strategy while building new relationships. It also offers a number of important lessons that easily generalize to other settings. First, in American Express we saw a company that pursued both a digital and a social strategy. The digital strategy entailed having an active Facebook page and a set of Twitter accounts to broadcast messages to American Express cardholders, and to obtain feedback from them. The social strategy entailed building connections between cardholders as well as between cardholders and potential cardholders in a way that generated business benefits for the company, and ultimately steered the company's strategy in a new direction. American Express integrated these two strategies by using its digital strategy to advertise and power many of its social strategies.

Second, American Express showed us that large established firms rarely launch a set of fully developed social strategies. Instead, the company started with smaller-scale projects, with fairly limited social and economic potential. Learning from these projects, it then developed new initiatives that had much bigger social and economic potential. As it did so, it actively sought to increase its competitive advantage. For example, initial projects, such as Members Project, started as public relations efforts. Subsequent ones, such as Members Know, began to leverage the company's competitive advantage to build social strategies, but did not really contribute to that competitive advantage. It is only the later developments, such as the Link, Like, Love integrations, that both leverage the competitive advantage and also actively contribute to it. Finally, programs such as GoSocial leverage and contribute to competitive advantage, and also seek to change the nature of the company's competitive advantage.

Third, this chapter foreshadows an important organizational process that allows social strategies to come to fruition. Because this is the first chapter documenting the existence and the success of social strategies at large established corporations, I focused on the content of these strategies rather than the people who facilitated this process and the manner in which they did so. Nonetheless, the people, roles, and processes are critically important, and the way in which American Express went about designing and implementing its social strategies is instructive.

My research indicates that, as of 2013, many companies were suffering from a really big organizational problem for social strategies. Specifically, the people who truly understand the various capabilities afforded by social media and know how to link social media to business objectives are in their twenties and early thirties and therefore hidden in the lower echelons of organizations. In contrast, people who have decision rights over investments and firm strategy are usually in their fifties and many layers removed from those who understand how to make a social strategy work. A successful process for developing and implementing a successful social strategy involves connecting these 20-year-olds with the 50-year-olds, without upsetting those in the middle levels of the organization. Creating and implementing such a process is incredibly hard, and I have seen a number of social strategies die (in favor of digital strategies) the second they hit the directors and vice presidents of marketing in those midmanagement levels. They die because these directors are too senior to understand the power of social platforms, but also too junior to make a decision on a fundamental change in how business gets done. Without having very senior executives connecting with very junior ones, social strategies have very little chance of being fully developed and implemented.

American Express has overcome these challenges. Gilligan, the company's vice chairman, with explicit consent from Ken Chenault, the company's CEO, initiates the process of building social strategy. But right there, too, is Leslie Berland, who runs the Twitter account. Leslie Berland is young. She knows the technology; she has friends at Facebook, and she is not afraid to experiment. Gilligan gives Berland a lot of air cover, and his support signals her credibility. Gilligan then also connects her with people like Gebb who really understand the technology. Together, this team acts fast—and generates results just as quickly. They upset a lot of people; they bypass traditional channels and sidestep procedure, but they keep going. And in the end, they win.

CHAPTER 12

Social Strategy at Nike

Nike is a publicly traded clothing, footwear, sportswear, and equipment producer and one of the top ten advertisers in the United States. The company's overall marketing budget, as of 2012, stood at more than $2.5 billion. Importantly, a few years prior, Nike started reallocating much of that massive expenditure away from TV and print toward digital and social marketing. In fact, between 2009 and 2012, the company cut traditional media expenditures by 40 percent, and allocated more than eight hundred million dollars to digital and social marketing—more than any other U.S.-based advertiser.

Most of this chapter will document what Nike did with this money. Some of Nike's choices exemplify a type of social strategy we have not yet studied—one that increases customers' willingness to pay in return for helping them build closer relationships with people they already know. But the chapter will also show how the company built its own ecosystem to implement and support all four types of social strategies concurrently.

The data for this chapter come from qualitative analysis of the firm strategy and interviews with company executives and Nike product users. For competitive reasons, the chapter does not contain any proprietary information from the company.

Background

Nike was founded in 1964 by Phil Knight, a University of Oregon track athlete, and Bill Bowerman, his coach, as a small, custom running shoe producer called Blue Ribbon Sports. The company adopted its famous swoosh logo in 1972 and renamed itself Nike in 1978. By then, it had developed shoes with innovative rubber "waffle" soles and had marketed them to great effect, capturing more than half of the U.S. running shoe market. The company filed for an IPO in 1980, and continued to launch new products successfully, broadening its offerings to target basketball, baseball, football, tennis, and cross-training athletes. All of these products were backed by strong marketing campaigns, perhaps the most notable of which was the widely recognized "Just Do It" and "If you have a body, you are an athlete" initiatives.

The company's success continued into the 1990s and 2000s, with investments in new sports and "brand name" teams and athletes including the Brazilian National Team (soccer), Tiger Woods (golf), and Lance Armstrong (cycling). Nike's connection with iconic athletes allowed the company to claim that its footwear significantly improved athletic performance. During this time, the company also acquired a few other brands, such as Cole Haan, Converse, Hurley, and Umbro. By 2012, the company, headquartered in Beaverton, Oregon, was the world's top manufacturer of athletic footwear and apparel, with twenty-one billion dollars in revenue across 160 countries and thirty-five thousand employees. It operated 690 retail stores worldwide, managed twenty-three thousand retail accounts in the United States, and worked with multiple distributors and licensees around the world.

Nike's Digital Strategy

Nike's digital strategy tracks back to 1998, when the company launched its website, Nike.com. Two years later, it launched its first sport-specific website, NikeFootball.com. Then, in 2004, it started to port its digital strategies onto existing platforms. For example, early that year, Nike challenged fifteen filmmakers to interpret the idea of speed, and promised to feature short films they created on a dedicated blog called *Art of Speed*. The idea was received with enthusiasm, and the blog attracted more than five hundred thousand visitors every month for a couple of months, showing Nike that its customers welcomed the idea of interacting with the company through content, and spurring its senior management team to seek similar opportunities.

One such opportunity was suggested by Jesse Stollak, then a digital manager working on Nike Football. Stollak floated the idea of creating a channel on YouTube and uploading ads there. The first video, titled "Touch of Gold," received nearly twenty million views in just a few weeks. In an interview, Stollak, who at the time this book was written was the global digital director for brand and innovation at Nike, recalled: "We were the first company to really leverage YouTube with branded content. When I posted the 'Touch of Gold' video people were a little freaked out here, they said 'Are you crazy? Why isn't this on Nike's website? How are people going to know it is Nike?' Once we saw this success, we began to understand how to use social platforms to communicate with the young consumer in their context, in their language."

Building on that insight, Nike launched a set of Facebook pages, one for the company as a whole, and one for every major sport that it focused on. Many customers flocked to these pages, and by 2012 Nike had garnered more than 10 million fans for the main page, 13 million fans for Nike Football, and 4.5 million for Nike Basketball. The company used the main page to inform its fans about upcoming product launches, while sport-related pages included pictures and videos of examples of products in use, and sport challenges and tricks that users could try. As time progressed, these Facebook pages became increasingly central to the company's digital strategy. For example, in May 2010, Nike launched a major commercial for the World Cup called "Write the Future," which featured many of soccer's biggest stars. The commercial launched exclusively on Facebook and could be seen only by Nike's Facebook fans. The video quickly went viral, setting a record for the largest audience with 7.8 million views and doubling the number of Nike Soccer Facebook page fans all in just one week.

The company also built an extensive presence on Twitter, with handles that included "Nike" (with about 700,000 followers in mid-2012), "NikeStore" (with about 450,000 followers), "NikeSoccer" (380,000 followers), "NikeBasketball" (350,000 followers), "NikeSportsWear" (140,000 followers), and "NikeRunning" (100,000 followers). Nike used these accounts to announce new product releases and interact with customers, posting various tips and challenges, and offering encouragement to continue training. Nike also integrated Twitter into its other campaigns. For example, when the company rented Life Center in Johannesburg,

South Africa, for the 2010 World Cup, it displayed Twitter-submitted messages to the whole city via the center's enormous LED ticker.

Around the same time, Nike started building applications inside the Facebook environment, effectively adding still more social elements to its digital strategy. For example, in June 2010, the company announced a program called "The Chance"—a global search for talented soccer players to join the Nike Academy, a high-performance training program supported by the Premier League in England. To participate, teens registered online and uploaded a video showing their potential for success. They then were encouraged to create their own Facebook page to get more notoriety. Within six months, nearly seventy-five thousand players had created profiles for themselves, each attracting numerous friends and fans. Eventually, Nike selected the top one hundred players, based on their performance and Facebook presence, and invited them to compete in a tryout in England, where eight spots at the academy were awarded. Stollak commented:

> With those eight kids becoming professionals, we created a new path to professional [soccer] in countries as diverse as Australia and South Africa. We also learned that social media was more than a marketing mechanism, but it is all about connecting people to each other and to us. If you look at it now, our [soccer] community is close to 14 million people. Most recently we were able to leverage it again when we launched The Chosen for Action Sports, where young players were able to use Facebook to create a video of themselves and then we selected the best videos. The winners received money and gear and almost a professional contract through Nike.

Nike's Social Strategies

At the same time the company was building its digital strategy on social platforms, it was also developing a very distinct social strategy. Already in 2006, the company had partnered with Google's "friend" platform, Orkut, to launch a site called Joga.com targeted at "the soccer-obsessed teen." The platform featured discussion groups focused on teams and players, and encouraged users to talk about football and the upcoming World Cup online. To spur such discussions, the site hosted an online TV channel called JogaTV, and featured well-known soccer stars performing tricks, as well as soccer analysis.

Joga.com was rolled out in 140 countries and fourteen languages and attracted a million members in its first five months. Despite that initial success, however, Nike stopped managing the site as soon as the World Cup ended. Trevor Edwards, Nike's vice president of global brand and category management, reflected on the decision and on how the Joga experience changed the company's approach to social strategy:

> We had a great ramp-up, we attracted a lot of people to the site, we had real conversations and user-generated content through which we created a community and learned about our consumers. . . . But the content we created was for people who were rabid about [soccer] and the site was where they would come to talk with others about their passion. On Facebook and other social networks, content is more about your broader life. So, moving forward, instead of trying to bring them into our world, we wanted to go and be part of their daily lives; we wanted to be pervasive and help the consumer in ways that they already connect with things and others.

To achieve this goal, in mid-2006, Nike launched a tightly interconnected proprietary ecosystem, illustrated in figure 12.1. The ecosystem embedded measurement and communication technologies in a range of Nike products. These could transmit physical activity data to Nike software that was deployed on portable devices produced by other companies, such as Apple iPod, iPad, or iPhone. The software passed the data over the Internet to Nike's proprietary online social platform, NikePlus.com, which then posted status updates to Facebook or Twitter. Upon clicking on these updates, users would be taken to the NikePlus platform, where they would see more data about their friends' sport achievements as well as advertisements for the equipment with embedded chips.

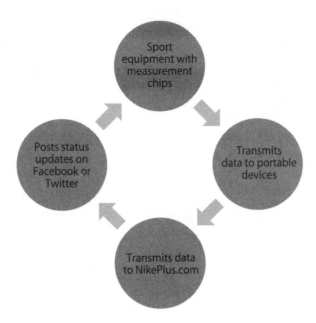

Figure 12.1. NikePlus.com ecosystem

This ecosystem became the center of the company's social strategy (it still was at the time of this writing), even as Nike continued to innovate on its individual pieces.

Nike's Devices and Their Integration with Portable Devices

Nike's first device, branded Nike+ and released in 2006, featured a thirty-dollar sensor placed inside running shoes that monitored the runner's speed, distance, and calories burned. The sensor connected wirelessly to the runner's Apple iPod and transmitted the data to a dedicated Nike application. The application informed the runner about his or her average speed and remaining distance, and played a "power song" if the runner was slowing down. After the run was complete, the athlete could transmit the data to NikePlus.com. In 2008, the company simplified the system by releasing Nike+ Sportband, which consisted of a rubber strap worn around the wrist, and a USB-based device that could be plugged directly into a computer, and, with the help of Nike software, upload workout data to NikePlus.com. Two years later, Nike upgraded its software on Apple products by releasing an application called Nike+ GPS. This app tracked data on pace, distance, time, and calories burned, but it also recorded an athlete's locations during a run, thereby constructing precise route maps. As before, all of these data could be uploaded to NikePlus.

In 2010 Nike also created a new division, called Nike Digital Sport, tasked with developing more products that track performance. The first product developed by this division was FuelBand, released in January 2012 and retailing for $149. The device was a wristband that tracked movement of the wearer throughout the day, and captured and displayed three metrics: calories, steps, and "NikeFuel." NikeFuel used algorithms based on oxygen kinetics to compare activity regardless of the user's sex, body type, and sport (or general movement) of choice. To use the device, an athlete would first plug it into a computer via a USB port, and synchronize it with proprietary Nike software to establish daily activity goals, as measured by NikeFuel. Then, as the user wore the band throughout the day, a series of LED lights on the band would appear, shifting from red to yellow to green to show progress toward the user's stated daily goal. At any point, users could press a button on the FuelBand to send the data to their iPhones, which would then relay the information to the NikePlus.com site. Alternatively, they could plug the band into their computer to achieve the same goal.

Later that year, the company released Nike+ Training and Nike+ Basketball, both of which used pressure sensors built into the soles of shoes to collect data on how quickly users moved, how high they jumped, and how many NikeFuels they burned and send it wirelessly to dedicated applications on their mobile devices, which then uploaded the information to NikePlus.com. Nike+ Training, for example, helped users create daily workout programs and then used the data from the shoes to monitor user progress. Nike+ Basketball allowed users to set achievement goals and, upon reaching those goals, receive prerecorded messages from Nike+ Basketball stars and coaches on their phone. The application also allowed users to record videos of themselves slam dunking, or doing other impressive basketball moves, and superimposed data on how high they jumped and how fast over the video. As always, users could easily share such videos with others.

NikePlus.com

All of the devices listed above transmitted athletic data to Nike's proprietary social platform, NikePlus.com. In the words of one Nike executive: "We built this platform on the insight that you can use digital technology to enhance someone's performance, and then add [a] community and social interaction layer to it to make the experience more powerful.... [E]very category has something where both the use of data and the use of social interaction can be used to create products no-one has created before."

Put another way, with this approach, Nike was able to perform on each of the elements of our familiar breadth, display, search, and communication framework.

BREADTH

Anyone on the Internet could sign up for a NikePlus platform and establish a profile there to establish new relationships as well as strengthen existing ones. Nike engaged in little explicit advertising of its platform—most users registered because they purchased a product that integrated with the platform, for example, an iPod or a shoe, or saw one of their friends use the platform, for example, by seeing a status update. This strategy paid off handsomely for Nike and attracted more than five million users to NikePlus, making it the largest online running and sporting destination.

To help users establish online interactions with people they knew, users had the option to connect their registration to their Facebook or their Twitter profile. When they did so, they could import their lists of online friendships to NikePlus, and then choose if they want to re-establish relationships with these friends on the Nike's platform. By importing their list of Facebook or Twitter friends, users could also easily find out which of their friends synchronized their Nike devices with the platform.

Display

Beyond posting a single picture, their name, and location, the platform offered limited ability for users to disclose personal information. Instead, it prompted users to synchronize their Nike device with the platform, so that it could start displaying the data from the device on the user's profile. For example, if the user was a runner, the profile would display data such as total amount of NikeFuel burned, total distance run, the number of runs, as well as a list of the user's achievements, such as having run ten, fifteen, or twenty miles. The profile would feature a fairly detailed graphic documenting the user's last three runs. NikePlus also collected the data on the route users took and aggregated those data with information about other runners' routes. If a route proved to be particularly popular, Nike would provide a leaderboard for that route displaying the fastest or the most committed runners. Users could then reach out to those individuals to establish an online relationship and perhaps run together. Indeed, one NikePlus user I spoke with attested to this important "meet" functionality: "I train quite heavily and you would be surprised how difficult it is to find someone who is as serious about running as I am. You know … it's less about running itself, but more about nutrition, how to avoid injuries, and pace your training well. … So when I was checking out various routes online I found this guy who seemed as committed as I was and now he and I actually talk and train together to get ready for the [Boston] Marathon."

Integration with Facebook or Twitter provided a separate set of display functionalities. For example, using the platform, runners could post a status update on Facebook announcing that they were starting to run. Similarly, when they finished their run, they could post a status update to Facebook informing their friends how far they ran and what route they took. Every time users achieved their daily or monthly fitness goals, they could also share that information with their Facebook friends, often eliciting praise. One of the NikePlus users I interviewed underscored the importance of this display solution in the context of a "friend" solution: "I am always quite surprised how many people 'like' my Facebook posts with my runs or leave comments. Perhaps the most unexpected part of all of this is that a few of the people I know reached out to me and said they wanted to run together. . . . I'd say now every other day I would run with one of them."

Finally, Nike+ Basketball platform allowed users to upload their videos to Facebook, and company executives believed that this functionality was critical to encouraging people to use Nike products and recruit their friends to do so. In the words of LeBron James, a famous basketball player and a Nike athlete: "When you're growing up and playing the game of basketball, your friends are your competition. Young players will be excited to track their stats to earn bragging rights or showcase their best plays on video. They'll be anxious to get back out on the court to improve their stats."

SEARCH

Once the data were online, it was easy for users to view their own achievements, and to go to their friends' profiles to examine theirs. At the time I was writing this book, Nike did not offer explicit functionalities to allow users to search for other athletes on the basis of observable criteria, such as age, location, or the sport. Users could, however, use leaderboards to identify strangers who might be of interest to them, and then go see some of their performance data, and potentially establish an online relationship. Nike also allowed users to browse its extensive running route map data. Indeed, Nike boasted the largest such database in the country, and many avid runners consulted it frequently when choosing or updating their runs.

COMMUNICATION

NikePlus did not explicitly offer users the ability to message each other independently through the site, but it did enable messaging within the context of athletic activity. Specifically, users could create sporting challenges and send them to their friends to complete. For example, a user could challenge a couple of friends to run a total of one hundred miles, and include a personal message saying that the last person to complete the goal would have to buy dinner for everyone involved. The Nike-Plus application would then monitor progress and make it visible to all runners involved and finally declare a winner. One NikePlus user I interviewed opined on the communication solutions provided by the "friend" solution:

> Challenges are fantastic because they really motivate me to get out of bed and do my exercise. And best thing about them is that allow me to engage with people I would not have run with or interacted with otherwise. Some of them live far away, some of them it's just too awkward to walk up to them and challenge them. . . . But then when we are all done we end up hanging out. . . . I was actually very sad when Nike took the functionality down from the site to upgrade it. Can't wait for it to come back.

Friends could also click on a link embedded in users' Facebook status updates that announced that the user was out for a run; the click would automatically trigger an audible cheer on top of the music that the runner was listening to on his or her iPhone while exercising. One of the NikePlus users I interviewed described how this functionality affects his athletic performance and offline relationships:

> I get a lot of motivation when friends cheer me on when I am running. You are going to laugh . . . but I went out for a run this morning and I only got three cheers, and I wanted to cry. It's like my friends do not like me anymore. . . . A few days ago I got like 15 and I was on top of the world. It really makes a difference for me and motivates me to run more and faster, because I know my friends have my back. We talk about it later, and it's all good fun.

Summary

Ultimately, NikePlus created both a "meet" and a "friend" platform in which athletic activities became the centerpiece of breadth, display, search, and communication solutions. Embedding athletic activities in the context of a social platform had the dual function of motivating people to exercise more or more frequently, and at the same time helped them identify other people with similar interests and develop relationships in ways they would otherwise find difficult. Although the lack of data from the platform prohibits us from understanding its exact efficacy, the fact that the platform membership and usage grew by 55 percent in 2011 suggests that it did quite well on both fronts.

Tasks and Strategy Impact

These social benefits also created benefits for the company. Consider the kinds of corporate tasks the platform asked users to engage in and the impact those tasks have had on Nike's business outcomes. The NikePlus platform did not allow users to enter performance and activity data manually; only Nike devices could transfer such data. This put one major requirement on NikePlus users: in order to participate, they had to synchronize relevant devices with the platform. That meant that users had to buy Nike's shoes or devices. Put differently, users had to pay up front to be able to meet strangers or interact with friends. This approach is fairly typical for "meet" platforms—after all, users of many dating sites are expected to pay a monthly subscription to participate in them. But Nike extended the concept to include "friend" platforms, whereby users would have to purchase a device to be able to improve their friend relationships. Thus, one of Nike's social strategies can be described as:

(1) Nike increases willingness to pay for its products
(2) by allowing people to meet new people and strengthen their friendships
(3) when they connect the product to Nike's social platform

The results of such integration have been impressive. For example, some analysts have estimated that growth in NikePlus membership played a very significant role in the growth of Nike's overall running division, which grew 30 percent in 2011. To be clear, the connection with the social platform did not generate all of the willingness to pay for a Nike product. Users still derived value from the shoes and devices they bought. They also probably derived value from the tracking activities and recording abilities that the devices and the platform gave them. But the ability to interact—and by doing so become more committed to exercising and better acquainted with friends and strangers—generated additional value.

In addition to creating willingness-to-pay benefits, the NikePlus platform also featured two social strategies aimed at reducing cost. Both of those strategies will be familiar, as one resembles Zynga's strategy while the other one is somewhat akin to Yelp's approach. The Zynga-like strategy involves getting users to post status updates—and videos, in the case of Nike+ Basketball—on their own Facebook pages. As discussed earlier, such status updates and videos allow individuals to display their athletic information to their friends, and at the same time advertise Nike products to them. This social strategy takes the familiar form of:

(1) Nike lowers its customer acquisition costs
(2) by allowing people to strengthen their friendships
(3) when they post status updates and videos

In a Yelp-like approach, Nike also collected information on users' running routes and aggregated them to showcase the most popular, and therefore probably the most attractive routes. Without such contributions, Nike would have to incur substantial cost to obtain to obtain these data. To encourage users to contribute such data, Nike built leaderboards, which displayed the most active users. The platform had limited functionalities for users to easily find strangers, but being featured on the leaderboard gave users exposure so that others could approach them and establish new relationships with them. This approach is quite similar to what we saw in Yelp, where people were able to meet others if they contributed content. Nike's equivalent strategy can be summarized as:

(1) Nike lowers its cost of acquiring data
(2) by allowing people to meet new people
(3) when they run a lot and submit data about their runs

Conclusions

This chapter examined the final type of social strategy introduced in this book—one that allows companies to increase their customers' willingness to pay as it allows people to strengthen their interactions with their friends. As we trace the development of Nike's social strategy, we also saw how firms can embed their social strategies directly into their products. Compare Nike's approach to that of American Express. At AmEx, we saw a company that kept its existing product intact (i.e., the credit card), but then added auxiliary products (merchant discounts), which it then used to develop a social strategy. Nike also started the same way—keeping the main product (i.e., running shoe) intact, but adding an auxiliary product (the movement sensors), which it then used to develop a social strategy. With time, however, Nike started developing products, such as the FuelBand or Nike+ Basketball, that were designed with social strategy in mind, and whose value in large part was derived from social integration. As more firms come to understand the value of social strategy, we can expect to see more products that explicitly integrate social experiences into their design.

Nike's experience also powerfully illustrates that the four types of social strategies need not be developed in isolation. In fact, it is not difficult to develop a set of tools and capabilities and then create a number of different social strategies around those functionalities, as shown in table 12.1. Recognizing that fact, readers can begin thinking about

Table 12.1. Nike's Social Strategies

		Social impact	
		New relationships	Existing relationships
Business strategy impact	Higher willingness to pay	To meet new people need to buy a device	To strengthen relationships need to buy a device
	Lower costs	To meet new people need to contribute free content to Nike	To strengthen relationships need to post to Facebook and advertise Nike

introducing various complementarities between social strategies, such that the value of one social strategy increases because another social strategy is present. Although Nike has not explicitly built its social strategies in this way, in the next chapter we will encounter an organization, the *Harvard Business Review*, that explicitly sought to build such complementarities.

CHAPTER 13

Building Social Strategy at XCard and *Harvard Business Review*

When we studied Zynga and Yelp, we examined companies that built social strategy into their operations right from the inception. We spent very little time, however, thinking about how these companies *developed* their social strategies. Then we looked at American Express and Nike, where we traced processes of organic experimentation that allowed these companies to transition from a purely digital strategy to a combination of digital and social strategies. American Express and Nike both engaged in lengthy processes of building their social strategies, which may lead many readers to ask: I already have a digital strategy, but I don't have five years to experiment with social strategy. Is there anything I can do to accelerate the process and start integrating social platforms directly and effectively into my strategy now?

To explore some answers to that question, we'll now examine two companies' experiences tackling this exact issue. The first company is a credit card issuer, which for reasons of confidentiality we will refer to as XCard. Examining XCard's process will allow us to review three basic tests that any social strategy developer should use. The second is the *Harvard Business Review* (HBR), whose leaders' experiences will help reveal how firms use these tests and also seek to build complementarities between various social strategies they build.

XCard Develops a Social Strategy

XCard's process began in 2010, when an eight-person team including members from marketing, product development, and IT and two outside consultants was tasked with developing a social strategy for the company. The group was to report back to both the CMO and the CEO.

To help the team structure its process, the consultants initially took the lead, asking the team to use the framework (business impact, social impact, tasks) to develop at least two strategy statements for each of the four social strategy types (low-cost "meet," low-cost "friend," higher willingness-to-pay "meet," and higher willingness-to-pay "friend"). Over the course of several in-person meetings team members, brainstormed the various types of social failures they thought the company could solve and then tried to connect those ideas to XCard's business objectives.

What follows are some of the fruits of those initial brainstorming sessions—representing each of the four social strategy types. The ideas vary in their quality, illuminating the elements that distinguish a powerful social strategy from a mediocre one.

XCard's Low-Cost "Meet" Social Strategy Idea: Executive Women

To develop this low-cost meet strategy, the team leveraged the fact that although people often find it hard to identify others with whom to interact, consumption of a particular product can be used as an indicator of a potential match. For example, certain types of people who spend a substantial amount of money may be interested in other people who also spend a lot of money. A credit card company is in the unique position of knowing who spends a lot of money (at least on credit), and can use this information to help people find others who do likewise. When this happens, a credit card can potentially solve a "meet" social failure better than other social platforms or firms can.

Team members agreed that helping people meet on the basis of how much they spend also stood to benefit the company. They reasoned that people would be willing to charge their expenditures to XCard, rather than to a competitive product, to signal their ability to spend and thus have the ability to meet equally powerful spenders. These marginal decisions to use XCard would translate into higher revenues for the company.

To devise a way to put this theory to work, team members focused on XCard's top-of-the-line card and narrowed their sights to focus on one segment of the card's users: high-spending female customers, who were mainly consultants or executives traveling up to four days a week. The team believed that these female executives sought to connect to others to discuss issues of how to be successful as women in predominantly male office environments. They also posited that doing so was difficult. To solve the social failure, the team proposed to organize invitation-only events in large metropolitan areas, such as New York or San Francisco, and invite these women to come when they were visiting these cities, as long as they possessed and used the high-end charge card at least a fixed number of times per month.

The team believed that this program would encourage the cardholders to use the XCard card rather than a competitive product so that they could qualify to be invited to these special events. In turn, XCard would be able to reduce its expenditures on monetary rewards, such as special mileage promotions, that it had been offering to encourage card usage. The team called this strategy *executive women* and summarized it as:

(1) XCard's social strategy decreases customer retention costs
(2) by allowing executive women to connect to similar others
(3) if they continue to hold and use their exclusive credit card

XCARD'S DIFFERENTIATED "MEET" SOCIAL STRATEGY IDEA: MOMS

To develop this strategy, the team drew on the observation that people want to interact with strangers and talk about various purchases they made or want to make, but find it difficult to do so. Team members believed that their company possessed at least some data about cardholders' purchases that it could display to others (with permission) and hence facilitate mutually beneficial interactions.

To make this idea actionable, the social strategy team decided to focus on moms with young children. The team believed that these women sought to obtain a lot of information about products from other moms, but did not always know whom to trust when it came to reviews. To help alleviate this problem, the team wanted to introduce a specially branded card targeted at moms. The card would be connected to a dedicated online platform where moms could establish personal profiles and display some or all of the purchases they made with the card. Moms could also search for others who bought the same product to discuss their experience using it. Only moms who made themselves searchable and continued to make purchases on the card would be allowed to search, however.

The team believed that attaching this branded credit card to a social platform would allow XCard to charge more for the card than the company was able to charge for its regular branded offerings. The team called this strategy *moms* and summarized it as follows:

(1) XCard's social strategy seeks to increase willingness to pay
(2) by allowing cardholder moms to view strangers' information
(3) if they made their own information broadly available

XCard's Low-Cost "Friend" Social Strategy Idea: Social Discounts

In formulating this strategy, the team relied on the observation that people often want to refer certain businesses or business offers to their friends, but are often afraid to do so because they do not know if their friends are interested. As a consequence, many mutually beneficial interactions between friends do not take place. The team believed they could solve this failure by providing its cardholders with discounts to popular retailers that could only be used if the cardholders paid with XCard. Cardholders could also then share these discounts by posting them on their Facebook profiles for their friends to see. The team reasoned that this solution would allow cardholders to share money-saving opportunities with their friends without forcing them to consume these opportunities, much in the same way Facebook in general allows people to share content with others without forcing anyone to consume it.

The team believed that this strategy would primarily benefit the company in terms of cheaper customer acquisition. Specifically, suppose an XCard current cardholder shared a discount on Facebook, and one of her friends wanted to claim it, but she did not have a card from the company. She would then apply for the card. If accepted, this new customer would become an XCard customer at a fraction of the cost of what the company would normally spend to acquire a new customer. Although team members were not able to project the economic impact of this strategy, they were encouraged by the fact that eBay employed a very similar strategy and was able to lower its customer acquisition costs by doing so. The team called this strategy *social discounts* and summarized it as follows:

(1) XCard's social strategy seeks to reduce costs
(2) by allowing people to improve their interactions with friends
(3) if they post status updates advertising the card and the discounts it offers

XCard's Differentiated "Friend" Social Strategy Idea: Rewards with Friends

The team conceived of many differentiated friend strategies, but one in particular stood out as having potential. That strategy was based on the observation that people often choose not to interact with their friends regarding financial arrangements, even when those arrangements would be mutually beneficial, for fear they might derail and thereby undermine their friendships. The team believed that there were substantial opportunities in allowing friends to benefit from each other in a very consistent, equitable, and transparent fashion, which would then lead them to establish closer personal relationships.

To make this strategy actionable, the team devised a program that would allow customers of a particular card that had an annual fee of almost one hundred dollars per year to form a group with four other friends who also possessed that card or acquired one. All members of this group would obtain additional rewards in the form of airline miles if they *all* engaged in a minimum number of XCard transactions per month. They could also earn additional miles if they *all* used their XCard at the same retailer during the same month, with extra credit if they all used XCard at the same retailer at the same time, for example, if they *all* went to the same restaurant together.

Not only did team members believe that this social strategy would result in closer friend interactions, but they also felt it would generate substantial benefits for the firm in terms of cardholders' higher willingness to pay. First, cardholders could recruit others who did not hold the card to join them, resulting in additional revenues. Second, these cardholders would probably encourage each other to use XCard rather than competitors' cards and, by doing so, would improve the company's top line. Finally, in some cases, friends could talk their friends out of potentially abandoning the card in favor of a competitor's card, as doing so would undermine their joint benefits. The team called this strategy *rewards with friends* and described it as:

(1) XCard's social strategy increases willingness to pay
(2) by allowing people to better interact with friends
(3) when they ask them to use XCard more frequently

Choosing between the Strategies

Having identified several potential social strategies, the team's next step was evaluating what they had come up with. To do so, the consultants proposed three tests—a *social utility test*, a *unique social solution test*, and a *business value test*—and asked the team to put the proposed strategies through these tests. These tests allowed the team to identify the weakest areas of their strategies, which allowed them to identify the aspects needing most improvement.

SOCIAL UTILITY TEST

The social utility test seeks to make sure that a proposed social strategy solves a real social failure. To do so, it asks the following question: *Does this social strategy enable an important social interaction for a meaningful set of people who cannot engage in it on their own?*

This test has two very distinct parts. First, it asks that the social strategy identify a real *social* interaction that does not occur in the offline world. That might seem like an easy hurdle, but it is not. I have often heard social strategy designers describe "the need for insurance," "the need for a stroller" (or some other material good), or "the need for entertainment" as a social failure. All of these are examples of unmet *economic* needs, not unmet *social* needs. Whenever anyone is in doubt whether a particular need is social, I recommend testing whether it can be described as: "Someone wants to *meet* someone else, but cannot," or "Someone wants to *become a better friend with* someone else, but cannot." If the failure cannot be described thus, it probably is not a social failure.

The XCard team set out to rank each of the four ideas against this test, starting with executive women. Although some team members thought that this strategy does not solve a real social failure, two female members of the team were very excited about the idea. They explained to the rest of the team that high-powered women executives would really like to meet others like themselves, but that it was difficult to do because most companies have very few female executives. This problem is made even worse by the fact that these women travel a lot and have a lot of family obligations, making such valuable meetings almost impossible.

Their argument was compelling, and the team was persuaded that this is an important social relationship for their target group and one that is very difficult to establish offline, giving the firm an opportunity to step in and improve social relationships. Thus, the team gave this strategy high marks on the first part of the social utility test.

Next, the team considered its moms strategy. The team applied the logic it had used in the design process to conclude that moms want to connect to other moms to talk about childrearing, but for many moms this is difficult to do, opening up an opportunity for the firm to step in and help. One team member provided further evidence in support of this claim, showing that moms are the most active category on other sites facilitating new relationships. With this in mind, the team also gave this strategy high marks on the first part of the social utility test.

Then the team turned to its social discounts idea. Since this strategy was not targeted at a specific group of people, the team wanted to ascertain that reconnecting with friends was a broadly applicable unmet social need. As there was substantial difference of opinion among team members on this topic, some of the team members went to collect additional research evidence and found that in excess of 60 percent of XCard users would be grateful to their friends if they obtained discounts from them via Facebook. This persuaded the team to give this strategy high marks on the first part of the social utility test.

Finally, the team evaluated its rewards with friends strategy. Again, this strategy did not target a specific group of people and therefore required addressing a broadly felt unmet social need. Members of the team were not persuaded that the strategy actually solved a social failure. Indeed, most believed that this strategy had the potential to undermine social relationships. Some team members were concerned that some friendships could be undermined if people did not use the card sufficiently frequently for their friends to generate additional rewards. Others were concerned about what would happen to friendships if people started explicitly telling each other that they ought to use one product over another. With these considerations in mind, the team gave this strategy low marks on the first part of the social utility test.

The second part of the test examines whether the proposed social strategy actually *enables* these interactions. To do that we first need to ascertain that the proposed functionality actually solves the failure. To do so, it is important to follow the prescriptions in chapter 2, paying particular attention to make sure that the functionality does not aggravate the underlying social failure, or solves it, but creates many derivative failures. This latter scenario can sometimes occur when social strategy designers devise social solutions to fit the corporate jobs the company wants people to undertake. For example, I witnessed one company that designed a social strategy that allowed people to ask their friends for contributions to a charitable cause. Few people actually engaged in such behaviors, however. The company later discovered that the only people who felt comfortable posting such requests felt that their friends "owed" them a lot of favors. Everyone else felt that asking their friends for contributions amounted to using, rather than improving, their friendships to benefit the company. The company ended up developing a very different solution—one that allowed users to benefit, rather than use, their existing relationships.

Next, we need to test that the functionality solves the failure in the most effective manner possible. Suppose the social strategy called for a "meet" solution for people who face significant normative restrictions on reaching out to others. Thinking back to the lessons from the first part of the book, we see that such a strategy would have to use a broker or activity meet solution rather than a marketplace solution, as marketplaces rarely help people overcome normative restrictions on contact. Furthermore, the solution would need to address breadth, display, search, and communication interaction costs. In contrast, if the strategy called for a "friend" solution, it would be important to scrutinize the breadth of the solution and align all of the display, search, and communication functionalities appropriately. In both cases, appropriate tactical decisions would need to be made regarding integration with existing social platforms, such as LinkedIn or Facebook.

Adhering to those lessons from the first part of the book will help social strategy designers avoid a "knee-jerk" reaction to solving social failures—a phenomenon I have often witnessed. For example, when tasked with helping strangers meet, I have seen strategy designers recommend that the company set up a forum where people can show up and freely interact with each other. As we saw in the first part of the book, simply giving people a venue to interact with strangers is unlikely to solve failures for those who are most affected. Unless the "meet" platform provides functionalities to address all four interaction costs we discussed in the first part of the book, it is unlikely to work. In other cases, I have seen firms seeking to help people interact with their closest friends, but then making those interactions public. Rather unsurprisingly, such functionalities did not result in the intended behaviors, requiring the firms to alter their approaches significantly.

Finally, we need to confirm that the proposed social solution is unique. That is, the solution should be different from what users can already do on existing stand-alone social platforms such as Twitter or

Facebook. It should also be different from what competitors have offered and will be able to offer. Addressing this part of the question is the most stringent part of the test, as it requires that the social solution that the company wants to offer will not be copied. To ensure that it will not, it is best that the social solution draws on the unique resources that the company has or reinforces the firm's key point of differentiation.

The XCard team members, with these considerations in mind, examined the remaining three social strategies, starting with executive women. (Given that the rewards with friends strategy had not passed the first part of test of identifying a social failure, the team logically determined that it couldn't be tested further.) Team members believed that they were creating a solid social solution by creating a safe space for women to meet. They also believed that the strategy would induce few derivative failures here, as there probably were not many inappropriate social relationships that would be created by introducing women to women. The team also believed that they tackled at least three of the four aspects of creating a meet platform. Specifically, XCard's large membership base would probably take care of breadth solutions. The team also believed that the restricted nature of the platform would actually make women display a lot of content about themselves. Equally, they believed that XCard could take care of any search issues by asking women about their travel plans in advance and then coordinating the schedules.

The team stumbled a little when it came to communication solution. Initially, team members imagined that the women would simply come to a hotel function room to mingle and socialize. But as they thought about the solution, they became concerned that some women might shun the meetings because of the unstructured interaction process. Thus, they decided to organize these meetings around a theme or a speaker to help facilitate interactions. Finally, the team examined the solution against competitors and came to the conclusion that neither standalone sites nor other firms in their industry would be able to replicate such high-powered meetings with ease. Overall, the team gave the executive women strategy high marks for the second part of the test.

Next up was the moms strategy. Team members believed that the number of cards they would be able to issue would be a strength with regard to breadth. But they did not believe they could provide a display solution because XCard knew where cardholders made their purchases but did not know what they bought. Although moms could be asked to manually enter their purchases, the team members did not believe that much content would be delivered this way. They did believe that they could provide strong functionalities for the search and communication solutions. They knew, however, that the poor display solution would severely undermine the efficacy of these solutions. The concerns about display solutions became even more pronounced when the team considered alternatives. Specifically, the team was worried that large stores such as Target or Wal-Mart had much more detailed display data that they could use to create a better "meet" platform than XCard to help moms connect. With this in mind, the team gave moms a low mark for the second part of the test.

The team then turned to its social discounts strategy, quickly deciding, in this case, that the functionality provided appropriate solutions to the problem of sharing deal-related information with both close friends and acquaintances (breadth). Following eBay's example, the team also believed that the integration with Facebook was the best implementation of this solution. Some team members raised the concern that some competitors in the industry might possess better relationships with retailers that would then allow them to obtain better discounts from more places. Others on the team, however, believed that XCard possessed some retailer relationships that were not available to competitors, which should allow it to remain competitive. Overall, the team gave social discounts high marks for the second part of the test.

SOCIAL SOLUTION TEST

Having examined whether a social strategy identifies a meaningful social failure, the next test must determine whether it actually addresses the failure in a way that also benefits the business. The social solution test thus asks: *Do the tasks that help the company reach its competitive goals provide the most effective and unique way of enabling social interactions?*

This test is simultaneously quite straightforward and quite difficult. It seeks to ensure that the task that people undertake allows them to engage in better relationships and at the same time benefits the company. Getting this tight integration to work is the most difficult part of designing a workable social strategy. It is critical, however, because if the same task does not create social benefits for the customer and economic benefits for the company, a social strategy is bound to fail. Specifically, when the task allows people to enter into new interactions with others but does not benefit the company, individuals will undertake the task but it will not have any effect on corporate performance. Furthermore, when the task allows the company to benefit but it does nothing to help people establish better relationships, people will simply not undertake it, resulting in no changes to the company's competitive advantage.

With these considerations in mind, the XCard team set out to examine the two strategies that survived the previous tests. The team concluded that the executive women strategy appropriately connected the economic and social benefits. The only way in which the women could solve their failure and meet other women like them was to remain loyal to the card, which generated the business benefits. The social discounts strategy also passed the social solution test. It tightly aligned social and economic benefits: the social act of inviting a friend to participate in a discount offer also generates business benefits if the friend becomes a new card member and/or makes a purchase on the card. Encouraged by the outcome, the team moved to the business value test.

BUSINESS VALUE TEST

The business value test ensures that the solutions to social failures actually end up benefiting the business, by asking: *Does the social strategy meaningfully help the business improve competitive advantage over the long term?*

Here, it is important to ascertain that the social strategy promises a significant impact on profits. A social strategy that passes the social utility and social solution tests with flying colors is unfortunately not worth executing if it does not move the needle on the bottom line. In evaluating that potential impact, it is important to consider both the potential impact on willingness to pay and cost reductions. Specifically, if the social strategy calls for cost reduction, it is important to pay attention to the concomitant reduction in willingness to pay. Similarly, if the social strategy calls for increases in willingness to pay, it is important to understand the increase in cost. In my experience, social strategies that pass the business value test usually target parts of the value chain that are most responsible for generating the majority of willingness to pay or the majority of cost. After all, if a particular part of the value chain accounts for 40 percent of company cost, and social strategy can reduce that cost by 10 percent, that is already 4 percentage points that drop directly to the bottom line. These types of calculations are critical to picking the right strategies. For this reason, the best social strategy designers actually try to explicitly quantify the changes in willingness to pay and costs to see if the proposed strategy actually increases profitability.

With these considerations in mind, the XCard team set out to examine the two strategies that survived the previous tests. The team concluded that the executive women strategy had a very small target group: only 0.2 percent of total cardholders. Although reducing defection among this small but disproportionately profitable segment could have a measurable bottom line impact, it was not big enough for the team to justify the necessary investments. In contrast, the social discounts strategy met the business value test requirements. Here, because each new customer recruited by a card member in effect halves the customer acquisition costs, the team calculated that the strategy had great economic potential. As the social discounts strategy performed best on all three tests, the team decided to pilot it.

Harvard Business Review

Harvard Business Review's formal path toward determining and implementing a social strategy began in November 2011. By then, the HBR Group had established robust presences on Twitter, Facebook, LinkedIn, and YouTube, with more than 1.3 million fans in total, and had used these platforms to generate increased engagement and traffic to its website. Fifteen percent of all website traffic came from these sites. Even with these numbers, however, social platforms were seen as an important enhancement to core efforts, but not central to the HBR Group's business strategy. Josh Macht, the HBR Group's publisher, discussed the central problem with HBR's digital strategies on these social platforms: "We're Tweeting, and Facebooking, and it's a blast, and we see all of this engagement. . . . We could continue to get more fans and more people following us . . . but now we're scratching our heads, how can we make money with this? We have already started to look at who is influential in our audience and how we can tap them. But so far we have found it hard to convert influential users into increased sales. We needed a way to fundamentally transform the way we think about this."

Faced with this problem, HBR Group's leadership team started to look for a framework that would help the organization derive greater benefits from social platforms. In doing so, they realized that the organization's flagship publication, the *Harvard Business Review* magazine, had published parts of the social strategy framework described earlier in this chapter in its November 2011 issue. Macht recalled the leadership group's reaction to the social strategy framework: "[It] allowed us to think about two things. First, we started to think about the network of readers and followers that we have and the value each person has to all others in that network. . . . What if we started to really connect these people to each other and to others. . . . Second, instead of seeing social and profit as separate, we now see them as complementary. [The framework gave us] a much more deliberate way of thinking about this, and it can help us make a real connection to fundamentals of marketing, growing the brand and the editorial."

Within a month of starting to work on developing their social strategy, a few members of the HBR Group attended a research talk I gave in Boston. They told me that they were using the framework to develop their own social strategy, and I asked if they would let me observe and document the process. (Although most companies do not allow researchers to document the often-messy strategy development process, HBR leaders were generous enough to let me do it and document my findings in this chapter without exercising any editorial control. In particular, the experience of the team charged with developing a social strategy for the HBR Group may offer useful insights to managers and leaders at smaller and midsized businesses that do not have the resources to spend a great deal of time testing and researching social strategy options.)

Background

HBR was the leading research-based business magazine, focusing on management techniques and breakthrough ideas, with featured pieces written by some of the top business minds from all around the world. It was published ten times a year, reaching more than 250,000 subscribers in more than a dozen countries. There were also eleven licensed and independently run editions of the magazine, including two Chinese, one Italian, one German, one Japanese, and one Polish. HBR's origins date back to 1922, when Wallace Donham, the dean of the Harvard Business School, founded it as a magazine for the school's community. From its first issue, though, focusing as it did on macroeconomic trends as well as on important developments within specific industries, the magazine was circulated outside the school. Following World War II, its emphasis changed to new management techniques that were developed during this period in large corporations, such as General Motors. And in the 1980s, its feature articles were shortened and the scope of the magazine was expanded to include a wider range of topics and to make it more accessible to a general audience.

In 1994, Harvard Business School Publishing became an independent entity, first financially and then editorially. After several reorganizations, it emerged with three divisions: Higher Education, which distributed cases, articles, and book chapters for business education materials; Corporate Learning, which provided standardized online and tailored offline leadership development courses; and the HBR Group, which included the *Harvard Business Review* magazine and its online version, as well as a book press.

In 2009, the organization recruited Adi Ignatius from his position as deputy managing editor of *Time* magazine to lead an intensive editorial transformation. Ignatius set out three key priorities. First, although he continued to publish research-based pieces, he determined to add articles on more current topics to broaden the audience and improve the magazine's reach. He also decided to give HBR a complete graphic makeover and to have each issue focus on a single theme and have a distinct personality, rather than publishing collections of unrelated articles. Second, he committed to increasing the company's digital and social presence, and integrating its print and digital divisions more closely. Finally, he articulated a desire to develop new business models for the brand that leveraged the digital and social spheres. The remainder of the chapter delves into these developments.

DIGITAL STRATEGY

The origins of the HBR Group's digital strategy date back to 1997, when the organization first launched hbr.org, featuring an online catalogue of previous issues of the magazine, books published by Harvard Business School Press, and article collections. Later, the magazine was digitized and made available for online consumption by subscribers. And over time HBR started adding new features. One was *IdeaCast*, launched in 2006, a weekly audio show that featured commentary and interviews with thought leaders from the business world. *IdeaCast* was accompanied by a short weekly video podcast, and within four years of its launch, those podcasts had been downloaded nine million times.

In 2007, HBR introduced a blog network, which featured contributions from established academic thought leaders and practitioners with extensive hands-on experience as well as blogs written by up-and-coming voices discussing recent news events in the business world. Initially, it was difficult to find bloggers to contribute, largely because the blog network was separate from the HBR magazine. When the blog network finally took off, however, it quickly began to log more than four million page views per month.

The following year, HBR started building presences on Facebook, Twitter, LinkedIn, and YouTube. The move toward these social platforms came about organically, with several employees gathering together to brainstorm ideas and then implement them. One employee recalled: "It was a self-organizing thing, and it started as brown-bag lunches—people who were just enthusiastic about it and really wanted to explore and test. We called it the 'volunteer army.' " One of the first topics the group discussed was the fit between the company and the platforms. Macht elaborated: "We wondered how the brand, which represents big management ideas through long articles in print and books, would translate into social media. We were all about heavy research and big ideas, and case studies, and management frameworks that could be applied to businesses and in academia. How could we be true to all that in a place where you're allowed 140 characters?"

The company soon found, however, that many of these concerns were unfounded. Many readers appreciated the short versions of complex ideas, as these were easily shared and discussed with others. Macht commented: "There's a whole ecosystem of people who create and use management ideas, and a whole group of people who are really passionate about being managers and executives. And there are not that many places that take it as seriously as the *Harvard Business Review*. They feel their ideas can carry more weight just by being associated with our brand. We have also learned [that it's] okay to be both playful and serious, and that the content actually lends itself to that."

These condensed versions of academic ideas were particularly central to HBR's presence on LinkedIn. Sarah McConville, a publisher at HBR, elaborated: "LinkedIn users like to feed and connect to others, and also share a lot of content. So when we post content there, it gets reposted and discussed with others, and this gets people interested in subscribing to the magazine or buying our books, once they've had a chance to explore what we publish."

HBR also played well on Twitter. Initially, the organization used the platform to post editorial comments together with links to content from the magazine, blog posts, and selected third-party websites. The editorial team also interacted with followers and handled other reader queries. This proved to be resource-intensive and required constant attention from editors, and concrete economic returns were mediocre. But then the organization cut out the interactive part of the process, and tweeted out links only to content on its main site. That approach proved to be much more successful, and within three months Twitter became hbr.org's second highest source of traffic.

Toward a Social Strategy

Following that initial success, HBR's leaders decided to create an official team tasked with leveraging social platforms. To balance both editorial and commercial goals, the team comprised fifteen people who came from the organization's editorial, PR, communication, and customer service departments. Soon after its formation, the team started to think about building interactions *between* its fans and followers, rather than merely broadcasting *to* them. To that end, team members conceived of a product that would allow HBR readers to seek and provide answers on pressing, real-life business and management issues. One team member summarized the theory of the product in this way: "There's a point in your career where you don't know everything you're supposed to know, but you can't ask anymore. You need to be able to ask those questions without risking much by asking. We wanted people to get answers to questions, in a safe place, where they're not showing weakness to their colleagues."

After exploring several possible forms for the product, the team eventually created the HBR Answer Exchange, using an off-the-shelf solution. Launched in March 2010, the service did not take off as expected, and was quickly retired. Reflecting on the causes, the team identified two key reasons why the product had floundered. First, team members believed that asking individuals to join a new and unfamiliar platform had been off-putting. They believed it would have been better to leverage an existing social platform and attract users there. Second, they believed that they had inadvertently mismanaged the product's implementation. To get the site off the ground, HBR had hired free-lancers to prepopulate with questions and answers. But doing so had created a mixed message, with users seeing "preapproved" questions and answers even as they were being asked to provide their own. This intimidated many potential users, who complained that the questions they had were much more complex and messy, and wouldn't have a textbook kind of answer.

SOCIAL STRATEGY OPTIONS

Armed with these experiences, HBR's leaders asked the team to work on connecting HBR's readers, fans, and followers to one another. It was by then November 2011, and this time the team was asked to use the social strategy framework described in this book. New team members were added to the team at that time as well, including an employee from HBR's IT department, and an individual who developed mobile apps for the organization. The group at that point was also split into two teams, one tasked with generating "meet" strategies, the other with "friend" strategies.

Initially, it was difficult for the teams to start thinking about their readers' social failures. When they considered the results of their own internal research, however, they were soon able to develop some educated guesses as to what these failures might be. Based on their work, the teams generated the following four ideas.

"MEET" SOCIAL STRATEGY TO INCREASE WILLINGNESS TO PAY

This first social strategy idea sought to solve a fairly basic social failure, most easily described as: "Many managers want to increase the size of their peer network, but they find it very difficult to do so." To solve this failure, the team proposed developing a "meet" platform that would allow people to find one another, meet online and offline, get feedback on questions or ideas, and provide and receive mentorship. To generate the large breadth needed to implement this solution, the team proposed advertising the new product to all existing HBR customers, fans, and followers. To ensure appropriate levels of display, the product would ask users what they were willing to offer and what they were looking for. To provide an element of profile veracity, users would also be asked to link their presence on the platform to their LinkedIn profile. To facilitate search, the product would allow users to search for others freely, on the basis of geography, industry, and needs and wants. Communication would take place through in-platform messaging, like the approach they would use on a dating site. Taking the dating-site analogy even further, the team recommended charging users for access to this new product. Indeed, team members affectionately (and internally) called this solution "Match.com for Business" though formally they called it the *Connection Platform*.

The team believed that this product leveraged HBR's unique resources and had the potential to attract skilled people and businesses from all around the world, in ways that HBR's competitors could not copy. At the same time, the team realized that in order to implement and sustain the platform successfully, they would need additional—and continuous—help from a number of colleagues beyond the core social media team. As one team member remarked, "This is not just a 'set it and let it go' opportunity. It would have to be actively monitored, managed, and measured. It would be a significant undertaking for our organization to launch this."

Phrased to fit the social strategy template, this idea can be described as follows:

(1) HBR's social strategy increases willingness to pay
(2) by allowing people to meet other HBR readers and fans
(3) when they pay to join the service

"MEET" SOCIAL STRATEGY TO REDUCE THE COST OF ACQUIRING CONTENT

The second "meet" social strategy sought to address the following social failure: "I often need answers to my work/business questions from like-minded individuals, but I find it difficult to ask safely." This failure was closely related to that which HBR had tried to address with Answer Exchange. This time, however, the team proposed a very different solution: building an application that would integrate tightly with the LinkedIn platform. It would be launched as a new version of the *Answer Exchange*.

To provide breadth for this solution, HBR would advertise the new product to all current subscribers to the magazine and to its followers on LinkedIn. To create a display solution, the application would allow users to post their questions and contribute answers. To give users greater privacy, the application would use friendship data from LinkedIn, so that users had the option to display their questions and answers only to people who were *not* the user's LinkedIn friends, or did *not* work at the user's company. This way, users would be able to ask sensitive questions or give frank answers without having to worry that their friends or coworkers would see them. To populate the platform, users would be given the capability to convert whatever they contributed on LinkedIn groups into questions and answers on the new Answer Exchange. To facilitate search, the new Answer Exchange would also provide extensive search capabilities that included keyword and topic searches. To encourage interaction, users would be able to comment on one another's entries, vote on the ones they thought were useful, and contact each other directly through an internal messaging system.

The team members believed that this new iteration of the Answer Exchange had a better chance of succeeding than the original initiative because it leveraged existing social platforms. The team also believed that by giving users the option to hide posts from people they knew, they created sufficient differentiation from LinkedIn in ways that LinkedIn would not emulate. Finally, team members believed that the questions and answers posted on the Answer Exchange could be easily published on the HBR blogs or the main HBR web property (after some editing to remove personally identifiable information). This strategy would therefore lower costs by allowing users to generate appropriate content, and potentially increase conversions by generating conversation around HBR-related topics. The template description was as follows:

(1) HBR's social strategy reduces the cost of acquiring inputs
(2) by allowing people to interact with relevant strangers
(3) when they contribute career-related questions and answers

"FRIEND" SOCIAL STRATEGY TO INCREASE WILLINGNESS TO PAY

The third social strategy idea sought to address a failure that can be summarized as: "I want a better way to keep in touch with my colleagues from school and work, but I find it very difficult to do that." To solve this failure, the team wanted to give users the ability to develop an *HBR Briefcase* that would contain all of their favorite HBR and HBR blog pieces. The Briefcase could then be shared with friends and acquaintances.

Existing research suggested that there would be substantial interest in this idea—many subscribers told stories of keeping shelves of back issues in their offices that moved with them from job to job. "I never throw an issue away," was a common remark. They were proud to consume HBR content and wanted to demonstrate their affinity with HBR because of what it said about them as intelligent, idea-engaged professionals. The team opted for a "wide" breadth product here, and proposed a display solution that would let users create a newsletter filled with articles containing pieces from their HBR Briefcase combined with more recent and topical pieces. The team believed that such content could become a great excuse for people to keep in touch and benefit their acquaintances. To facilitate search, the team also proposed that the platform allow users to search through their friends' briefcases. Users would also be able to comment on the favorite pieces and ask their friends questions, with the intent of starting interaction.

Many on the team believed that this solution leveraged HBR's unique content assets in ways that could not be copied by others easily. At the same time, they believed that the briefcase idea would help the organization drive more traffic to hbr.org, and generate more sales and subscriptions. In template language:

(1) HBR's social strategy increases willingness to pay
(2) by allowing people to reestablish connections to others
(3) when they share HBR's content with others

"FRIEND" SOCIAL STRATEGY TO REDUCE THE COST OF INPUTS

The final social strategy concept sought to alleviate a social failure that can be summarized as: "People want to show that they are participating in the exchange of intelligent ideas with colleagues and business associates, but often find it very socially awkward to do so." To help alleviate this failure, the second team proposed to develop detailed profiles of HBR users that would automatically display all of their comments and contributions across various HBR online properties. If users achieved and sustained certain levels of activity on the platform, they would be able to obtain badges that would be prominently displayed at the top of their profile pages. Users would also be given the option of showcasing their achievements and badges on their LinkedIn and Facebook profiles for their friends to see. Users could also search through their friends' contributions and initiate interaction with them either publicly or privately.

The team members believed that such public display of contributions would motivate users to create more user-generated content on

HBR websites. They also thought that the badge idea had the potential to increase retention and generate long-term positive engagement with the brand, as badge owners would try to maintain their badge status. Although many people on the team liked the idea, they also wanted to make sure that the badge would not imply that the badge owner had graduated from Harvard Business School. For this reason, they determined to think very carefully about how to design the badges and how to award them. In template form, the *Badge* strategic idea read as follows:

(1) HBR's social strategy reduces its costs
(2) by allowing people to display their knowledge to others
(3) when they contribute content to HBR for free

Testing the Proposals

The two teams next got together to present their ideas to each other (see table 13.1 for a summary). The meeting was lively, and there was a lot of excitement about all of the ideas. But once all of the ideas were presented, the group decided to evaluate each one through the lens of the social utility, social solution, and business impact tests. To ensure objectivity, each team took it upon themselves to evaluate the other team's ideas.

The process started with the second team evaluating the Connection Platform social strategy. Team members quickly agreed that, for many professions, it is fairly difficult to meet work-related mentors or advisors. For this reason, they decided that this strategy passed the first social utility test (the one that tests for important social failures), in that it did seem to enable an important social interaction for a meaningful set of people who cannot engage in it on their own.

Next, the team examined the Answer Exchange social strategy. Here, team members also readily agreed that there are some real failures in people's ability to ask professional questions and get relevant responses to them. So this strategy passed the first part of the social utility test as well.

Table 13.1. HBR's Social Strategies

	"Meet"	"Friend"
Higher willingness to pay	Connection Platform	HBR Briefcase
Lower cost	Answer Exchange	Badges

Subsequently, the first team evaluated the HBR Briefcase strategy. Team members agreed that many people probably find it difficult to reach out to acquaintances and certain coworkers in ways that benefit them, and so this strategy, too, addressed a real social failure and thus passed the first part of the social utility test.

This team reached a different verdict, however, when considering the Badges strategy. Team members raised concerns about the breadth of the social failure the strategy aspired to solve, claiming that only a very narrow set of people want to receive badges for participating in the exchange of intelligent ideas to colleagues and business associates. Although they did not discount the social failure completely, they concluded that the social failure targeted by the Badges strategy was the weakest of all four failures identified.

Next, the group turned to the second part of the social solution test, once again starting with the second team looking at the Connection Platform. Here, the team very quickly reached the conclusion that the functionality offered did not effectively alleviate the social failure. One team member recalled: "We were very concerned that everyone was able to contact anyone else so easily. Say a well-known businessperson joined the platform wanting to mentor someone. It is likely that she would be inundated with messages, making it difficult for her to make a choice. Also, she might not have enough information to choose the right person both in terms of fit and commitment to the process." Another team member was concerned about the potential for derivative failures: "What if someone signs up and claims to be knowledgeable in a particular area, and they end up advising someone, but then it turns out that they are not an expert at all? This might actually make someone worse off than they would have been. Some people complain about this problem when it comes to dating sites, and this is not the kind of experience we want to create. We need some way for people to certify their skills."

Although the team that came up with this strategy initially pushed back on these concerns, it did eventually agree that allowing free and unfettered contact might not be an optimal solution. This led both teams to start thinking about other ways of solving the social failure underlying the Connection Platform. Drawing on the dating analogy, one team member suggested that perhaps they should adopt the eHarmony model. Users would enter what they could offer and what their needs were, and the site would then match them appropriately. The team liked the idea, because it solved many issues related to who should pair up with whom. They were still concerned, however, that this solution did not ensure that members represented their skills and needs correctly.

Connecting Social Strategies

Listening to this discussion, a team member who had participated in the development of the Answer Exchange social strategy chimed in with a potential solution. "What if we connect this idea with Answer Exchange," she asked, "and reward asking and answering questions with the ability to meet others? For example, users could elect to include their questions and answers on their Connection Platform profile. That way they could convey their interests and skills to others more truthfully." This idea generated a lot of enthusiasm, as many team members believed that the ability to display questions and answers strengthened the efficacy of the Connection Platform.

The discussion quickly turned to examining whether the users should be required to provide questions or answers before they would be allowed to use the Connection Platform. A few team members were concerned that asking users to contribute content before being able to meet others would be too burdensome and would thus limit the use of the Connection Platform. Others disagreed, and in fact saw that requirement as strengthening the power of Answer Exchange solution. One member recalled his reasoning: "One of the big concerns that I had about bringing Answer Exchange back is that we still did not give people enough reason to contribute questions and provide answers. So I worried that we would end up with the same result as we did before—no one would write. But linking this to the Connection Platform made a lot of sense to me. Now you have a greater incentive to write, because you care about people seeing your content, but you also care about being able to meet other people." Most group members were persuaded by this argument, and they decided to amend the strategy to require individuals who want to meet others through the HBR "meet" platform to contribute at least a few questions and answers to the Answer Exchange first.

Then, the team member who had come up with the Badges social strategy suggested another tweak. He said: "It makes complete sense to ask people to contribute content to our Answer Exchange, but what if we also monitored other activities that users undertake, and gave them badges to recognize what they do. They could then use these badges as a way of signaling what they can do on the meet platform." His recommendation met with immediate approval, and also sparked further discussion, during which the group decided to develop badges for reading HBR online articles and blogs, providing comments on them, and purchasing a magazine subscription or books from the organization.

At this point, almost everyone in the group recognized a natural synergy between the revised Connection Platform strategy and the HBR Briefcase concept. Users who consumed and passed along a lot of HBR content, and generated and shared more do-it-yourself newsletters, would be rewarded with additional badges.

A team member later commented on why she believed that the integration was critical to the viability of the Briefcase and the Badges social strategies:

> I am glad we integrated all of this together. My team developed the HBR Briefcase idea, but I was really unsure how many people would really share their newsletters with others. Now that we reward them for doing so I think they will do more of that. . . . This was even more important for Badges. I can see how you can get teenagers do something for an electronic badge, but I really did not believe that we could get a typical HBR reader do that. But with this integration,

we turned badges into something highly relevant—ability to meet people. This should make a big difference!

At this point, the team took some time to reflect on the results of the meeting thus far. One team member raised a question: "So, we started with some of the problems that we had with the Connection Platform. And we ended up with adding badges for contributing content on the Answer Exchange and sharing one's Briefcase. But did we really solve the problems we identified?" Team members went back to their original notes and quickly agreed that their badging solution went a long way toward ascertaining that people would properly display their skills and commitment to participating in the Connection Platform. The group did worry, however, that some users might still be inundated with messages. With the badge system in place, would it not be all too easy to identify the most prolific and engaged contributors, who might then receive too many unwanted requests for contact?

That question sparked another vigorous debate, which culminated in the group deciding that users possessing a certain number and combination of badges would be awarded placement in a particular tier: bronze, silver, gold, or platinum. Tiers would be important because users could then decide whether to limit the type of user who could initiate a conversation with them. A gold-tier user, for example, could choose to be contacted only by other users of his tier and higher, as well as those holding silver status. Those holding bronze, and those without badge status, would not be able to contact that user, and would have to wait for the user to contact them. The group liked this solution because it would limit unwanted contact on the Connection Platform. At the same time, the solution would give users an additional incentive to ask and answer questions, share HBR content with others, and buy HBR products to advance to higher tiers and be given the opportunity to interact with more and more committed users. The group agreed to leave the decisions about what exactly would qualify users for a given tier for another day.

The team began to wrap up the meeting. Overall, team members noted that they were pleased with their accomplishments—and also very surprised by the outcome. They had thought that they would apply the social failure, social solution, and business value tests to each of the four ideas in a linear fashion and keep eliminating ideas until they settled on the one that worked. Instead, as it turned out, they identified a problem with one of the proposed social solutions and then generated a better solution by integrating solutions developed for other social strategies, in a way that also strengthened those other solutions. This sophisticated approach to evaluating social strategies allowed the group to generate a powerful set of mutually reinforcing social strategies.

Just as the team was getting ready to disband for the day, however, two additional issues emerged. First, one of the team members who had led the development of the Connection Platform idea reminded everyone that they still had to run the augmented strategies through the lens of the business value test. As she put it: "Our original specification of the Connection Platform asked people to pay directly for the privilege of meeting others. Now we replaced this direct payment with contributions to forums and sharing our content. Are we sure that this is actually a good business decision for us? Or would we be better off staying with direct payment?" Group members were grateful for this comment, as in the fever of creating their strategies they had paid less attention to immediate business considerations. Very quickly, however, they identified substantial business benefits of the social strategies they proposed, pointing to the additional content created for free and reduced acquisition and retention costs generated by members sharing content with others. One group member also pointed out that the strategy calls for users to purchase an HBR subscription in order to be able to connect with many others through the Connection Platform. It was that last comment that persuaded the questioner that the strategy has a great chance of affecting profitability.

That same comment, however, caused another team member to make an astute observation. She said: "Notice how central the Connection Platform has become to the success of the other strategies. For example, we think that people will be more willing to contribute to the Answer Exchange because that gives them the ability to meet others. Same goes for sharing the Briefcase and earning Badges. But what if no one really cared about meeting others? Then our intricate plan falls apart." This comment generated some consternation in the group, mainly because everyone knew that their colleague was right, but they simply did not know how to tackle this. To resolve the problem, team members agreed to reach out to me to see if there was anything they could do to prove a real need for people to meet each other. I had no magic answer to their question, but I did recommend to them a process of interviewing their customers that convinced them that meeting others is something that their customers want.

CHAPTER 14

Conclusions

We began by considering the choices LinkedIn faced in 2005, and we discovered pretty quickly that to understand the implications of each choice we needed to identify some underlying social failures and the kinds of solutions that LinkedIn could provide to those failures, which led us to the concept of social strategy.

There is very little doubt in my mind that at this point, readers will be able to revisit LinkedIn's dilemma and offer much more robust input than they could previously. More importantly, I hope that the foregoing chapters have also been helpful in developing a more general set of principles to guide readers on their own path to developing vibrant and profitable social strategies. Although each reader will probably have his or her own set of takeaways, I would like to review the three key ideas in the book—social failures, social solutions, and social strategy—and spell out what I believe to be their key implications for scholars and for practicing managers.

Social Failures

The concept of social failures has implications in the fields of sociology, economics, and strategy. As I suggested in chapter 1, we have many theories in sociology about how networks work and how they are often better than other social arrangements (Nohria and Eccles 1992; Powell 1990). We know little, however, about why people fail to engage in mutually beneficial interactions with each other. This is where the discussion of social failures comes in handy to help us understand why these interactions do not arise. To my mind, two features of our discussion are particularly useful to sociologists. First, social failures arise not only because people are too busy or too far from each other to interact, but also because there exists a host of normatively prescribed rules that stop us from engaging with each other. Second, by proposing four different types of interaction costs, the discussion in the book reveals that social failures relate not just to two or more people communicating with each other, but also to people participating in certain social environments to display information about themselves or to collect information about others.

The distinction between the four different types of interaction costs has some immediate applications to the current debate in sociology related to whether the Internet makes us more or less connected in the offline world. On the one hand, scholars such as Turkle (2011) argue that the Internet reduces the frequency of our face-to-face interaction in the offline world. On the other hand, another set of scholars have shown that social platforms actually increase that offline interaction (Hampton, Sessions, and Her 2011; Rainie and Wellman 2012). The concept of social failures immediately recognizes that the debate is too narrow in that it focuses only on the last type of interaction costs—those related to communication. People also care about breadth, display, and search interaction costs, implying that any discussion of what the Internet does to social structure should examine all four dimensions and then call for a verdict. I hope that future researchers in sociology will pick up on these distinctions and examine them further to help us glean deeper insight into the phenomenon.

The concept of social failures has also implications for economic theory, and particularly for the concept of market failures. Social failures and market failures share the common core of mutually beneficial interactions that do not take place. They differ, however, in their domain and the kinds of explanations they emphasize. Market failure theories assume that people do not engage in economic exchanges because of information asymmetry problems (Hart 1995; Spence 1974). In contrast, our discussion of social failures has consistently emphasized normative reasons why people choose not to interact socially. Nothing weds one type of explanation to one kind of domain, however. Indeed, our analysis has drawn extensively on nonsocial reasons why people do not interact socially. There is now an opportunity to do the same with market failures and bring normative restrictions to the analysis of why some economic exchanges do not take place. Our example of LinkedIn has already illustrated some of the benefits of doing so in the context of labor markets. I hope that future work in economics will develop similar norm-based theories of failures in other types of markets.

Finally, the concept of social failures has implications for our understanding of firm strategy. Most analyses in strategy start with the assumption that people have unmet economic needs that firms can step in and fulfill, and then proceed to theorize when differences in these needs can give rise to unique strategic positions in the marketplace (Porter 1985). The concept of social failures adds unmet social needs to the consideration set, and I dedicated most of the book to understanding how firms can meet such needs. In doing so, I have, however, not discussed how these unmet social needs may interact with unmet economic needs. Such interactions between economic and social needs should not surprise us—after all, a lot of what we consume takes place in the context of socializing with others, and a lot of what we purchase is for others. It is my hope that future students of strategy will pick up on this interaction and help us understand how firm strategy may change when meeting people's economic needs takes place within the context of meeting their social needs.

The concept of social failures should also help teachers and students understand that there exists a set of unmet social needs that affect many people and give rise to social platforms. If that is true, then social platforms are not a "flash in the pan" that will fizzle quickly as users move onto another entertainment source. Instead, this means that these platforms are here to stay as a permanent fixture on the Internet. It should also help students understand and appraise their own social situation better and ask, "What kinds of social failures am I facing? And where is there an opportunity for a social platform to step in and help me?" Equally, I hope the concept will lead some of my fellow academics who do not use social platforms to ask why they find them of limited use, while hundreds of millions of people engage on them daily. Perhaps you will find that the social environment you face as an academic is fairly devoid of social failures that others face. Or perhaps you will discover that you simply have not had the time to engage online with others yet, but would find it very useful to do so.

Finally, I hope that the concept of social failures will help practitioners—executives in established companies, managers in up-and-coming start-ups, and fledgling entrepreneurs who are just starting their companies. I am very grateful for your willingness to engage in depth with this topic. I could have made your task easier by simply describing what various companies and decision makers did as they developed their strategies. Doing so ran the risk, however, that you would consider much of what I would say out of date by the time the book was published. For this reason, I have focused on providing you with principles that I believe are enduring and will serve you well in the long run.

Specifically, I hope that the concept of social failures will help you sharpen the value proposition that you can provide in at least three distinct ways. First, it will give you a clear yardstick for what is an unmet social need. Being unable to obtain insurance is not a social failure. Being unable to meet new people or reconnect with existing friends is. Second, I often hear executives and entrepreneurs identify social processes they are going to improve on the basis of what they observe happening, for example, "people already exchange business cards, let's help them do so more efficiently." Although you can always improve the efficacy of any social process, the idea of social failures alerts you to pay attention to the mutually beneficial interactions that do *not* occur, and largely ignore the interactions that already take place. Granted, identifying interactions that should take place, but do not, is hard, but if you do manage to identify such a missing interaction, the payoff will be high.

Third, the notion of social failures should also sensitize you to the fact that we often do not interact because there is a norm that prevents us from doing so. Again, all too often I hear executives and entrepreneurs identify social failures by saying, "You know how it is very inefficient when you try to …," referring to some mechanical or time friction that prevents individuals from interacting. In my experience, however, a more powerful set of ideas come from people who start their sentences by saying, "You know how it is very awkward when you try to . . . ," referring to a normative restriction we face when interacting. To the extent that you can reframe your thinking about the problem and focus on the norms first, you might actually be more successful at identifying real social failures.

Social Solutions

The concept of social solutions is interesting to sociologists both at the descriptive and at the prescriptive levels. At the descriptive level, it helps us refocus the debate on whether or not social platforms make us more lonely. Specifically, if we accept that the offline face-to-face interaction is the right criterion on which to judge social platforms, the concept of social solutions argues that these platforms have the potential to do both. Those platforms that do not provide social solutions are likely to make us more disconnected from each other, while those that provide social solutions will connect us. Put differently, we cannot uniformly state that social platforms will make us more or less connected—it all depends on whether or not the Internet platforms provide solutions to the underlying social failures.

At the prescriptive level, it allows sociologists to start designing institutions to help people interact. With rare exceptions, sociologists have not spent a lot of time explicitly thinking about how to help individuals meet new people or interact with people they already know (Ingram and Morris 2007). The concept of social solutions explicitly asks sociologists to start doing so in a way that clearly helps people without introducing new derivative failures. This clearly is new territory for sociologists, one that some may actually resist, claiming that sociology has no business in actively shaping the social structure of our society. Although I am sympathetic to this view, I am also aware that many companies, Facebook included, already have a huge impact on how we interact with each other, and do so without our input.

By way of comparison, economists have made tremendous progress in researching economic solutions and put them to work helping companies and governments build auctions and other types of markets. I believe the time has come for sociologists to do more research on how to build these social solutions, and use this knowledge to help companies to shape how we interact with others in the online and offline worlds.

The concept of social solution also has a number of interesting implications for strategy. First, it sharpens our understanding of how competition between social platforms will probably play out. This becomes particularly salient once we start asking questions such as whether Facebook will encroach on LinkedIn's territory. Without thorough understanding of the concept, we might conclude that there are no limits on what Facebook can do, and LinkedIn is at risk of being subsumed by Facebook. Once we understand how social solutions work, however, we quickly see that Facebook faces real strategic trade-offs in introducing a "meet" solution to its platform, which will probably stop the company from building it. Similarly, given the size of Facebook, we might conclude that no other company will be able to provide "friend" solutions. Yet, once we understand what kind of social solution Facebook is, we can easily predict the rise of competing solutions that Facebook will not be able to emulate easily.

More broadly, the concept has implications for existing theories in strategy, particularly those that relate to competition between multi-sided platforms in which numerous people or other entities interact with one another. A number of influential papers in the field have suggested that these platforms should grow as large as possible and facilitate as many connections as possible to outcompete others (e.g., Caillaud and Jullien 2003; Rochet and Tirole 2003). The concept of social solution warns us that this is not always the case when these platforms seek to connect people to each other. This was particularly salient in the eHarmony and OkCupid comparison, where restricted choice actually allowed eHarmony to flourish and even charge a higher price. Similarly, the comparison of mixi and Facebook revealed that the platform offering more limited choice actually might succeed at facilitating deeper friendship connections than the one offering more choice. I hope that future research will continue to identify such patterns both with respect to theory and data.

I also hope that practitioners will find the idea of social solutions helpful. The book provided a number of specific "lessons," for example, you must attend to all four types of interaction costs, or if you want people to produce a lot of content to share with others, social functionality has to allow them to restrict the size of their audience. To my mind, however, the most important part of the social solution idea is that it has to address both economic and social causes of interaction costs, which often implies developing alternative forms of interaction to what you already see in the offline world. This is a difficult task in that it asks you to develop alternative means of interacting, when a ready-made template is already available to you in the offline world. Recognizing the inherent difficulty of this task, I still hope that you will give it serious consideration, as doing so will allow you to differentiate your offerings from competitive offerings.

Social Strategy

In devising the concept of social strategy I sought to keep it aligned with one of the key frameworks for understanding strategy—one advanced by Michael Porter—which argues that firms can pursue either low-cost or high willingness-to-pay strategies. In this framework, firms achieve a competitive advantage to the extent they can lower their costs without losing a commensurate amount of their customers' willingness to pay, or increase their willingness to pay without enduring a commensurate increase in costs. With this in mind, most theories in strategy examine how firms can achieve this goal in ways that cannot be easily replicated by competitors.

Typically, to achieve these strategic goals, firms have to incur direct costs. My key innovation here was to argue that the goals can be achieved indirectly, and firms can lower their costs or increase their willingness to pay by investing to build social solutions that get people to undertake corporate tasks for free. As long as people undertake these tasks and their value exceeds the costs of building and operating the social solution, this more indirect way of executing strategy will improve the company's competitive position. I dedicated the second part of the book to helping us understand when people are likely to do this, and when these tasks will actually benefit the company.

I hope that future scholars of strategy will develop the ideas presented here to answer questions that still remain unanswered. To my mind, it is particularly important to examine how firms protect their social strategies from imitation by others. Suppose, for example, that two firms build very similar "meet" platforms to lower their costs. What factors determine which one of them will attract more people who are more willing to undertake corporate tasks for free, thereby leading to a more powerful competitive advantage? Some of the examples I have discussed begin to give us some answers. For example, Nike developed a number of different strategies around a shared resource, thereby reducing the average cost of building the social solutions. American Express developed its social strategy around its unique resource, thereby protecting its strategy from being copied by Visa or MasterCard. *Harvard Business Review* developed many social strategies and connected them to make each one of them more valuable in the presence of other strategies. In this case, competitors who copied just one of the strategies, but not all of them, would be at a disadvantage. Clearly, a more overarching framework is needed to combine all of these conditions.

Finally, I hope that practitioners will be able to get tremendous mileage out of the concept of social strategy and the process for developing one. All too often I hear executives complain that they do not see much return on their investments in "social media" and relegate it to the "nice-to-have-but-not-really-important" category. A quick inquiry into the nature of these efforts reveals that most of these executives have pursued a digital strategy on social platforms and have not really explored the possibilities afforded by connecting people to each other and getting them to do tasks for free in return. A short description of what American Express and Nike are doing in this arena is usually sufficient to pique their interest to reorient their approach to social platforms. I hope that the frameworks and the examples advanced here will get you to start experimenting with social strategies, so that when I sit down to write the next version of this book, I will be able to use your company as the exemplary case of how to leverage online social platforms for profit!

ACKNOWLEDGMENTS

To me, there is nothing more enjoyable than writing about human relationships, particularly when these interactions happen online. I get this astonishing surge of energy just thinking about the billions of people who every day interact with one another in ways they could not even fathom twenty years ago. To write a book about these people, however, I had to sit alone in front of my computer day in and day out for months on end. Sometimes this felt as if I had been banished to a deserted island with no human contact allowed. I was fortunate, however, to be surrounded by an incredibly supportive offline and online social network of friends and colleagues. Without them, I would never have finished the book. I want to take a second to thank them here.

First, I am incredibly grateful to numerous executives who took time from their busy schedules to talk with me about their companies, and some of whom subsequently entrusted me with their company data. As the list is very long, I need to constrain myself to key decision makers, and I list them roughly in the order their companies are discussed in the book. These are: Greg Waldorf, Greg Steiner, and Joseph Essas at eHarmony; Sam Yagan and Christian Rudder at OkCupid; Douglas Atkin and Scott Heiferman at MeetUp; Dennis Crowley at foursquare; Kenji Kasahara at mixi; Elliot Schrage at Facebook; Reid Hoffman, Konstatin Guericke, and Adam Nash at LinkedIn; Kent Lindstrom and Jonathan Abrams at Friendster; Angela Courtin and the crew at MySpace; Mark Pincus at Zynga; Jimmy Wales at Wikipedia; Ed Gilligan and Leslie Berland at American Express; Trevor Edwards and Stefan Olander at Nike; Adi Ignatius and Josh Macht at Harvard Business Review; and Karen Webster from Market Platform Dynamics.

I am equally indebted to my friends and colleagues who have supported me throughout the process. I am especially grateful to my longtime advisor, Nitin Nohria, who insisted that I write this book; Bharat Anand, Felix Oberholzer-Gee, Sean Safford, and Toby Stuart, who read the early versions of the manuscript; and my friend Isabel Fernandez-Mateo, who meticulously read every line in this book when it was finished and provided extensive feedback. Along the way, Juan Alcacer, Ravi Bapna, Ron Burt, Ramon Casadesus-Masanell,

Tiziana Casciaro, Michael Cusumano, John Deighton, Kathleen Eisenhardt, Tom Eisenmann, Joshua Gans, David Garvin, Giovanni Gavetti, Andreea Gorbatai, Sanjeev Goyal, Boris Groysberg, Sunil Gupta, Hanna Hałaburda, Rebecca Henderson, Marco Iansiti, Tarun Khanna, Rakesh Khurana, Paweł Korzyński, Karim Lakhani, Hong Luo, Daniel Malter, Bill McEvily, Mark Mizruchi, Jan Rivkin, Martin Ruef, Olav Sorenson, Jerzy Surma, Woody Powell, Magnus Torfason, Brian Uzzi, Dennis Yao, and David Yoffie provided invaluable feedback on some or all ideas presented in this book.

I was also very fortunate to benefit from extensive feedback from over 750 students who took Competing with Social Networks, my second-year elective at Harvard Business School. They generously listened to my still half-baked ideas and patiently worked with me to improve the frameworks and make sure that they met managerial realities. Without their commitment and their positive attitude, this book would have lost most of its appeal. I would be equally lost without my research team, comprising David Chen, Jeff deBeer, Kerry Herman, Sara Hunt, Carin Knoop, John Sheridan, Aaron Smith, Sarah Woolverton, and Mayuka Yamazaki, as well as my editorial team: Madeleine Adams, Kathleen Cioffi, Regina Maruca, Ryan Mulligan, Rafe Sagalyn, and Eric Schwartz. All of you have given all you could to make this book happen and I cannot thank you enough!

The entire book writing process would have been miserable if I could not regularly hang out with my friendsies (as I call them). Thank you, David Ager, Yasemin Akçakaya, Scott Belsky, Julie Bershadsky, Emilio Castilla, Chris Dexter, Ty Dowell, James Forren, Cindy Gallop, Volkan Gurel, Tim Hayes, Daniel Heller, Chad Hildal, Pedro Jaile, Adam Kleinbaum, Roger Kraus, Melissa Leimbach, Charlene Li, Pai Ling-Yin, Merlina Manocaran, Alejandro Morales, Aldo Musacchio, Sunil Nagaraj, Paul Nelson, Hubert Roberts, Metin Sengul, Clara Shih, Troy Smith, Kaisa Snellman, Silviya Svejenova Velikova, my bestie Tomek Rozwadowski, Rui and Scooby, and Carla Tishler, for keeping my spirits up!

I am also beyond grateful to my two biggest fans, Kasia Piskorska and Charles Fletcher. They both consoled me on days when the book was "just not working out" and celebrated those little victories on days when I thought I was "making some progress." I love both of you so much, and I could not be luckier to have you both in my life!

Last but not least, I want to thank my mom and dad, Maria and Krzysztof, for letting me leave home so early in my life. Although we have had to face geographic separation for more than twenty-three years, we have managed to make our relationship grow stronger and stronger! I love you and I dedicate this book to both of you.

NOTES

Chapter 1. The Arc of the Book

1. Alex Wilhelm, "Facebook: Our 1 Billion Users Have Uploaded 240 Billion Photos, Made 1 Trillion Connections," http://thenextweb.com/facebook/2013/01/15/facebook-our-1-billion-users-have-uploaded-240-billion-photos-made-1-trillion-connections/.

2. Sophie Estienne, "Twitter Seeks Up to $1.61 Billion in IPO," http://news.yahoo.com/twitter-hikes-amount-raised-ipo-1-61-bn-202150593.html.

3. "Study: 542 People Married Every Day in U.S., on Average, through eHarmony," http://www.eharmony.com/press-release/31/.

4. Matt Schiavenza, "WeChat—Not Weibo—Is the Chinese Social Network to Watch," *Atlantic*, July 30, 2013, http://www.theatlantic.com/china/archive/2013/07/wechat-not-weibo-is-the-chinese-social-network-to-watch/278212/.

5. The URL for the book's social platform is www.socialstrategybook.com.

Chapter 3. "Meet" Solutions: eHarmony and OkCupid

1. Tim Ghose, "Online Date Game: 1 in 10 Americans Have Tried It," http://www.pewinternet.org/Media-Mentions/2013/1-in-10-Americans-have-tried-it.aspx.

2. "Study: 542 People Married Every Day in U.S., on Average, through eHarmony, http://www.eharmony.com/press-release/31/.

Chapter 4. "Meet" Solution: Twitter

1. I collected the data together with the Harvard Business School MBA student Bill Heil in 2009.

2. The data from Pinterest were initially collected by the Harvard Business School MBA students Joshua Yang, Kevin Chuang, and Amy Chan in 2012 and subsequently were augmented by my own data collection.

3. Estimating the number of Twitter users is always problematic because only a certain proportion of Twitter users post and read tweets through the Twitter website.

4. It is also instructive to note that once we cross the fifty-tweet threshold, the pattern reverses. For example, there is at least 1 percent more Twitter users who have more than one hundred tweets than OkCupid users with profiles equivalent to one hundred tweets. This is consistent with our earlier discussion according to which Twitter experiences substantial usage by its power users.

Chapter 5. "Friend" Solutions: Facebook and mixi

1. Lars Backstrom, "Anatomy of Facebook," https://www.facebook.com/notes/facebook-data-team/anatomy-of-facebook/10150388519243859.

Chapter 6. "Meet" and "Friend" Solutions: LinkedIn and Friendster

1. Orkut, Google's online friend platform, which also ran into performance problems, failed in the United States, but was able to succeed in Brazil for exactly the same reasons.

2. In an auxiliary analysis I took a 10 percent sample of all users, and identified all of the pictures and profiles they examined, and then constructed a list of unique identification numbers of these profiles. For the ID numbers not connected to the focal user, I examined the path length between the viewer and the target user, and found that 35 percent of users who were viewed were friends of friends, 35 percent were friends of friends of friends, and the remaining 30 percent were fourth degree of separation or higher.

Chapter 7. "Meet" and "Friend" Solution: MySpace

1. This calculation assumes that Internet penetration within a state is distributed uniformly, but this may not be the case. To counteract this problem, I used data on Internet use from the USDA Census of Agriculture, which reports farm Internet access at the county level; only in Arizona, Nevada, and New Mexico does this assumption not hold. This is not a problem for us, because few MySpace users hail from these states anyway.

Chapter 9. Social Strategy at Zynga

1. As I discussed earlier, social actions also have an important retention effect. To quantify this effect, I would need to know how many users who

could be considered lapsed were brought back in by an existing user, and how many users who are still playing the games do so only because of their friends. Unfortunately, I do not have any data that speak to these issues so I omit them from the analysis here. Since social strategy will have an effect on both customer acquisition and retention, all analyses in the main text should be considered lower-bound estimates of the effects of social strategies.

REFERENCES

Akerlof, George. 1970. "The Market for 'Lemons': Qualitative Uncertainty and the Market Mechanism." *Quarterly Journal of Economics* 84:488–500.

Bator, Francis M. 1958. "The Anatomy of Market Failure." *Quarterly Journal of Economics* 72:351–379.

Burt, Ronald S. 1982. *Toward a Structural Theory of Action: Network Models of Social Structure, Perception, and Action*. New York: Academic Press.

———. 1992. *Structural Holes: The Social Structure of Competition*. Cambridge, MA: Harvard University Press.

———. 2001. "Bandwidth and Echo: Trust, Information and Gossip in Social Networks." In *Markets and Networks: Contributions from Economics and Sociology*, ed. A. Casella and J. E. Rauch. New York: Russell Sage Foundation.

———. 2005. *Brokerage and Closure: An Introduction to Social Capital*. Oxford: Oxford University Press.

Buskens, Vincent, and Arnout van de Rijt. 2008. "Dynamics of Networks if Everyone Strives for Structural Holes." *American Journal of Sociology* 114:371–407.

Caillaud, Bernard, and Bruno Jullien. 2003. "Chicken and Egg: Competition among Intermediation Service Providers." *RAND Journal of Economics* 34:309–328.

Casciaro, Tiziana. 2008. "When Competence Is Irrelevant: The Role of Interpersonal Affect in Task-Related Ties." *Administrative Science Quarterly* 53:655–684.

Cate, Rodney M., and Sally A. Lloyd. 1992. *Courtship*. Newbury Park, CA: Sage.

Coase, Ronald. 1937. "The Nature of the Firm." *Economica* 4:386–405.

Coleman, James Samuel. 1990. *Foundations of Social Theory*. Cambridge, MA: Harvard University Press.

Collins, Randall. 2004. *Interaction Ritual Chains*. Princeton, NJ: Princeton University Press.

Dickson, Fran C., Patrick C. Hughes, and Kandi L. Walker. 2005. "An Exploratory Investigation into Dating among Later-Life Women." *Western Journal of Communication* 69:67–82.

Fernandez, Roberto M., Emilio J. Castilla, and Paul Moore. 2000. "Social Capital at Work: Networks and Employment at a Phone Center." *American Journal of Sociology* 105:1288–1356.

Fischer, Claude S. 1973. "Urban Malaise." *Social Forces* 52:221–235.

Goffman, Erving. 1967. *Interaction Ritual: Essays in Face-to-Face Behavior*. New York: Anchor Books.

Granovetter, Mark. 1974. *Getting a Job: A Study of Contacts and Careers*. Cambridge, MA: Harvard University Press.

Grossman, S., and Oliver Hart. 1986. "The Costs and Benefits of Ownership: A Theory of Vertical and Lateral Integration." *Journal of Political Economy* 94:691–719.

Hałaburda, Hanna, and Mikołaj Jan Piskorski. 2013. "Competing by Restricting Choice: The Case of Search Platforms." Harvard Business School Working Paper no. 10–098.

Hampton, Keith N., Lauren F. Sessions, and Eun Ja Her. 2011. "Core Networks, Social Isolation, and New Media: Internet and Mobile Phone Use, Network Size, and Diversity." *Information, Communication and Society* 14:130–155.

Hampton, Keith N., Lauren Sessions Goulet, Cameron Marlow, and Lee Rainie. 2012. "Why Most Facebook Users Get More Than They Give." Pew Internet. http://pewinternet.org/Reports/2012/Facebook-users.aspx.

Hart, Oliver. 1995. *Firms, Contracts, and Financial Structure*. New York: Oxford University Press.

Hart, Oliver, and John H. Moore. 1990. "Property Rights and the Nature of the Firm." *Journal of Political Economy* 98:1119–1158.

Hitsch, Günter J., Ali Hortaçsu, and Dan Ariely. 2010. "Matching and Sorting in Online Dating." *American Economic Review* 100:130–163.

Ingram, Paul, and Michael W. Morris. 2007. "Do People Mix at Mixers? Structure, Homophily, and the 'Life of the Party.'" *Administrative Science Quarterly* 52:558–585.

Ingram, Paul, and Peter Roberts. 2000. "Friendships among Competitors." *American Journal of Sociology* 106:387–423.

Katz, Michael, and Carl Shapiro. 1986. "Technology Adoption in the Presence of Network Externalities." *Journal of Political Economy* 94:822–841.

Khurana, Rakesh. 1998. "The Changing of the Guard: Causes, Process and Consequences of CEO Turnover." Ph.D. dissertation, Harvard University.

Kollock, Peter. 1994. "The Emergence of Exchange Structures." *American Journal of Sociology* 100:313–345.

Kossinets, Gueorgi, and Duncan J. Watts. 2009. "Origins of Homophily in an Evolving Social Network." *American Journal of Sociology* 115:405–450.

Lawler, Edward J., and Jeongkoo Yoon. 1996. "Commitment in Exchange Relations: Test of a Theory of Relational Cohesion." *American Sociological Review* 61:89–108.

Marsden, Peter V. 1983. "Restricted Access in Networks and Models of Power." *American Journal of Sociology* 88:686–717.

Marsden, Peter V., and Noah E. Friedkin. 1993. "Network Studies of Social-Influence." *Sociological Methods and Research* 22:127–151.

McElhany, L. J. 1992. "Dating and Courtship in the Later Years." *Generations* 16:21–23.

McPherson, Miller, Lynn Smith-Lovin, and Matthew E. Brashears. 2006. "Social Isolation in America: Changes in Core Discussion Networks over Two Decades." *American Sociological Review* 71:353–375.

McPherson, M., L. Smith-Lovin, and J. M. Cook. 2001. "Birds of a Feather: Homophily in Social Networks." *Annual Review of Sociology* 27:415–444.

Miller, Rowland S., Daniel Perlman, and Sharon S. Brehm. 2009. *Intimate Relationships*. Boston: McGraw-Hill Higher Education.

Molm, Linda D. 1997. *Coercive Power in Social Exchange*. Cambridge: Cambridge University Press.

Molm, Linda D., Noboyuki Takahashi, and Gretchen Peterson. 2000. "Risk and Trust in Social Exchange: An Experimental Test of a Classical Proposition." *American Journal of Sociology* 105:1396–1427.

Nohria, Nitin, and Robert G. Eccles, eds. 1992. *Networks and Organizations: Structure, Form, and Action*. Boston: Harvard Business School Press.

Piskorski, Mikołaj Jan, and Tiziana Casciaro. 2006. "When More Power Makes You Worse Off: Turning a Profit in the American Economy." *Social Forces* 85:230–265.

Porter, Michael E. 1985. *Competitive Advantage: Creating and Sustaining Superior Performance*. New York: Free Press.

———. 1996. "What Is a Strategy?" *Harvard Business Review*, November–December: 61–78.

Powell, W. W. 1990. "Neither Market Nor Hierarchy—Network Forms of Organization." *Research in Organizational Behavior* 12:295–336.

Powell, Walter W., Douglas R. White, Kenneth W. Koput, and Jason Owen-Smith. 2005. "Network Dynamics and Field Evolution: The Growth of Inter-organizational Collaboration in the Life Sciences." *American Journal of Sociology* 110:1132–1205.

Putnam, Robert D. 2000. *Bowling Alone: The Collapse and Revival of American Community*. New York: Simon & Schuster.

Rainie, Lee, and Barry Wellman. 2012. *Networked: The New Social Operating System*. Cambridge, MA: MIT Press.

Rochet, Jean-Charles, and Jean Tirole. 2003. "Platform Competition in Two-Sided Markets." *Journal of the European Economic Association* 1:990–1029.

Safford, Sean. 2008. *Why the Garden Club Couldn't Save Youngstown: The Transformation of the Rust Belt*. Cambridge, MA: Harvard University Press.

Schrank, Andrew, and Josh Whitford. 2013. *When Networks Fail: Uncovering the Hidden Weaknesses in the Global Economy*. Princeton, NJ: Princeton University Press.

Simmel, Georg. 1970. "The Metropolis and Mental Life." In *Neighborhood, City, and Metropolis: An Integrated Reader in Urban Sociology*, ed. Robert Gutman and David Popenoe. New York: Random House.

Spence, A. M. 1974. *Market Signaling: Informational Transfer in Hiring and Related Screening Processes*. Cambridge, MA: Harvard University Press.

Turkle, Sherry. 2011. *Alone Together: Why We Expect More from Technology and Less from Each Other*. New York: Basic Books.

Ugander, Johan, Brian Karrer, Lars Backstrom, and Cameron Marlow. 2011. "The Anatomy of the Facebook Social Graph." http://arxiv.org/abs/1111.4503v1.

Uzzi, Brian. 1997. "Social Structure and Competition in Interfirm Networks: The Paradox of Embeddedness." *Administrative Science Quarterly* 42:35–67.

Williamson, Oliver E. 1985. *The Economic Institutions of Capitalism*. New York: Free Press.

———. 1996. *Mechanisms of Governance*. Oxford: Oxford University Press.

INDEX

The letter *f* or *t* following a page number indicates a figure or table on that page. The letter *n* following a page number indicates a note on that page. The number following the *n* indicates the number of the note. A link to the online appendix can be found at http://press.princeton. edu/titles/10190.html.